MPLS for Cisco Networks

A CCIE v5 guide to Multiprotocol Label Switching

By Stuart Fordham

Copyright

Notice of Rights

Copyright © 2014 Stuart Fordham.

All rights reserved. This book or any portion thereof may not be reproduced or used in any manner whatsoever without the express written permission of the publisher except for the use of brief quotations in a book review.

Front cover image copyright of Studiojumpee / Shutterstock, Inc.

Notice of Liability

Although the author and publisher have made every effort to ensure that the information in this book was correct at press time, the author and publisher do not assume and hereby disclaim any liability to any party for any loss, damage, or disruption caused by errors or omissions, whether such errors or omissions result from negligence, accident, or any other cause.

Trademarks

CCNA, CCNP, CCIE and Cisco are registered trademarks of Cisco Systems, Inc.

To my wonderful wife Nicky, you now have two computer books dedicated to you, the first one by a geeky father, and this one by a geeky husband. Technology has moved and changed a lot over those thirty-something years, giving us so much in the way of innovation and improvement to better our lives.

You have given me the best life and family possible.

To my mum, it's only because of you and Dad that I have the dedication and drive to do this. The pride you show in me keeps me trying to make you proud.

There is a fine line between being pushy and being encouraging. I think you nailed it; I'll try and do the same.

MPLS for Cisco Networks 1
Copyright 2
Notice of Rights 2
Notice of Liability 2
Trademarks 2

1. About 7
1.1 About the Author 7
1.2 About this series of books 7
1.3 Following this book 9
1.4 About the reader 11
1.5 About the Technical Editor 11
1.6 Cisco IOS basics 11

2. A (very) brief history of MPLS 13

3. Topology 14

4. The basics of MPLS 17
4.1 The problem with packets 17
4.2 Enter label switching 21
4.3 MPLS Roles 22
  Label Switch Router (LSR) / Provider (P) 22
  Label Edge Router (LER) / Provider Edge (PE) 22
  Customer Edge Router (CE) 23
4.4 MPLS Requirements 23
4.5 MPLS packet flow 24

5. Initial MPLS VPN configuration 26
Goal 1: Creating the MPLS cloud IGP 28
Goal 2: LDP adjacencies 29
Goal 3: Creating the MP-BGP process 32
Goal 4: Creating VRFs, RDs and RTs 34
Goal 5: Adding our VRFs to BGP 38
Goal 6: Customer to Provider IGP 38
Goal 7: Redistribution between MP-BGP and Customer network 39
Confirming MPLS VPN connectivity 40
Addtional VRFs 44
  VRF WHITE 44
  VRF BLUE 48

6. Inside the LSP 51
Implicit Null 62
TTL Propagation 63
Penultimate Hop Popping 67

Explicit Null 69

7. Inside the Service Provider Network 72
7.1 The BGP-free core 77

8. Customer to Provider Routing 84
8.1 CE-PE routing with OSPF 84
    OSPF Sham-links *84*
8.2 CE-PE Routing with RIP 92
8.3 CE-PE Routing with EIGRP 97
8.4 CE-PE Routing with BGP 101
8.5 CE-PE Routing with static routing 107
8.6 CE-PE Routing with IS-IS 111

9. Services within an MPLS Cloud 115
9.1 Customer Route Leaking 115
9.2 Central Services within MPLS 120
9.3 Customer Internet Access 128
    Providing Internet Access using a separate connection *129*
    Providing Internet Access through route leaking *130*
    Providing Internet Access through a dedicated VRF *138*
    Completing Internet Access through a dedicated VRF *155*

10. Filtering and loop prevention 161
10.1 Label Filtering using the Site-of-Origin 161
10.2 MP-BGP Prefix Filtering 171
10.3 Label filtering 174

11. VRF-Lite 179
11.1 Basic VRF-Lite configuration 179
11.2 An expanded VRF-Lite scenario 186
11.3 The DN bit and capability vrf-lite 201

12. MPLS and Layer 2 209
12.1 L2TPv3 210
12.2 AToM 217
12.3 VPLS and OTV 233

13. IPv6 over MPLS 236
13.1 6VPE 236
13.2 6PE 243
13.3 IPv6 and VRF-Lite 248

14. Tweaking MPLS 255

14.1 Tweaking MLPS labels.. 255
14.2 Tweaking MPLS timers 261
14.3 Tweaking MPLS security 262
14.4 Tweaking MPLS performance 265

15. Troubleshooting MPLS 267
Troubleshooting the Core 268
Ticket 1 ....*268*
Ticket 2 ....*273*
Ticket 3 ....*279*
Ticket 4 ....*283*
Troubleshooting the Customer environment... 288
Ticket 1 ....*288*
Ticket 2 ....*292*
Ticket 3 ....*297*

16. This book and the CCIE v5.0 304
Alternative syllabi 305

17. Further reading 307

1. About

1.1 About the Author

I have been working in IT for about 12 years - starting off in desktop support, moving up the chain to third line and more recently and specifically finding my "home" within networking. I have worked for a number of companies, including local health authorities, Hedge Funds, and software houses. My current role is looking after the global network for a SaaS company.

I studied Psychology at university; however, at the end of the degree, I really didn't fancy spending years and years studying in order to progress up the ladder. So, I moved into IT, and have spent years and years studying on order to progress up the ladder. I have a number of qualifications including; CCNP, CCNA, JNCIP, CEH, RHCSA, MCITP, MCSE, MCSA: Security, Network+, Security+, A+ and I think that's about it. I tend to collect certifications; some I have purposefully let lapse in order to concentrate more on the Cisco side of things. Others are still current. I released my first book, BGP for Cisco Networks, in March 2014. I enjoyed the process of creating it so much that I continued with Volume II right away.

I am married with twin sons, and I live in Bedfordshire in the UK.

I can be contacted at stu@802101.com. I am always happy to hear feedback and suggestions.

My website address is http://www.802101.com.

1.2 About this series of books

It seems that as the number of certifications being passed grows, so does the recommended reading list of books that need to be purchased. For the CCNA it was two books, for the CCNP it's three books. The technical jump from CCNP to CCIE is vast. With that so is the required reading list. The publicized reading list from Cisco is a whopping 21 books[1]. Even with judicious purchasing of second hand books (via the likes of eBay or Amazon marketplace), you would still end up paying in the region of $15 (if very lucky) or more. So buying the entire book list even at this minimum price, would total about $300 (about £200). I have bought a large number of the books on the reading list, but a number

---

[1] http://www.802101.com/2013/05/ccie-book-list.html

of them will go untouched. Large portions of others will go unread (at least until I need to cover bits I have missed). With twenty-odd books, time is a significant factor. If you figure, at best, you would be able to finish one book a month, that's still nearly two years just to complete the reading list. Granted, not all books are created equal in length, and some people have more time than others to go through the reading. Even so, there is still a lot of reading to be done. Let's face it; no one really wants to spend two years reading for one exam.

That said, finding a book that is affordable, contains all the relevant information, but at the same time can be precise and short enough (but without lacking the detail) to finish within a week or so can be a bit of a mission.

After more than 10 years of being in this industry, I have read a large number of computer books on a variety of subjects, from the very best to the very worst. There are a number of things that, in my mind, make for a good networking book.

Networks are by their very nature constantly evolving, by that token, any book that teaches anything about networks should also follow this evolutionary path. It should build and scale as the book progresses in the same way that someone faced with a network. They will first start from the ground up, such as basic connectivity. Their skills and knowledge grow as the network grows and additions to the network are added. This including more complex routing, access rules and redundancy. The types of books that don't present an evolutionary network to the reader are also, in my experience, one of two types. Type A is full of tables of commands, with little actual examples of the commands and their results. Type B is slightly better and offers the commands within the context of a network, showing the results and effects of the commands. Generally, type B uses singular examples, each is self-contained. Example X bears no relevance to example Y. Therefore, the reader cannot actually see the evolution of the network, and how the intricacies of pathways are built and changed as the network grows.

With this in mind I decided to write one myself. The hope is that the end result would serve two purposes. The first being to solidify my own knowledge towards the CCIE certification. The second being to start a series of Cisco-centric networking books that will:

- Be affordable
- Be easy to read within a couple of weeks
- Be of use at any level of networking competency
- Follow a topology to show how a network is built and evolves
- Allow the reader to follow using either physical or virtual (i.e. GNS3) equipment

This is the second book in this series. Due to trying to keep the costs as low as possible I have had to opt for black and white printing for the paperback version. Please see the links in the topology chapter to download the full color images.

1.3 Following this book

I have used GNS3 for the majority of the topology, primarily as this is the virtual environment that many people studying Cisco exams (after packet tracer for CCNA of course) are familiar with, it is free and easy to use.

Hopefully, by the time this book is ready for publishing, Cisco will have released VIRL/CML. If and when it is released, I will rebuild the topology and publish the files on my website. Links for IOU will also be published.

For more information on Cisco IOU and Cisco VIRL, please have a look at my site.

The initial router configurations and topologies used can be downloaded from:

http://l.802101.com/802books

Please refer to chapter 3 for the main topology that will be used through the majority of this book.

There are a couple of scenarios where I have had to move away from the main topology and set up smaller examples. Although this goes against the evolutionary style I hope to accomplish with this book, I hope you'll understand the reasoning behind not pushing it all into one topology.

During the book, you will encounter a number of different exercises. Not all of these actually require all the routers to be switched on. Therefore, I will include a smaller picture (without the IP address details) indicating which routers are in use, the routers will look like this:

Router
(In use)

Router
(turned off)

Edge Label
Switch Router

For example, let's say we were working on the left hand side of the topology with no dependencies on IGW, P2, R2, R4 and R6. Then, these can be safely turned off without any negative effects.

The associated image would look like this in the book:

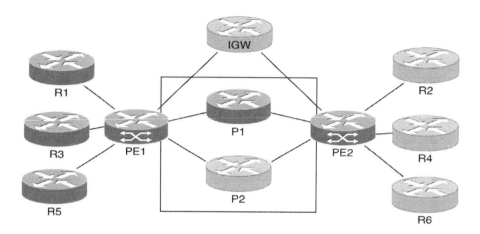

The reason for doing this is to preserve some host computer memory. These routers are all 7200 series running a later IOS version; 15.1(4)M4, therefore the memory requirements are greater than a 3600 router running an older 12.4 image. I am using an IOS 15 image, as this is more closely aligned with the CCIE lab exam which uses 15.3T. There are only few features that require an IOS 15 image, and here is a break down of the relevant changes since IOS 12.4:

    15.0.1M - IS-IS VRF Support
    15.1(1)T - MPLS MTU command for GRE tunnels
    15.2(1)T - MPLS-TE-TE over GRE
    15.2(2)T - MPLS VPN over mGRE

In order to ensure a stable topology that will run on the majority of computers, we can turn off some of the routers that are not in use. Obviously, if you can run all the routers then go for it, but the mini-topology diagrams are meant to show the minimum routers required.

The idea that the exercises within the book could be performed with a degree of router selection was as a result of some feedback I received on my first book, from Tyler on Facebook:

"It's very well written book, and has helped a lot. I would highly recommend it to be honest. I can turn on a few routers at a time, and easily do labs for a variety of reasons, without turning all of them on " – Tyler P, on Facebook

I didn't need to include the first two sentences to illustrate the gist. It's nice to get positive feedback, so I thought I would include it. Back to the point in hand, memory wasn't so much of an issue with the first volume as that used an older, less memory intensive router and image, but it is more of a consideration with this volume. So you can all thank Tyler if you meet him for saving your computer memory! It did mean a bit more work to make all the associated images, but I hope it'll make for a better over-all experience.

1.4 About the reader

The hope with this book is that anyone looking to get a good grounding in MPLS can find this book useful without a large amount of prerequisite knowledge about Cisco commands or networking in general. That said, this is primarily designed for readers with at least a basic knowledge of Cisco routers and their basic commands. Similarly, as the examples given in this book are all based around the use of GNS3, I hope that you are familiar with this as well. The series is designed for those pursuing the CCIE certification, and as the CCIE has no prerequisites, I have tried hard to start with the basics and then to advance as the book progresses. Hopefully, you as the reader will have had previous exposure to Cisco networking and know your way around the IOS CLI. By the end of this book, you will feel like you have a firm understanding of MPLS.

1.5 About the Technical Editor

Beau Jones (CCNP, CCNA-Sec, Sec+, JNCIS-ENT) joined the efforts of this volume as the technical editor. He has both a B.S. and M.S. in Applied Mathematics from the University of Central Arkansas. After five years of teaching high school and college mathematics courses, he stumbled into networking, and it was love at first sight. He currently works as a Network Engineer for a global financial provider. Being the technical editor allows Beau to combine his love for teaching with his love of networking.

Beau lives in Little Rock, Arkansas, with his wife and daughter.

1.6 Cisco IOS basics

There is a lot of command truncation in this book. Although this book is aimed at CCIE level readers, I do hope that anyone at any level can pick it up and get going. So a few quick words about the commands used.

Most of the show commands will be truncated to "sh" and will use further truncation such as "neigh" being the short version of neighbor. I also use the output modifier a lot. This is the bar, or "pipe" character | . I follow this by an "i" for include, an "e" for exclude, and "beg" for begin [at]. If you have never even looked at the Cisco IOS before, there are plenty of guides around to get you going. If you know a bit about the Cisco IOS and are looking for a good MPLS resource, hopefully this is the right place for you.

When entering configuration mode IOS always adds "Enter configuration commands, one per line. End with CNTL/Z", I have removed these lines from all output. Occasionally, due to space requirements, I will truncate GigabitEthernet to Gi in console output as well. Generally, I will remove interface up notifications, and where we use a ping to confirm reachability, I will remove the round-trip statistics as well.

2. A (very) brief history of MPLS

As far as age of routing protocols goes, MPLS is the new kid on the block. In 1994, only twenty years ago, which is recent in terms of routing, Toshiba presented a paper on Cell Switch Routers (CSR) that used label switching with ATM interfaces[2]. Two years later, Cisco released a paper on Label Switching, but this time it was not tied to ATM, which by then was experiencing a bit of a downturn. Cisco turned this over to the IETF for Open Standardization, in 1997 the IETF MPLS Working Group was formed.

It wasn't until 2001 that the first RFC for MPLS was released. RFC 3031 specified the MPLS architecture, and RFC 3032 specified its label stack encoding. AToM (Any Transport over MPLS) followed a year later, along with Layer 3 VPN in 2004 and Label Switching Multicast in 2009.

So, as you can see, the history of MPLS is pretty brief. It's still considered a new technology, but its popularity and uptake has been massive.

Historically, the reason for the popularity of MPLS was the fact that it is protocol independent, eliminating the reliance on Frame-Relay, SONET or Ethernet. MPLS neither operates (solely) at Layer 2 (data link) or Layer 3 (network) of the OSI model. Instead, I sits somewhere in between, which is why it is often referred to as a layer 2.5 protocol.

MPLS has played a significant part in the downturn in popularity of both Frame Relay and ATM, though it does share some characteristics (i.e. increased reliability and performance, traffic engineering and out-of-band control). The major similarities regarding packet handling with MPLS will be discussed shortly.

---

[2] http://hiroshi1.hongo.wide.ad.jp/hiroshi/papers/spie97.doc

3. Topology

For the first few chapters, we will be using the following topology:

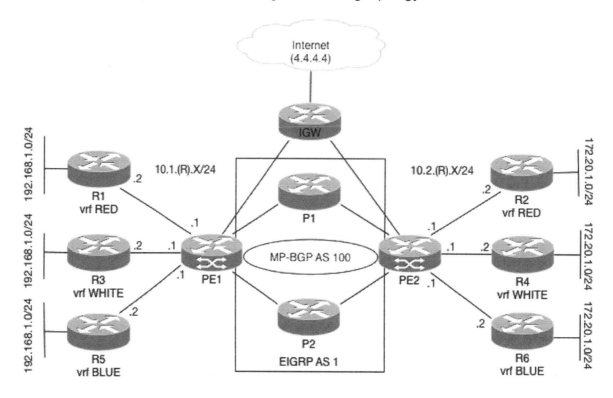

Because the majority of the CCIE focuses on MPLS VPN we will also spend most of the book looking at this. For the most part, we will be using the aforementioned topology; however we will use different topologies later on when we discuss VRF-lite and other MPLS technologies.

You are the Senior Network Engineer for "802 ISP Limited". We have three clients. These are denoted by their VRF (Red at the top, White in the middle and Blue at the bottom). The Red company on the left hand side will connect to their other office on the right hand side. The same goes for the White company (White to White) and the Blue company (Blue to Blue). Initially, each client will be advertising the same internal prefixes from each side, 192.168.1.0/24 from the left hand side and 172.20.1.0/24 on the right hand side. Both company prefixes will be advertised through the MPLS core and will need to be kept separate from other each other.

Each of the company routers connect to the MPLS providers PE routers using the following format: 10.1.R.X for the left hand side, 10.2.R.X for the right hand side. The "R" will be the company's router number, and the "X" is the number denoted on the topology. For example, Red company's R1 router will connect to PE1 using the IP addresses 10.1.1.2 on R1 and 10.1.1.1 on PE1. The White company's R3 router will connect to PE1 using the IP address 10.1.3.2 on R3 and 10.1.3.1 on PE1.

Each customer will (initially) run OSPF between itself and the PE router. The OSPF instance will be consecutive;

> OSPF 1 for RED
> OSPF 2 for WHITE
> OSPF 3 for BLUE

Each router has a loopback interface defined. For the customer routers (R1-6) these loopback interfaces are to emulate the customer networks (192.168.1.0/24 on the left hand side and 172.20.1.0/24 on the right hand side). Our biggest challenge will be to pass the customer traffic through our core without mixing their traffic up despite the use of the same address scheme.

The MPLS core routers have the following interface configurations:

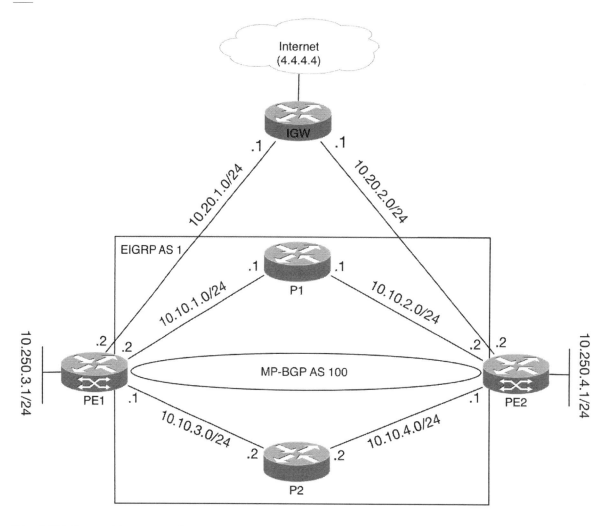

The MPLS provider network routers will be connected through EIGRP, and we will run MP-BGP between the two PE routers. These will use their loopback interfaces (10.250.3.1/24 and 10.250.4.1/24) to form the BGP peering. We also have a router named "IGW," which we will use to supply a default route to our customers for internet access.

Full color images, initial configurations, and topology files can be downloaded from:

http://l.802101.com/802books

4. The basics of MPLS

So far we have seen how MPLS came about, the technologies it is based on, and those it left by the wayside due to its high adoption rate. We have not, however, discussed what kind of issues it overcomes, which also explains why it became so popular. We will do that in this chapter.

4.1 The problem with packets

To illustrate the issues MPLS overcomes, we will start off small using static routing, with just PE1, R1, and R3 configured (as follows):

```
PE1#sh ip int bri | i up
GigabitEthernet2/0        10.1.1.1         YES manual up          up
GigabitEthernet3/0        10.1.3.1         YES manual up          up
Loopback0                 10.250.3.1       YES manual up          up
PE1#ping 10.1.1.2
Type escape sequence to abort.
Sending 5, 100-byte ICMP Echos to 10.1.1.2, timeout is 2 seconds:
.!!!!
Success rate is 80 percent (4/5)
PE1#ping 10.1.3.2
Type escape sequence to abort.
Sending 5, 100-byte ICMP Echos to 10.1.3.2, timeout is 2 seconds:
.!!!!
Success rate is 80 percent (4/5)
PE1#sh run | i route
ip source-route
ip route 192.168.1.0 255.255.255.0 10.1.1.2
ip route 192.168.1.0 255.255.255.0 10.1.3.2
PE1#

R1#sh ip int bri | i up
GigabitEthernet1/0        10.1.1.2         YES manual up          up
Loopback0                 192.168.1.1      YES manual up          up
R1#

R3#sh ip int bri | i up
GigabitEthernet1/0        10.1.3.2         YES manual up          up
Loopback0                 192.168.1.1      YES manual up          up
R3#
```

We have very basic connectivity between three routers. The loopback addresses simulate the 192.168.1.0/24 "network" that we intend to use.

Can PE1 reach the 192.168.1.0 network?

```
PE1#ping 192.168.1.1
Type escape sequence to abort.
Sending 5, 100-byte ICMP Echos to 192.168.1.1, timeout is 2 seconds:
.....
Success rate is 0 percent (0/5)
PE1#
```

No, it cannot.

We have the routes installed in our routing table as we can see here:

```
PE1#sh ip route | beg Gate
Gateway of last resort is not set

      10.0.0.0/8 is variably subnetted, 6 subnets, 2 masks
C        10.1.1.0/24 is directly connected, GigabitEthernet2/0
L        10.1.1.1/32 is directly connected, GigabitEthernet2/0
C        10.1.3.0/24 is directly connected, GigabitEthernet3/0
L        10.1.3.1/32 is directly connected, GigabitEthernet3/0
C        10.250.3.0/24 is directly connected, Loopback0
L        10.250.3.1/32 is directly connected, Loopback0
S     192.168.1.0/24 [1/0] via 10.1.3.2
                     [1/0] via 10.1.1.2
PE1#
```

But in order to reach the 192.168.1.0/24 network we must specify the source:

```
PE1#ping 192.168.1.1 so G3/0
Type escape sequence to abort.
Sending 5, 100-byte ICMP Echos to 192.168.1.1, timeout is 2 seconds:
Packet sent with a source address of 10.1.3.1
!!!!!
Success rate is 100 percent (5/5)
PE1#
```

And even then, that only fixes the issue for one interface:

```
PE1#ping 192.168.1.1 so G2/0
Type escape sequence to abort.
Sending 5, 100-byte ICMP Echos to 192.168.1.1, timeout is 2 seconds:
```

```
    Packet sent with a source address of 10.1.1.1
    .....
    Success rate is 0 percent (0/5)
    PE1#
```

In order to reach the 192.168.1.0/24 network hosted by R1, we must shut down our connection to R3:

```
    PE1(config)#int g3/0
    PE1(config-if)#shut
    PE1(config-if)#do ping 192.168.1.1
    Type escape sequence to abort.
    Sending 5, 100-byte ICMP Echos to 192.168.1.1, timeout is 2 seconds:
    !!!!!
    Success rate is 100 percent (5/5)
    PE1(config-if)#do sh ip route | beg Gate
    Gateway of last resort is not set

          10.0.0.0/8 is variably subnetted, 4 subnets, 2 masks
    C        10.1.1.0/24 is directly connected, GigabitEthernet2/0
    L        10.1.1.1/32 is directly connected, GigabitEthernet2/0
    C        10.250.3.0/24 is directly connected, Loopback0
    L        10.250.3.1/32 is directly connected, Loopback0
    S     192.168.1.0/24 [1/0] via 10.1.1.2
    PE1(config-if)#
```

And now, we can see that with just the one entry in our routing table PE1 can see the 192.168.1.0/24 network on R1. If the G3/0 interface is brought back up, PE1 can no longer get to the network on R1.

Extending this network out slightly, imagine that PE1 is connected to another router, and this router needs to access the 192.168.1.0/24 network. This router just has a default route via PE1 and leaves the routing decisions to PE1. Even if both customer networks were simultaneously available to and reachable by PE1, PE1 would have no way of differentiating packets destined for one company from packets destined for the other. How does PE1 know that the traffic sent to the 192.168.1.0/24 network should be sent to R3 and not R1? Is there something in the packet to differentiate?

We can look at the packet itself by telnetting from PE1 to the loopback:

```
    PE1#telnet 192.168.1.1 /source-interface g3/0
    Trying 192.168.1.1 ... Open


    Password required, but none set
```

```
[Connection to 192.168.1.1 closed by foreign host]
PE1#
```

Using Wireshark to capture the traffic flow, we can see the contents of the packet from the layer 2 frame through to the application layer information:

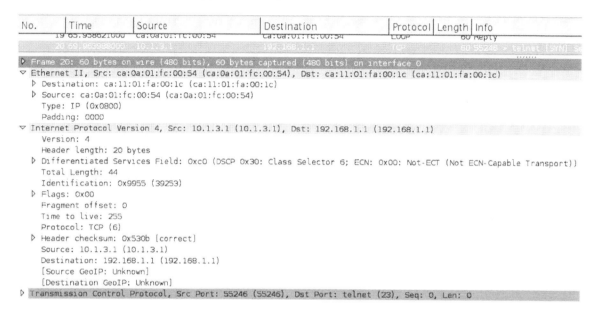

There isn't anything in the packet itself to distinguish R1 from R3, apart from the MAC address at layer 2. However, recall that the MAC address is only as good as the ARP cache. Even then, only one IP-to-MAC binding will live in the ARP cache.

Similarly, running IGPs, or even BGP, between PE1, R1 and R3 is equally unfeasible. They would still advertise the same loopback interfaces into the IGP (or BGP) and PE1 would still have no way of distinguishing traffic destined for the Red company from that destined for the White Company. There is not even any room within either of the different layers of the packet for any additional information in which we can distinguish traffic destined for R1 from that destined for R3.

Clearly, the standard packet is not well suited for this scenario.

So what alternatives are there? Well, we have two. The first is the basis for MPLS. The second is to create additional routing tables, called Virtual Routing Forwarding (VRF). VRFs are used in conjunction with MPLS, or by itself, which is called VRF-Lite. We will look at VRF-Lite a bit later. For the moment we will look at the MPLS option, which involves the assigning of labels to packets. The routers can then look at the labels to make routing decisions. The packets are therefore referred to as being label switched.

4.2 Enter label switching

We have seen that the standard packet does not contain the right information in our scenario, nor can we add the required information into it. We can however place information on top of the packet. This information is called a label. The label sits on top of the existing packet, and this is where the packet-forwarding decisions now take place, rather than the destination IP address located inside the packet.

An MPLS header, which is 32 bits in length, is prefixed to a packet. This header contains one or more labels, known as the label stack. Each label in the stack contains a 20-bit label value and a 3-bit EXP (experimental) field for QoS. The next bit is the bottom-of-stack (BOS) flag which, if set to 1, signals that the current label is the last one in the stack and that the IP header will follow. The final 8 bits are the TTL field.

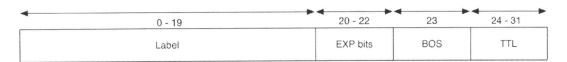

0 - 19	20 - 22	23	24 - 31
Label	EXP bits	BOS	TTL

The most labels we can have in a stack is three. We can have an LDP label, a VPN label, and a TE (Traffic engineering) label. The first label in the stack is referred to as the Top label, and the last one is called the Bottom label. As each MPLS header is 32 bits, and that we can have a maximum of three of them, it can be wise to set the MTU to a number greater than 1512 (1500 being the "standard" MTU, 32 bits equaling 4 bytes, and 3 times 4 = 12). Increasing the MTU setting is not essential, and I have not tweaked any default MTU during the writing of this book. However, should you wish to adjust the interface MTU settings, the appropriate interface command would be "mpls mtu 1512".

Labels are represented by numbers, which range from 16 to 100,000. The numbers 0 to 15 are reserved for MPLS operations, with 0 to 3 actually currently being used:

> Label 0 - IPv4 Explicit Null
> Label 1 - Router alert - This can appear anywhere in the stack apart from at the bottom of the stack. The router alert notifies the device that the packet needs to be treated separately. That is, it is not forwarded in hardware but, rather, at the software level. The router alert is removed, and the lookup is base on the next label in the stack.
> Label 2 - IPv6 Explicit Null
> Label 3 - Implicit null

Null labels control how a packet is treated as it exits the MPLS network, We will discuss this further in Chapter 6.

From a customer perspective, MPLS all happens within the service provider's equipment and network. How the customer packet moves through the provider's network is at the discretion of the service provider. It is for this reason that MPLS networks are often referred to as MPLS "clouds," which is a phrase used throughout this book.

Before we can start attaching MPLS labels to our traffic, we need to look at the different roles played by routers within an MPLS network and the requirements of MPLS.

4.3 MPLS Roles

There are a couple of basic required roles within an MPLS network, and there is a certain amount of overlap in the terminology and roles played by the routers in an MPLS network.

Label Switch Router (LSR) / Provider (P)

In the core of the network is the Label switch router (LSR). This sits at the heart of the provider network (in our case this would be P1 and P2). LSRs, as the name might suggest, switch the labels are they come in from the periphery of the MPLS network and cross the core on their way to the other side. As a packet enters the LSR, the router will use the label to determine the next hop for the packet. This sequence of next-hops forms the label-switched path (LSP). The LSR will remove the old label that has been added by the LER (or PE) router and replace that with a new label before forwarding the packet on. This action is referred to as a *swap*.

In the context of MPLS based VPN, this is also known as a Provider, or "P" router.

Label Edge Router (LER) / Provider Edge (PE)

Connecting the customer to the MPLS network are the Label Edge Routers (LER). These operate at edge of MPLS network and act as entry (ingress) and exit (egress) points. LERs add an MPLS label onto a packet coming into the MPLS network (this is known as a "*push*" or imposition) and will remove a label from an outgoing packet (or a "*pop*", or label disposition) as it exits the MPLS network and enters the customers network.

In the context of an MPLS based VPN, this is known as a Provider Edge router (or "PE").

Customer Edge Router (CE)

The customer edge router connects to the LER or PE router, this does not have any MPLS configuration on it. Customer routes are passed into the MPLS network, usually through an IGP.

4.4 MPLS Requirements

MPLS (on Cisco hardware) has a few requirements. Firstly, the routers must be running Cisco Express Forwarding (CEF) on the LER / PE routers. CEF is used to match label to prefix in order that labels may be pushed onto or popped off a packet. For more information about CEF, check out my blog entry: http://www.802101.com/2014/03/all-about-cef.html. CEF is only a requirement on Cisco routers; other vendors will have their own method. CEF is enabled by default on Cisco IOS.

The second requirement is a method to attach the labels. This comes in the form of either Tag Distribution Protocol (TDP), which is Cisco's proprietary method, or the Label Distribution Protocol (LDP). LDP is the industry standard.

The other requirements are routing protocols. Firstly, they will carry the customer prefixes across the MPLS cloud (MP-BGP if we are talking about MPLS VPN) and secondly, they will advertise and receive the customer routes via the MPLS cloud from the CE to the PE routers.

So as we have discussed so far, with MPLS, we are adding one or more labels onto the packet passed to us from the customer. We have also seen that the "standard" unicast-routing method does not allow for distinction between customer and prefix, where the prefix is used more than once. In our topology, we are dealing with the same set of prefixes at each side of the customer networks, so how do we get around this limitation?

We use the concept of VRFs (which either stand for Virtual Routing Forwarding in a purely IP based environment, or it stands for VPN Routing and Forwarding when used with MPLS). VRFs enable us to have multiple instances of a routing table. Each customer can therefore have a unique forwarding information base (FIB), which tells the router which interfaces are used to forward the packet, along with which label is to be used to identify it.

It is these labels that allow for the separation of overlapping prefixes. MPLS adds another set of numbers in front of the original NLRI (Network Layer Reachability Information), which is a fancy term for a network prefix. This set of numbers is known as the route distinguisher (RD). Usually, and in our examples, the RD is a mixture of BGP AS number and a unique customer reference. The RD is 64 bits in length, and has three fields: a 2-byte Type field, an administrator field, and a value field. Depending on the type (0, 1 or 2), the length of the final two fields can vary. For type 0, the administrator (ASN) field is 2 bytes and the value is 4 bytes. For type 1, the administrator field is a 4-byte IP address, and the value field is 2 bytes. For the final type 2, the administrator field is a 4-btye ASN field, followed by a 2-byte value field.

Examples of the different formats are:

> Type 0 – 65000:300
> Type 1 – 199.200.200.1:300
> Type 2 – 100.200:300

Where route distinguishers are used to match endpoint to a particular VPN, thus maintaining a level of uniqueness, Route Targets (RT) values can do the opposite and enable routes from one VPN to be added into another VPN, which we will look at when we cover route leaking and central services. The RT is an 8-byte field.

4.5 MPLS packet flow

In a very simplified example, a customer's packet is passed from the customer edge router (CE) to the provider edge router (PE). The PE router determines the Forwarding Equivalency Class (FEC). The FEC is set of packets that share characteristics, and are forwarded in the same way. Often, because of this, they will share the same MPLS label.

In the next step, the packet has an MPLS header pushed onto it. It is this header that is read throughout the Label Switching Path (LSP), which is the path the packet will take across the MPLS cloud. The FECs next hop will be the exit point out of the MPLS cloud (such as the destined customer edge router on the other side of the MPLS cloud). CEF uses the FIB to build the Label Forwarding Information Base (LFIB), which is a table of label-to-FEC associations. This table is advertised along the LSP. The LSR (or P) routers store labels in the LIB.

Once the packet has moved across the MPLS cloud, the MPLS header is "popped" off as it exits the MPLS network and into the customer's network.

Hopefully, you should have a good overview of how packets flow within an MPLS network and the requirements. In the next chapter, we will put this newfound information to practice and create an MPLS VPN network with our three different customers.

5. Initial MPLS VPN configuration

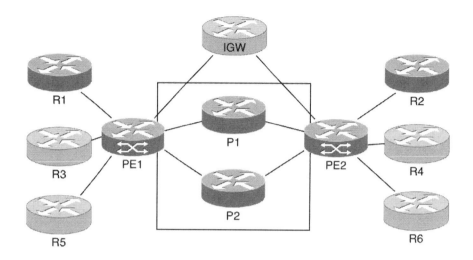

Now that we have got the majority of the discussion of MPLS roles and requirements out of the way, we can start to configure our network.

There are several steps to creating and MPLS cloud, and I have broken them down into key goals for this chapter. These goals are:

1: Create the IGP within our MPLS cloud
2: Form LDP adjacencies within our MPLS cloud
3: Create the MP-BGP link between PE1 and PE2
4: Create our VRFs (Red initially, followed by White and Blue)
5: Assign our VRFs to the respective interfaces and add them into our BGP process
6: Create the IGP between the customer and provider routers
7: Redistribute between the IGPs created in step 6 and our MP-BGP process

As we go through the chapter, we will cover the key components, which include the creation of basic IGPs, BGP address-families, VRFs, route-distinguishers, route targets, and redistribution.

We start by removing our static routes on PE1:

```
PE1#conf t
PE1(config)#no ip route 192.168.1.0 255.255.255.0 10.1.1.2
PE1(config)#no ip route 192.168.1.0 255.255.255.0 10.1.3.2
```

The interfaces of the routers in our cloud have had their IP addresses assigned, and we have reachability. We can see that P1 can reach PE1 and PE2:

```
P1#sh ip int bri | i up
Interface              IP-Address      OK? Method Status                Protocol
GigabitEthernet1/0     10.10.1.1       YES manual up                    up
GigabitEthernet2/0     10.10.2.1       YES manual up                    up
Loopback0              10.250.1.1      YES manual up                    up
P1#ping 10.10.1.2
Type escape sequence to abort.
Sending 5, 100-byte ICMP Echos to 10.10.1.2, timeout is 2 seconds:
.!!!!
Success rate is 80 percent (4/5)
P1#ping 10.10.2.2
Type escape sequence to abort.
Sending 5, 100-byte ICMP Echos to 10.10.2.2, timeout is 2 seconds:
.!!!!
Success rate is 80 percent (4/5)
P1#
```

P2 can also reach PE1 and PE2:

```
P2#sh ip int bri | i up
Interface              IP-Address      OK? Method Status                Protocol
GigabitEthernet1/0     10.10.3.2       YES manual up                    up
GigabitEthernet2/0     10.10.4.2       YES manual up                    up
Loopback0              10.250.2.1      YES manual up                    up
P2#ping 10.10.3.1
Type escape sequence to abort.
Sending 5, 100-byte ICMP Echos to 10.10.3.1, timeout is 2 seconds:
.!!!!
Success rate is 80 percent (4/5)
P2#ping 10.10.4.1
Type escape sequence to abort.
Sending 5, 100-byte ICMP Echos to 10.10.4.1, timeout is 2 seconds:
.!!!!
Success rate is 80 percent (4/5)
P2#
```

As per the requirements of MPLS, we should make sure that CEF is enabled on all our routers. We can issue "sh run | i cef" to verify CEF is enabled. If needed, we will issue the global command "ip cef" to globally enable CEF. CEF is enabled by default, but it is wise to check that it is enabled (especially in an exam scenario):

```
P1#sh run | i cef
ip cef
no ipv6 cef
P1#
```

With our checks done we can start with our first goal.

Goal 1: Creating the MPLS cloud IGP

We need to create our MPLS provider IGP, and, for this, we will be using EIGRP. We will want our LDP adjacencies to bind to the local loopback address, so this must therefore be advertised into the IGP. Any IGP will do; so we could have just as easily used OSPF, ISIS, or even RIP.

The router configurations are below starting with our P routers:

```
P1#conf t
P1(config)#router eigrp 1
P1(config-router)#network 10.10.1.0 0.0.0.255
P1(config-router)#network 10.10.2.0 0.0.0.255
P1(config-router)#network 10.250.1.0 0.0.0.255
P1(config-router)#

P2#conf t
P2(config)#router eigrp 1
P2(config-router)#network 10.10.3.0 0.0.0.255
P2(config-router)#network 10.10.4.0 0.0.0.255
P2(config-router)#network 10.250.2.0 0.0.0.255
P2(config-router)#
```

Once we move on to configuring EIGRP on our PE routers, we can start to see the adjacencies form:

```
PE1(config)#router eigrp 1
PE1(config-router)#network 10.10.1.0 0.0.0.255
PE1(config-router)#
*Mar 29 12:23:39.091: %DUAL-5-NBRCHANGE: EIGRP-IPv4 1: Neighbor
10.10.1.1 (GigabitEthernet1/0) is up: new adjacency
PE1(config-router)#network 10.10.3.0 0.0.0.255
PE1(config-router)#
*Mar 29 12:23:52.315: %DUAL-5-NBRCHANGE: EIGRP-IPv4 1: Neighbor
10.10.3.2 (GigabitEthernet5/0) is up: new adjacency
PE1(config-router)#network 10.250.3.0 0.0.0.255
PE1(config-router)#
```

```
PE2(config)#router eigrp 1
PE2(config-router)#network 10.10.2.0 0.0.0.255
*Mar 29 12:27:36.171: %DUAL-5-NBRCHANGE: EIGRP-IPv4 1: Neighbor
10.10.2.1 (GigabitEthernet1/0) is up: new adjacency
PE2(config-router)#network 10.10.4.0 0.0.0.255
PE2(config-router)#
*Mar 29 12:27:43.959: %DUAL-5-NBRCHANGE: EIGRP-IPv4 1: Neighbor
10.10.4.2 (GigabitEthernet5/0) is up: new adjacency
PE2(config-router)#network 10.250.4.0 0.0.0.255
PE2(config-router)#
```

Now that we have an IGP running within our provider network, we can start on prepping our routers for MPLS. We start this by forming label distribution adjacencies.

Goal 2: LDP adjacencies

With our IGP in place, which is required by LDP (Label Distribution Protocol), we move on to enable MPLS on the interfaces. We will only enable MPLS on the internal cloud facing interfaces, not the PE router to customer interfaces. We are using LDP because this is the industry standard. The alternative to LDP is TDP (Tag Distribution Protocol), which is the Cisco proprietary version. Without specifying a label protocol to use the system will default to LDP. Both LDP and TDP can be specified on either a global or interface level. Therefore, we could make the global default to be TDP, whilst specifying LDP for the specific interfaces. If we were to bring another interface into the MPLS configuration and not specify LDP on the interface, it would use our new system default of TDP. The command we would use is "mpls label protocol <ldp|tdp>":

```
Router(config)#mpls label protocol ?
  ldp  Use LDP (default)
  tdp  Use TDP
```

At an interface level, we can actually have both protocols running:

```
Router(config)#int g1/0
Router(config-if)#mpls label protocol ?
  both Use LDP or TDP (Adapt to peer on multiaccess interface)
  ldp  Use LDP (default)
  tdp  Use TDP

Router(config-if)#mpls label protocol
```

We shall use LDP. Therefore, we will not specify anything and will let the system default to LDP. We use the interface command "mpls ip" to enable MPLS first on the P routers and next on the PE routers, at which point we can start to see LDP seeing the other routers:

```
P1(config-router)#int g1/0
P1(config-if)#mpls ip
P1(config-if)#int g2/0
P1(config-if)#mpls ip
P1(config-if)#

P2(config-router)#int g1/0
P2(config-if)#mpls ip
P2(config-if)#int g2/0
P2(config-if)#mpls ip
P2(config-if)#

PE1(config-router)#int g1/0
PE1(config-if)#mpls ip
*Mar 29 12:34:36: %LDP-5-NBRCHG: LDP Neighbor 10.250.1.1:0 (1) is UP
PE1(config-if)#int g5/0
PE1(config-if)#mpls ip
PE1(config-if)#
*Mar 29 12:34:41: %LDP-5-NBRCHG: LDP Neighbor 10.250.2.1:0 (2) is UP
PE1(config-if)#

PE2(config-router)#int g1/0
PE2(config-if)#mpls ip
*Mar 29 12:35:01: %LDP-5-NBRCHG: LDP Neighbor 10.250.1.1:0 (1) is UP
PE2(config-if)#int g5/0
PE2(config-if)#mpls ip
PE2(config-if)#
*Mar 29 12:35:06: %LDP-5-NBRCHG: LDP Neighbor 10.250.2.1:0 (2) is UP
PE2(config-if)#
```

Now, we can see that they have formed LDP neighbor relationships between each other. We can confirm this using the command "sh mpls ldp neighbor":

```
P1#sh mpls ldp neigh
    Peer LDP Ident: 10.250.3.1:0; Local LDP Ident 10.250.1.1:0
    TCP connection: 10.250.3.1.31790 - 10.250.1.1.646
    State: Oper; Msgs sent/rcvd: 14/16; Downstream
    Up time: 00:02:42
    LDP discovery sources:
      GigabitEthernet1/0, Src IP addr: 10.10.1.2
        Addresses bound to peer LDP Ident:
          10.10.1.2       10.1.1.1        10.1.3.1        10.10.3.1
```

```
            10.250.3.1
      Peer LDP Ident: 10.250.4.1:0; Local LDP Ident 10.250.1.1:0
        TCP connection: 10.250.4.1.39959 - 10.250.1.1.646
        State: Oper; Msgs sent/rcvd: 13/15; Downstream
        Up time: 00:02:17
        LDP discovery sources:
          GigabitEthernet2/0, Src IP addr: 10.10.2.2
              Addresses bound to peer LDP Ident:
                10.10.2.2       10.2.2.1        10.2.4.1        10.10.4.1
                10.250.4.1
   P1#

   P2#sh mpls ldp neigh
        Peer LDP Ident: 10.250.3.1:0; Local LDP Ident 10.250.2.1:0
        TCP connection: 10.250.3.1.45831 - 10.250.2.1.646
        State: Oper; Msgs sent/rcvd: 14/16; Downstream
        Up time: 00:03:06
        LDP discovery sources:
          GigabitEthernet1/0, Src IP addr: 10.10.3.1
              Addresses bound to peer LDP Ident:
                10.10.1.2       10.1.1.1        10.1.3.1        10.10.3.1
                10.250.3.1
        Peer LDP Ident: 10.250.4.1:0; Local LDP Ident 10.250.2.1:0
        TCP connection: 10.250.4.1.39797 - 10.250.2.1.646
        State: Oper; Msgs sent/rcvd: 13/16; Downstream
        Up time: 00:02:40
        LDP discovery sources:
          GigabitEthernet2/0, Src IP addr: 10.10.4.1
              Addresses bound to peer LDP Ident:
                10.10.2.2       10.2.2.1        10.2.4.1        10.10.4.1
                10.250.4.1
   P2#
```

As you can see, the MPLS routers are using the loopback interface addresses as their LDP router ID. When the router chooses the LDP identifier, it will first examine all the IP addresses in operation. If there is a loopback interface, the router will use this IP address. If there is more than one loopback interface, it will use the highest loopback interface IP address as its LDP identifier. If the router does not have any loopback interfaces, the router will pick the largest IP address from any physical interface.

We could change this if we wanted to and assign our own ID using the command "mpls ldp router-id GigabitEthernet 1/0 force" which would make the router use the IP address configured on the specified interface. If we do not use the force keyword, we would need to wait for an event that would cause the router to select a router-id, such as when the interface is shut down and brought back up again, or following a reboot. If the specified interface is operational, the force keyword will cause the router to tear down existing LDP connections and release all bindings, which will cause an interruption to MPLS activity on that router. If the interface specified in the "mpls ldp router-id" command is not operational, the router will only transition to using the new IP address when the interface is brought up.

Using the loopback interface makes sense, because they are pretty much guaranteed to be always accessible from our PE's, as they are advertised through the IGP.

Goal 3: Creating the MP-BGP process

Between PE1 and PE2 we have an MP-BGP connection. Because of the EIGRP process running within our MPLS cloud, we have connectivity between the two PE routers. We can confirm this by pinging the loopback of PE2 from PE1's loopback interface:

```
PE1#ping 10.250.4.1 so 10.250.3.1
Type escape sequence to abort.
Sending 5, 100-byte ICMP Echos to 10.250.4.1, timeout is 2 seconds:
Packet sent with a source address of 10.250.3.1
!!!!!
Success rate is 100 percent (5/5)
PE1#
```

Our BGP setup will not be very complex. In fact, the only major addition for the MPLS VPN is to add in the vpnv4 address family identifier (AFI) statements, but these are very straightforward. We will be using ASN 100, and the peer will form between the loopback addresses, which we have just confirmed reachability between.

```
PE1(config)#router bgp 100
PE1(config-router)#neighbor 10.250.4.1 remote-as 100
PE1(config-router)#neighbor 10.250.4.1 update-source lo0
PE1(config-router)#
*Mar 29 12:51:13.891: %BGP-5-ADJCHANGE: neighbor 10.250.4.1 Up
PE1(config-router)#
*Mar 29 12:51:44.939: %BGP-5-ADJCHANGE: neighbor 10.250.4.1 Down Peer closed the session
*Mar 29 12:51:44.939: %BGP_SESSION-5-ADJCHANGE: neighbor 10.250.4.1 IPv4 Unicast topology base removed from session  Peer closed the session
PE1(config-router)#
*Mar 29 12:51:46.831: %BGP-5-ADJCHANGE: neighbor 10.250.4.1 Up
```

We will form an adjacency at this stage, but the prefixes and label information needs to be carried through VPN. Therefore we create the AFI for vpnv4, and assign our neighbor to it:

```
PE1(config-router)#address-family vpnv4
```

```
PE1(config-router-af)#neigh 10.250.4.1 activate
PE1(config-router-af)#
*Mar 29 12:52:00.059: %BGP-5-ADJCHANGE: neighbor 10.250.4.1 Down
Capability changed
*Mar 29 12:52:00.063: %BGP_SESSION-5-ADJCHANGE: neighbor 10.250.4.1
IPv4 Unicast topology base removed from session  Capability changed
*Mar 29 12:52:00.935: %BGP-5-ADJCHANGE: neighbor 10.250.4.1 Up
PE1(config-router-af)#

PE2(config)#router bgp 100
PE2(config-router)#neigh 10.250.3.1 remote-as 100
*Mar 29 12:51:13.983: %BGP-5-ADJCHANGE: neighbor 10.250.3.1 Up
PE2(config-router)#neigh 10.250.3.1 update-source lo0
PE2(config-router)#address-family vpnv4
PE2(config-router-af)#neigh 10.250.3.1 activate
PE2(config-router-af)#
*Mar 29 12:51:45.011: %BGP-5-ADJCHANGE: neighbor 10.250.3.1 Down
Capability changed
*Mar 29 12:51:45.011: %BGP_SESSION-5-ADJCHANGE: neighbor 10.250.3.1
IPv4 Unicast topology base removed from session  Capability changed
PE2(config-router-af)#
*Mar 29 12:51:46.719: %BGP_SESSION-5-ADJCHANGE: neighbor 10.250.3.1
VPNv4 Unicast topology base removed from session  Capability changed
*Mar 29 12:51:46.723: %BGP-5-ADJCHANGE: neighbor 10.250.3.1 Up
PE2(config-router-af)#
*Mar 29 12:52:00.471: %BGP-5-ADJCHANGE: neighbor 10.250.3.1 Down Peer
closed the session
*Mar 29 12:52:00.475: %BGP_SESSION-5-ADJCHANGE: neighbor 10.250.3.1
IPv4 Unicast topology base removed from session  Peer closed the
session
*Mar 29 12:52:01.219: %BGP-5-ADJCHANGE: neighbor 10.250.3.1 Up
PE2(config-router-af)#
```

If we look at our BGP configuration in the running config of PE1 we can see that it has added an extra line:

```
PE1#sh run | section bgp
router bgp 100
 bgp log-neighbor-changes
 neighbor 10.250.4.1 remote-as 100
 neighbor 10.250.4.1 update-source Loopback0
 !
 address-family vpnv4
  neighbor 10.250.4.1 activate
  neighbor 10.250.4.1 send-community extended
 exit-address-family
PE1#
```

PE2 also shows this extra line (send-community extended), which is required by MPLS to carry the Route Target information, as we will see shortly.

Because BGP is multi protocol, in that it can carry IPv4 and IPv6 unicast, IPv4 and IPv6 multicast, VPNv4 and CLNP (Connectionless-mode Network Protocol), we use address families in order to create a form of separation. Neighbors are defined under a particular address family, and it is this grouping of neighbor to address family that allows us to exchange the routes we need to. A simplified example of this would be to have a dual-stack router running IPv4 and IPv6. Without using address families, a neighbor would receive both the IPv4 and IPv6 routes, even though it may only want the IPv4 routes. In regard to MPLS VPNs, we use the address family vpnv4 in order to be able to pass our customer traffic.

We can check that our MP-BGP adjacency is running correctly using the following command:

```
PE1#sh bgp vpnv4 unicast all summary
BGP router identifier 10.250.3.1, local AS number 100
BGP table version is 1, main routing table version 1

Neighbor     V   AS MsgRcvd MsgSent TblVer InQ OutQ Up/Down  Sta/PfxRcd
10.250.4.1   4  100       8       8      1   0    0 00:03:01          0
PE1#
```

With our MPLS cloud connectivity set up, we can concentrate on the individual routing requirements for the individual MPLS VPNs.

Goal 4: Creating VRFs, RDs and RTs

With our IGP and BGP base in place, the next step is to create the VRFs that our MPLS VPNs will use. We will keep it small for the moment, concentrating on just the Red Company. We first create the VRF "RED", then we will specify the route-distinguisher and the route-target, each of which we will discuss next.

VRFs allow routes to be stored on a per CE (Customer Edge) basis. Each VRF has its own routing table, which means that routes can be stored within different VRFs without worrying whether they overlap or not.

Route Distinguishers (RD) allow the PE to advertise routes, even if they do overlap. We are going to use the format ASN:OSPF process, therefore the RD for VRF RED will be 100:1, VRF WHITE will be 100:2 and BLUE will be 100:3.

Route Targets (RT) specify which routes are added to each VRF, which can be on a one-to-one basis, such as VRF RED to VRF RED. We can also allow for multiple connectivity, such as VRF RED having access to VRF WHITE. RTs are advertised as a BGP extended community path attribute (hence the addition of "send community-extended" when we created our vpnv4 address family in the previous goal). The extended community PA can contain one or more RT values. If you want more information on BGP communities, they are explained in the first volume of this series; BGP for Cisco Networks. RT values follow the same format as the RD. Yet, whilst a route prefix can only have one RD, the same prefix can have more than one RT assigned to it. This will be explained in the chapter 9 when we look at route leakage.

To create a VRF, we begin by using the command "ip vrf <VRF name>", followed by specifying the RD and RT:

```
PE1#conf t
PE1(config)#ip vrf RED
PE1(config-vrf)#rd 100:1
PE1(config-vrf)#route-target 100:1
```

The route-target command actually takes options; export, import or both:

```
PE2#conf t
PE2(config)#ip vrf RED
PE2(config-vrf)#rd 100:1
PE2(config-vrf)#route-target ?
  ASN:nn or IP-address:nn  Target VPN Extended Community
  both                     Both import and export Target-VPN
community
  export                   Export Target-VPN community
  import                   Import Target-VPN community

PE2(config-vrf)#route-target
```

On PE1, we did not specify any options; on PE2, we will specify both import and export:

```
PE2#conf t
PE2(config)#ip vrf RED
PE2(config-vrf)#rd 100:1
PE2(config-vrf)#route-target ?
  ASN:nn or IP-address:nn  Target VPN Extended Community
  both                     Both import and export Target-VPN
community
  export                   Export Target-VPN community
```

```
    import                        Import Target-VPN community
PE2(config-vrf)#route-target export 100:1
PE2(config-vrf)#route-target import 100:1
PE2(config-vrf)#
```

How does the end result compare on our routers?

```
PE1(config-vrf)#do sh run | beg vrf
ip vrf RED
 rd 100:1
 route-target export 100:1
 route-target import 100:1
!
PE2(config-vrf)#do sh run | beg vrf
ip vrf RED
 rd 100:1
 route-target export 100:1
 route-target import 100:1
!
```

They actually look the same, as the default option, i.e., not specifying an option, is to both import AND export the Target-VPN community. The key with route-targets is that each VRF must import and export at least one RT, which does explain why this is the default behavior. It is best to think about the action (import or export) from the viewpoint of the VRF. To export means that the data flows out of the VRF into BGP, and to import means that the data flows into the VRF from BGP.

Next we must instruct our router which interface is associated with which VRF:

```
PE1#conf t
PE1(config)#int g2/0
PE1(config-if)#ip vrf forwarding RED
% Interface GigabitEthernet2/0 IPv4 disabled and address(es) removed due to enabling VRF RED
PE1(config-if)#ip address 10.1.1.1 255.255.255.0
PE1(config-if)#exit
PE1(config)#exit
```

The important thing to note here is that once we tell the interface that it will be forwarding for a particular VRF, the router will automatically remove the IP address. Therefore, we must add it back.

We do the same on PE2:

```
PE2#conf t
PE2(config)#int g2/0
PE2(config-if)#ip vrf forwarding RED
% Interface GigabitEthernet2/0 IPv4 disabled and address(es) removed
due to enabling VRF RED
PE2(config-if)#ip add 10.2.2.1 255.255.255.0
PE2(config-if)#exit
PE2(config)#exit
```

We can check that our interfaces are forwarding the correct VRF using the command "sh ip vrf interfaces":

```
PE1#sh ip vrf interfaces
Interface              IP-Address         VRF           Protocol
Gi2/0                  10.1.1.1           RED           up
PE1#

PE2#sh ip vrf interfaces
Interface              IP-Address         VRF           Protocol
Gi2/0                  10.2.2.1           RED           up
PE2#
```

Even though we have created our VRF, we need to make our BGP process aware of it.

Goal 5: Adding our VRFs to BGP

We must next add our newly created VRF to our existing BGP process. To do this we create a new IPv4 address-family within BGP for our VRF:

```
PE1(config)#router bgp 100
PE1(config-router)#address-family ipv4 vrf RED
PE1(config-router-af)#no synchronization

PE2(config)#router bgp 100
PE2(config-router)#address-family ipv4 vrf RED
PE2(config-router-af)#no synchronization
```

We are nearly finished. We just need to get our CE and PE routers talking and start to pass this data across our MP-BGP.

Goal 6: Customer to Provider IGP

In order for our customer routers to advertise their networks to the MPLS cloud, we need to create an IGP between R1 and PE1 and also between R2 and PE2. We are using a simple OSPF design. Note that there is no MPLS or VRF information added to R1 or R2 (which are our customer edge or CE routers):

```
R1#conf t
R1(config)#int g1/0
R1(config-if)#ip ospf 1 area 0
R1(config-if)#
*Mar 29 13:40:03.194: %OSPF-5-ADJCHG: Process 1, Nbr 10.250.3.1 on
GigabitEthernet1/0 from LOADING to FULL, Loading Done

PE1(config)#router ospf 1 vrf RED
PE1(config-router)#router-id 10.250.3.1
PE1(config-router)#interface g2/0
PE1(config-if)#ip ospf 1 area 0
PE1(config-if)#
*Mar 29 13:51:44.203: %OSPF-5-ADJCHG: Process 1, Nbr 192.168.1.1 on
GigabitEthernet2/0 from LOADING to FULL, Loading Done
PE1(config-if)#
```

On the provider edge routers, we create the OSPF process within the VRF and assign our interfaces to the OSPF area (and therefore to the VRF).

```
R2#conf t
R2(config)#int g1/0
```

```
R2(config-if)#ip ospf 1 area 0
R2(config-if)#
*Mar 29 13:54:01.194: %OSPF-5-ADJCHG: Process 1, Nbr 10.250.4.1 on
GigabitEthernet1/0 from LOADING to FULL, Loading Done

PE2(config)#router ospf 1 vrf RED
PE2(config-router)#router-id 10.250.4.1
PE2(config-router)#interface g2/0
PE2(config-if)#ip ospf 1 area 0
PE2(config-if)#
*Mar 29 13:54:01.375: %OSPF-5-ADJCHG: Process 1, Nbr 10.2.2.2 on
GigabitEthernet2/0 from LOADING to FULL, Loading Done
PE2(config-if)#
```

In order to achieve what we are setting out to do (access the 192.168.1.0/24 and 172.20.1.0/24 networks across our MPLS cloud), we must advertise the loopback interfaces of R1 and R2. As per RFC 2328 (OSPF v2), loopback interfaces are considered to be host routes and, as such, are advertised as a /32 subnet. We must, therefore, specify that the loopback is of a point-to-point type in order to get the correct subnet advertised.

```
R1(config-if)#int lo0
R1(config-if)#ip ospf 1 area 0
R1(config-if)#ip ospf network point-to-point

R2(config-if)#int lo0
R2(config-if)#ip ospf 1 area 0
R2(config-if)#ip ospf network point-to-point
```

Now that OSPF is talking between the CE routers and the PE routers, the last step is to get the routes from OSPF into BGP and the routes from BGP into OSPF.

Goal 7: Redistribution between MP-BGP and Customer network

We have one last step to take before we have completed our first MPLS VPN and that is to set up some redistribution between our protocols. To do this we will redistribute OSPF into BGP and BGP into OSPF.

```
PE1#conf t
PE1(config)#router bgp 100
PE1(config-router)#address-family ipv4 vrf RED
PE1(config-router-af)#redistribute ospf 1
```

```
PE1(config-router-af)#

PE2#conf t
PE2(config)#router bgp 100
PE2(config-router)#address-family ipv4 vrf RED
PE2(config-router-af)#redistribute ospf 1
PE2(config-router-af)#

PE1(config-router-af)#router ospf 1
PE1(config-router)#redistribute bgp 100 subnets
PE1(config-router)#

PE2(config-router-af)#router ospf 1
PE2(config-router)#redistribute bgp 100 subnets
PE2(config-router)#
```

Confirming MPLS VPN connectivity

Now that all of our goals have been reached, we need to confirm that we have visibility and reachability. We can check the routing tables on R1 and R2, and we should be able to see the loopback networks from the other side:

```
R1#sh ip route | beg Gate
Gateway of last resort is not set

         10.0.0.0/8 is variably subnetted, 3 subnets, 2 masks
C           10.1.1.0/24 is directly connected, GigabitEthernet1/0
L           10.1.1.2/32 is directly connected, GigabitEthernet1/0
O IA        10.2.2.0/24 [110/2] via 10.1.1.1, 00:00:34, Gi1/0
         172.20.0.0/24 is subnetted, 1 subnets
O IA        172.20.1.0 [110/3] via 10.1.1.1, 00:00:34, Gi1/0
         192.168.1.0/24 is variably subnetted, 2 subnets, 2 masks
C           192.168.1.0/24 is directly connected, Loopback0
L           192.168.1.1/32 is directly connected, Loopback0
R1#

R2#sh ip route | beg Gate
Gateway of last resort is not set

         10.0.0.0/8 is variably subnetted, 3 subnets, 2 masks
O IA        10.1.1.0/24 [110/2] via 10.2.2.1, 00:01:09, Gi1/0
C           10.2.2.0/24 is directly connected, GigabitEthernet1/0
L           10.2.2.2/32 is directly connected, GigabitEthernet1/0
         172.20.0.0/16 is variably subnetted, 2 subnets, 2 masks
C           172.20.1.0/24 is directly connected, Loopback0
L           172.20.1.1/32 is directly connected, Loopback0
```

```
O IA    192.168.1.0/24 [110/3] via 10.2.2.1, 00:01:09, Gi1/0
R2#
```

With visibility confirmed, we can check reachability by pinging R2's loopback interface from R1:

```
R1#ping 172.20.1.1
Type escape sequence to abort.
Sending 5, 100-byte ICMP Echos to 172.20.1.1, timeout is 2 seconds:
!!!!!
Success rate is 100 percent (5/5)
R1#
```

The beauty of MPLS is that, unless we start digging, all the action happens behind the scenes. We can capture (using Wireshark) a telnet conversation between R1 and R2. If we capture either on the cable between R1 and PE1, or between PE2 and R2, we do not see any new information. Everything looks the same as it did in the Wireshark output in chapter 4. However, if we sniff the packets within the MPLS cloud, we get to see the relevant information:

```
15 11.980079000    10.1.1.2              172.20.1.1              TCP    68 30952 > telnet
▷ Frame 15: 68 bytes on wire (544 bits), 68 bytes captured (544 bits) on interface 0
▽ Ethernet II, Src: ca:1a:0d:de:00:1c (ca:1a:0d:de:00:1c), Dst: ca:1c:0d:de:00:1c (ca:1c:0d:de:00:1c)
  ▷ Destination: ca:1c:0d:de:00:1c (ca:1c:0d:de:00:1c)
  ▷ Source: ca:1a:0d:de:00:1c (ca:1a:0d:de:00:1c)
    Type: MPLS label switched packet (0x8847)
▽ MultiProtocol Label Switching Header, Label: 17, Exp: 6, S: 0, TTL: 254
    0000 0000 0000 0001 0001 .... .... .... = MPLS Label: 17
    .... .... .... .... .... 110. .... .... = MPLS Experimental Bits: 6
    .... .... .... .... .... ...0 .... .... = MPLS Bottom Of Label Stack: 0
    .... .... .... .... .... .... 1111 1110 = MPLS TTL: 254
▽ MultiProtocol Label Switching Header, Label: 22, Exp: 6, S: 1, TTL: 254
    0000 0000 0000 0001 0110 .... .... .... = MPLS Label: 22
    .... .... .... .... .... 110. .... .... = MPLS Experimental Bits: 6
    .... .... .... .... .... ...1 .... .... = MPLS Bottom Of Label Stack: 1
    .... .... .... .... .... .... 1111 1110 = MPLS TTL: 254
▷ Internet Protocol Version 4, Src: 10.1.1.2 (10.1.1.2), Dst: 172.20.1.1 (172.20.1.1)
▷ Transmission Control Protocol, Src Port: 30952 (30952), Dst Port: telnet (23), Seq: 0, Len: 0
▷
```

Inserted nicely between the layer 2 and layer 3 is the MPLS header. It is for this reason that an MPLS header is sometimes referred to as a "shim".

In a graphical format, the packet from R1 would look like this:

Ethernet Header	IP Header	Data

When the packet leaves PE1, it looks like this:

Ethernet Header	IP Header	MPLS Label	MPLS VPN Label	Data

We can see from packet capture the header that as the packet arrives in PE1 it has label 17 inserted into the header, and when the packet reaches PE2 it has label 22 inserted. Label 22 is the last label in the stack, and we know this because the MPLS Bottom Of Label Stack flag is set to 1.

If we do a traceroute, we can see that we have some extra information:

```
R1#traceroute 172.20.1.1
Type escape sequence to abort.
Tracing the route to 172.20.1.1
VRF info: (vrf in name/id, vrf out name/id)
  1 10.1.1.1 68 msec 16 msec 24 msec
  2 10.10.1.1 [MPLS: Labels 17/22 Exp 0] 724 msec 96 msec 96 msec
  3 10.2.2.1 [MPLS: Label 22 Exp 0] 76 msec 64 msec 84 msec
  4 10.2.2.2 96 msec 92 msec *
R1#
```

We can also interrogate BGP and see more information about the routes and how they are handled:

```
PE1#sh ip bgp vpnv4 vrf RED 192.168.1.0/24
BGP routing table entry for 100:1:192.168.1.0/24, version 3
Paths: (1 available, best #1, table RED)
  Advertised to update-groups:
     1
  Local
    10.1.1.2 from 0.0.0.0 (10.250.3.1)
      Origin incomplete, metric 2, localpref 100, weight 32768,
valid, sourced, best
      Extended Community: RT:100:1 OSPF DOMAIN
ID:0x0005:0x000000010200
        OSPF RT:0.0.0.0:2:0 OSPF ROUTER ID:10.250.3.1:0
      mpls labels in/out 22/nolabel
PE1#

PE2#sh ip bgp vpnv4 vrf RED 192.168.1.0/24
BGP routing table entry for 100:1:192.168.1.0/24, version 11
Paths: (1 available, best #1, table RED)
```

```
    Not advertised to any peer
    Local
      10.250.3.1 (metric 131072) from 10.250.3.1 (10.250.3.1)
        Origin incomplete, metric 2, localpref 100, valid, internal,
best
        Extended Community: RT:100:1 OSPF DOMAIN
ID:0x0005:0x000000010200
          OSPF RT:0.0.0.0:2:0 OSPF ROUTER ID:10.250.3.1:0
        mpls labels in/out nolabel/22
    PE2#
```

Here on PE1, we can see that as traffic comes in to the 192.168.1.0/24 network (from PE1 to R1) it will be unlabeled. Traffic going out from that network (into the MPLS cloud) will have the label 22 attached. On PE2, we can see that traffic going to the 192.168.1.0/24 network from PE1 will have label 22 attached, but traffic exiting PE2 from that same network (towards R2) will have the label removed. We can see the same occurring with the 172.20.1.0/24 network.

```
    PE2#sh ip bgp vpnv4 vrf RED 172.20.1.0/24
    BGP routing table entry for 100:1:172.20.1.0/24, version 4
    Paths: (1 available, best #1, table RED)
      Advertised to update-groups:
         2
      Local
        10.2.2.2 from 0.0.0.0 (10.250.4.1)
          Origin incomplete, metric 2, localpref 100, weight 32768,
valid, sourced, best
          Extended Community: RT:100:1 OSPF DOMAIN
ID:0x0005:0x000000010200
            OSPF RT:0.0.0.0:2:0 OSPF ROUTER ID:10.250.4.1:0
          mpls labels in/out 22/nolabel
    PE2#

    PE1#sh ip bgp vpnv4 vrf RED 172.20.1.0/24
    BGP routing table entry for 100:1:172.20.1.0/24, version 7
    Paths: (1 available, best #1, table RED)
      Not advertised to any peer
      Local
        10.250.4.1 (metric 131072) from 10.250.4.1 (10.250.4.1)
          Origin incomplete, metric 2, localpref 100, valid, internal,
best
          Extended Community: RT:100:1 OSPF DOMAIN
ID:0x0005:0x000000010200
            OSPF RT:0.0.0.0:2:0 OSPF ROUTER ID:10.250.4.1:0
          mpls labels in/out nolabel/22
    PE1#
```

Addtional VRFs

Now that we have VRF RED, working let's add the other two VRFs.

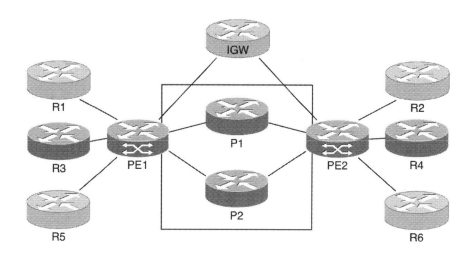

VRF WHITE

We confirm that R3 and R4 have the correct interfaces up and IP addresses assigned:

```
R3#sh ip int bri | i up
Interface              IP-Address       OK? Method Status  Protocol
GigabitEthernet1/0     10.1.3.2         YES NVRAM  up      up
Loopback0              192.168.1.1      YES NVRAM  up      up
R3#

R4#sh ip int bri | i up
Interface              IP-Address       OK? Method Status  Protocol
GigabitEthernet1/0     10.2.4.2         YES manual up      up
Loopback0              172.20.1.1       YES manual up      up
R4#
```

Because we have the major components of our MPLS cloud already in place, we can skip the first couple of steps and head straight to goal 4: creating our VRFs:

```
PE1#conf t
PE1(config)#ip vrf WHITE
```

```
PE1(config-vrf)#rd 100:2
PE1(config-vrf)#route-target 100:2
PE1(config-vrf)#exit
PE1(config)#int g3/0
PE1(config-if)#ip vrf forwarding WHITE
% Interface GigabitEthernet3/0 IPv4 disabled and address(es) removed
due to enabling VRF WHITE
PE1(config-if)#ip address 10.1.3.1 255.255.255.0
```

We can confirm that we are all set again using the command "sh ip vrf interfaces":

```
PE1(config-if)#do sh ip vrf interfaces
Interface              IP-Address      VRF            Protocol
Gi2/0                  10.1.1.1        RED            up
Gi3/0                  10.1.3.1        WHITE          up
```

We then make the BGP process aware of the new vrf:

```
PE1(config-if)#router bgp 100
PE1(config-router)#address-family ipv4 vrf WHITE
PE1(config-router-af)#no sync
PE1(config-router-af)#exit
PE1(config-router)#
```

Now, we will create our OSPF process between the customer and provider edge routers:

```
R3#conf t
R3(config)#int g1/0
R3(config-if)#ip ospf 2 area 0
R3(config-if)#int lo0
R3(config-if)#ip ospf 2 area 0
R3(config-if)#ip ospf network point-to-point
R3(config-if)#

PE1(config-router)#router ospf 2 vrf WHITE
PE1(config-router)#router-id 10.250.3.3
PE1(config-router)#int g3/0
PE1(config-if)#ip ospf 2 area 0
PE1(config-if)#
*Mar 30 11:42:04.851: %OSPF-5-ADJCHG: Process 2, Nbr 192.168.1.1 on
GigabitEthernet3/0 from LOADING to FULL, Loading Done
```

The last step is to set up redistribution between the two protocols:

```
PE1(config-if)#router bgp 100
PE1(config-router)#address-family ipv4 vrf WHITE
```

```
PE1(config-router-af)#redistribute ospf 2
PE1(config-router-af)#router ospf 2
PE1(config-router)#redistribute bgp 100 subnets
```

We can now move on to the other side of the cloud, first creating the VRF:

```
PE2#conf t
PE2(config)#ip vrf WHITE
PE2(config-vrf)#rd 100:2
PE2(config-vrf)#route-target 100:2
PE2(config-vrf)#exit
PE2(config)#int g3/0
PE2(config-if)#ip vrf forwarding WHITE
% Interface GigabitEthernet3/0 IPv4 disabled and address(es) removed
due to enabling VRF WHITE
PE2(config-if)#ip address 10.2.4.1 255.255.255.0
```

Adding our VRF to the BGP process:

```
PE2(config-if)#router bgp 100
PE2(config-router)#address-family ipv4 vrf WHITE
PE2(config-router-af)#no sync
PE2(config-router-af)#exit
```

We then create the OSPF process between our CE and PE routers, and redistribute between the two protocols:

```
PE2(config-router)#router ospf 2 vrf WHITE
PE2(config-router)#router-id 10.250.4.3
PE2(config-router)#int g3/0
PE2(config-if)#ip ospf 2 area 0
PE2(config-if)#router bgp 100
PE2(config-router)#address-family ipv4 vrf WHITE
PE2(config-router-af)#redistribute ospf 2
PE2(config-router-af)#router ospf 2
PE2(config-router)#redistribute bgp 100 subnets
PE2(config-router)#

R4(config)#int g1/0
R4(config-if)#ip ospf 2 area 0
R4(config-if)#int lo0
R4(config-if)#ip ospf 2 area 0
*Mar 30 11:52:07.551: %OSPF-5-ADJCHG: Process 2, Nbr 10.250.4.3 on
GigabitEthernet1/0 from LOADING to FULL, Loading Done
R3(config-if)#ip ospf network point-to-point
```

Now, we can see that R4 is aware of the 192.168.1.0/24 network:

```
R4#sh ip route | beg Gate
Gateway of last resort is not set

      10.0.0.0/8 is variably subnetted, 3 subnets, 2 masks
O IA     10.1.3.0/24 [110/2] via 10.2.4.1, 00:00:14, Gi1/0
C        10.2.4.0/24 is directly connected, GigabitEthernet1/0
L        10.2.4.2/32 is directly connected, GigabitEthernet1/0
      172.20.0.0/16 is variably subnetted, 2 subnets, 2 masks
C        172.20.1.0/24 is directly connected, Loopback0
L        172.20.1.1/32 is directly connected, Loopback0
O IA  192.168.1.0/24 [110/3] via 10.2.4.1, 00:00:14, Gi1/0
```

But, how do we know that we are getting to the correct router though? We should have a nice separation within the MPLS cloud, but let's just check. To do this, we can specify a telnet password on the vty lines on R3 and try to telnet from R5 to the 192.168.1.1 address:

```
R3(config)#line vty 0 4
R3(config-line)#password cisco
R3(config-line)#

R4#
R4#telnet 192.168.1.1
Trying 192.168.1.1 ... Open


User Access Verification

Password:
R3>
```

Great! We are on the correct router, and the MPLS cloud is doing exactly what it should do! Let's finish this chapter off by creating our last MPLS VPN.

VRF BLUE

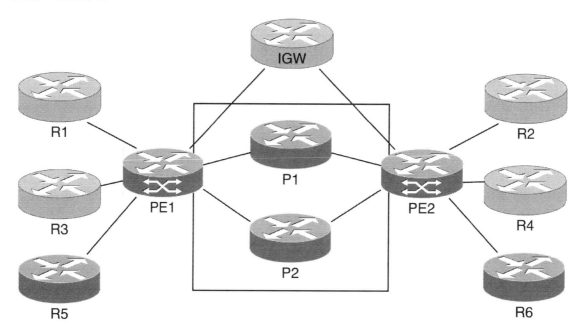

For this last section, some of the steps will be moved around just to show that you don't have to follow the steps exactly as I have laid them out. Only the commands are laid out below the overall process is the same as we have done for RED and WHITE:

```
PE1(config)#ip vrf BLUE
PE1(config-vrf)#rd 100:3
PE1(config-vrf)#route-target 100:3
PE1(config-vrf)#exit
PE1(config)#int g4/0
PE1(config-if)#ip vrf forwarding BLUE
% Interface GigabitEthernet4/0 IPv4 disabled and address(es) removed
due to enabling VRF BLUE
PE1(config-if)#ip add 10.1.5.1 255.255.255.0
PE1(config-if)#router bgp 100
PE1(config-router)#address-family ipv4 vrf BLUE
PE1(config-router-af)#no sync
PE1(config-router-af)#exit
PE1(config-router)#router ospf 3 vrf BLUE
PE1(config-router)#router-id 10.250.3.5
PE1(config-router)#int g4/0
PE1(config-if)#ip ospf 3 area 0
```

```
PE1(config-if)#router bgp 100
PE1(config-router)#address-family ipv4 vrf BLUE
PE1(config-router-af)#redistribute ospf 3
PE1(config-router-af)#router ospf 3
PE1(config-router)#redistribute bgp 100 subnets
PE1(config-router)#

R5#conf t
R5(config)#int g1/0
R5(config-if)#ip ospf 3 area 0
R5(config-if)#int lo0
R5(config-if)#ip ospf 3 area 0
R5(config-if)#ip ospf network point-to-point

PE2(config)#ip vrf BLUE
PE2(config-vrf)#rd 100:3
PE2(config-vrf)#route-target 100:3
PE2(config-vrf)#int g4/0
PE2(config-if)#ip vrf forwarding BLUE
% Interface GigabitEthernet4/0 IPv4 disabled and address(es) removed
due to enabling VRF BLUE
PE2(config-if)#ip add 10.2.6.1 255.255.255.0
PE2(config-if)#router bgp 100
PE2(config-router)#address-family ipv4 vrf BLUE
PE2(config-router-af)#no sync
PE2(config-router-af)#redistribute ospf 3
PE2(config-router-af)#exit
PE2(config-router)#router ospf 3 vrf BLUE
PE2(config-router)#router-id 10.250.4.4
PE2(config-router)#redistribute bgp 100 subnets
PE2(config-router)#int g4/0
PE2(config-if)#ip ospf 3 area 0
PE2(config-if)#

R6#conf t
R6(config)#int lo0
R6(config-if)#ip ospf network point-to-point
R6(config-if)#ip ospf 3 area 0
R6(config-if)#int g1/0
R6(config-if)#ip ospf 3 area 0
R6(config-if)#
*Mar 30 12:13:15.035: %OSPF-5-ADJCHG: Process 3, Nbr 10.250.4.4 on
GigabitEthernet1/0 from LOADING to FULL, Loading Done
R6(config-if)#

R6#sh ip route | beg Gate
Gateway of last resort is not set
```

```
         10.0.0.0/8 is variably subnetted, 3 subnets, 2 masks
O IA     10.1.5.0/24 [110/2] via 10.2.6.1, 00:01:32, Gi1/0
C        10.2.6.0/24 is directly connected, GigabitEthernet1/0
L        10.2.6.2/32 is directly connected, GigabitEthernet1/0
         172.20.0.0/16 is variably subnetted, 2 subnets, 2 masks
C        172.20.1.0/24 is directly connected, Loopback0
L        172.20.1.1/32 is directly connected, Loopback0
O IA  192.168.1.0/24 [110/3] via 10.2.6.1, 00:00:08, Gi1/0
R6#ping 192.168.1.1
Type escape sequence to abort.
Sending 5, 100-byte ICMP Echos to 192.168.1.1, timeout is 2 seconds:
!!!!!
Success rate is 100 percent (5/5)
R6#telnet 192.168.1.1
Trying 192.168.1.1 ... Open


User Access Verification

Password:
R5>
```

Now, we have three fully functional MPLS VPNs. In the next chapter, we will look in greater depth at how the packets flow from CE router to CE router across our MPLS cloud and how the packets are changed as they pass from router to router at each step.

6. Inside the LSP

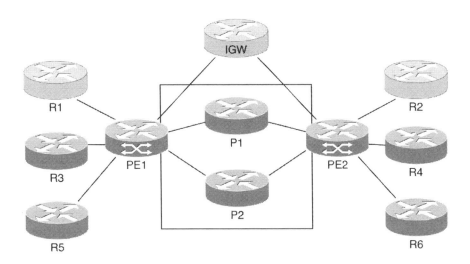

In the last chapter, we built three MPLS VPNs, each transporting the same IP prefixes over an MPLS cloud. But, what actually happens within the cloud?

Firstly, we know that we needed to enable the interfaces for use in our MPLS network, with the interface command "mpls ip". Also, our label switching protocol, LDP, was bound to the loopback interface assigned to the router. When we have done this, we start a process called LDP Discovery. We will focus on this more during some troubleshooting steps. However, during this stage we start to send out multicast HELLO packets to the address 224.0.0.2 at a default rate of 5 seconds. This is known as the LDP Hello Interval timer. LDP uses UDP port 646, which will allow LDP adjacencies to form with directly connected peers. For non-directly connected peers, unicast packets will be used instead of multicast. Non-directly connected LDP peers are referred to as "Targeted LDP session" or "extended discovery," and we will cover this when we look at Layer 2 VPNs.

Once the adjacencies have formed, we move into the session establishment phase. During this phase, the routers will negotiate the session parameters, such as the LDP version, label exchange method, and the timer values. This second stage occurs through TCP packets, rather that UDP, but, the port number remains the same at 646. If there is a failure to create a full session, the routers will use Error Negotiation Messages, and they will attempt to renegotiate. There is a 15 second initial back-off timer, and a maximum CDP back-off value of 120 seconds. Once a session is established, the HELLO packets are still sent. If a HELLO packet is not received during the LDP Hold Timer (for which the default is 15 seconds), the session will be torn down. Though, hopefully our session will not be torn down, and we should see a healthy MPLS network, ready to exchange labels!

If we look at the output of a traceroute between R5 and R6, we can see that we have some labels added to the packets as they go through the MPLS network (the Label Switching Path):

```
R5#traceroute 172.20.1.1
Type escape sequence to abort.
Tracing the route to 172.20.1.1
VRF info: (vrf in name/id, vrf out name/id)
  1 10.1.5.1 20 msec 20 msec 24 msec
  2 10.10.1.1 [MPLS: Labels 19/26 Exp 0] 112 msec 60 msec 100 msec
  3 10.2.6.1 [MPLS: Label 26 Exp 0] 72 msec 88 msec 60 msec
  4 10.2.6.2 88 msec 100 msec *
R5#

R6#traceroute 192.168.1.1
Type escape sequence to abort.
Tracing the route to 192.168.1.1
VRF info: (vrf in name/id, vrf out name/id)
  1 10.2.6.1 8 msec 16 msec 36 msec
  2 10.10.2.1 [MPLS: Labels 17/25 Exp 0] 120 msec 84 msec 120 msec
  3 10.1.5.1 [MPLS: Label 25 Exp 0] 88 msec 52 msec 88 msec
  4 10.1.5.2 108 msec 104 msec *
R6#
```

At hops 2 and 3, we can see MPLS label information. At hop 2, we have two labels 19 and 26 for the traceroute from R5 to R6; and 17 and 25 for R6 to R5. At step 3, we only have one label, 26 in the case of R5 and 25 for R6. We know that the path from R5 to R6 is to PE1, then to P1 and then to PE2 before reaching its destination.

Firstly, from our traceroute, we will take label 19. We know that all our traffic must cross P1 or P2 to get to PE2 (which is our MP-BGP neighbor). If we look at our BGP neighbor details, we can confirm that we are peered to an address in the 10.250.4.0/24 range:

```
PE1#sh ip bgp neighbors | i internal
BGP neighbor is 10.250.4.1,  remote AS 100, internal link
PE1#
```

Next, if we look at the MPLS label bindings, we can confirm that label 19 is attached to anything going into the MP-BGP network with a next-hop address of 10.250.4.1:

```
PE1#sh mpls ldp bindings 10.250.4.0 24
  lib entry: 10.250.4.0/24, rev 16
```

```
       local binding:  label: 20
       remote binding: lsr: 10.250.2.1:0, label: 19
       remote binding: lsr: 10.250.1.1:0, label: 19
    PE1#
```

We can also look at the forwarding table to get the same information:

```
    PE1#sh mpls forwarding-table 10.250.4.0
    Local    Outgoing   Prefix           Bytes Label   Outgoing   Next Hop
    Label    Label      or Tunnel Id     Switched      interface
    20       19         10.250.4.0/24    0             Gi1/0      10.10.1.1
             19         10.250.4.0/24    0             Gi5/0      10.10.3.2
    PE1#
```

We can confirm that this is the case by performing another traceroute to the same address on R3, which is in VRF WHITE:

```
    R3#traceroute 172.20.1.1
    Type escape sequence to abort.
    Tracing the route to 172.20.1.1
    VRF info: (vrf in name/id, vrf out name/id)
      1 10.1.3.1 12 msec 36 msec 24 msec
      2 10.10.1.1 [MPLS: Labels 19/24 Exp 0] 140 msec 96 msec 88 msec
      3 10.2.4.1 [MPLS: Label 24 Exp 0] 104 msec 76 msec 64 msec
      4 10.2.4.2 144 msec 56 msec *
    R3#
```

Again the first label is 19, which is our BGP traffic label.

R3 had a different second label to R5, so this would signify the VRF traffic (VPN label), but how can we confirm this?

If you recall from chapter 4, we said that for MPLS VPNs to work on Cisco routers we must have CEF enabled. Well, we can use CEF to confirm which labels our VRFs are being tagged with. We need to specify the VRF and the prefix that we want to check:

```
    PE1#sh ip cef vrf BLUE 172.20.1.0
    172.20.1.0/24
      nexthop 10.10.1.1 GigabitEthernet1/0 label 19 26
      nexthop 10.10.3.2 GigabitEthernet5/0 label 19 26
    PE1#
```

So, here we have label 26, which is the VRF specific label. Again, we can confirm this is the case by comparing the same command output using VRF WHITE, where we would expect to find label 24:

```
PE1#sh ip cef vrf WHITE 172.20.1.0
172.20.1.0/24
  nexthop 10.10.1.1 GigabitEthernet1/0 label 19 24
  nexthop 10.10.3.2 GigabitEthernet5/0 label 19 24
PE1#
```

We can check the entire forwarding table on PE1 and confirm this again:

```
PE1#sh mpls forwarding-table
Local   Outgoing   Prefix             Bytes Label  Outgoing Next Hop
Label   Label      or Tunnel Id       Switched     interface
16      Pop Label  10.10.4.0/24       0            Gi5/0    10.10.3.2
17      Pop Label  10.250.2.0/24      0            Gi5/0    10.10.3.2
18      Pop Label  10.10.2.0/24       0            Gi1/0    10.10.1.1
19      Pop Label  10.250.1.0/24      0            Gi1/0    10.10.1.1
20      19         10.250.4.0/24      0            Gi1/0    10.10.1.1
        19         10.250.4.0/24      0            Gi5/0    10.10.3.2
21      No Label   10.1.1.0/24[V]     0            aggregate/RED
22      No Label   192.168.1.0/24[V]  \
                                      0            Gi2/0    10.1.1.2
23      No Label   10.1.3.0/24[V]     0            aggregate/WHITE
24      No Label   192.168.1.0/24[V]  \
                                      0            Gi3/0    10.1.3.2
25      No Label   10.1.5.0/24[V]     2640         aggregate/BLUE
26      No Label   192.168.1.0/24[V]  \
                                      0            Gi4/0    10.1.5.2
PE1#
```

The bracketed V ([V]) denotes that the label is a VPN label. We can see from the LDP bindings database (below) that the lib entry for 10.250.4.0/24 has a local label of 20. This is then changed to 19 (as shown above) as it exits PE1 towards P1 (or P2).

```
PE1#sh mpls ldp bindings local
  lib entry: 10.10.1.0/24, rev 2
   local binding:  label: imp-null
  lib entry: 10.10.2.0/24, rev 12
   local binding:  label: 18
  lib entry: 10.10.3.0/24, rev 4
   local binding:  label: imp-null
  lib entry: 10.10.4.0/24, rev 8
   local binding:  label: 16
  lib entry: 10.250.1.0/24, rev 14
   local binding:  label: 19
  lib entry: 10.250.2.0/24, rev 10
   local binding:  label: 17
```

```
  lib entry: 10.250.3.0/24, rev 6
   local binding:  label: imp-null
  lib entry: 10.250.4.0/24, rev 16
   local binding:  label: 20
PE1#
```

If we repeat the process on PE2, we should see that 17 is its BGP label, and 25 is the VRF specific label. Firstly, let's confirm which prefix we should be looking at for the BGP peering:

```
PE2#sh ip bgp neighbors | i internal
BGP neighbor is 10.250.3.1,  remote AS 100, internal link
PE2#
```

Again, we can confirm against the entry in the forwarding table:

```
PE2#sh mpls forwarding-table 10.250.3.0
Local   Outgoing   Prefix          Bytes Label  Outgoing Next Hop
Label   Label      or Tunnel Id    Switched     interface
20      17         10.250.3.0/24   0            Gi1/0    10.10.2.1
        17         10.250.3.0/24   0            Gi5/0    10.10.4.2
PE2#
```

Then, we look at the label bindings for that prefix:

```
PE2#sh mpls ldp bindings 10.250.3.0 24
  lib entry: 10.250.3.0/24, rev 14
   local binding:  label: 19
   remote binding: lsr: 10.250.1.1:0, label: 17
   remote binding: lsr: 10.250.2.1:0, label: 17
PE2#
```

Again, we can confirm this by performing a traceroute from R4, where the first label we see should be 17 again:

```
R4#traceroute 192.168.1.1
Type escape sequence to abort.
Tracing the route to 192.168.1.1
VRF info: (vrf in name/id, vrf out name/id)
  1 10.2.4.1 48 msec 16 msec 24 msec
  2 10.10.4.2 [MPLS: Labels 17/26 Exp 0] 140 msec 84 msec 108 msec
  3 10.1.3.1 [MPLS: Label 26 Exp 0] 88 msec 88 msec 72 msec
  4 10.1.3.2 116 msec 92 msec *
R4#
```

Which leaves 25 as the VRF specific label, again we can confirm this with CEF:

```
PE2#sh ip cef vrf BLUE 192.168.1.0
192.168.1.0/24
  nexthop 10.10.2.1 GigabitEthernet1/0 label 17 25
  nexthop 10.10.4.2 GigabitEthernet5/0 label 17 25
PE2#

PE2#sh ip cef vrf WHITE 192.168.1.0
192.168.1.0/24
  nexthop 10.10.2.1 GigabitEthernet1/0 label 17 26
  nexthop 10.10.4.2 GigabitEthernet5/0 label 17 26
PE2#
```

We can also confirm this in the forwarding table:

```
PE2#sh mpls forwarding-table
Local   Outgoing   Prefix              Bytes Label  Outgoing    Next Hop
Label   Label      or Tunnel Id        Switched     interface
16      Pop Label  10.10.3.0/24        0            Gi5/0       10.10.4.2
17      Pop Label  10.250.2.0/24       0            Gi5/0       10.10.4.2
18      Pop Label  10.10.1.0/24        0            Gi1/0       10.10.2.1
19      17         10.250.3.0/24       0            Gi1/0       10.10.2.1
        17         10.250.3.0/24       0            Gi5/0       10.10.4.2
20      Pop Label  10.250.1.0/24       0            Gi1/0       10.10.2.1
21      No Label   10.2.2.0/24[V]      0            aggregate/RED
22      No Label   172.20.1.0/24[V]    0            Gi2/0       10.2.2.2
23      No Label   10.2.4.0/24[V]      0            aggregate/WHITE
24      No Label   172.20.1.0/24[V]    0            Gi3/0       10.2.4.2
25      No Label   10.2.6.0/24[V]      0            aggregate/BLUE
26      No Label   172.20.1.0/24[V]    0            Gi4/0       10.2.6.2
PE2#
```

Similar to PE1, we can see, from the LDP bindings database below, that the lib entry for 10.250.3.0/24 has a local label of 19. This is then changed to 17 (as shown above) as it exits PE2 towards P1 (or P2).

```
PE2#sh mpls ldp bindings local
  lib entry: 10.10.1.0/24, rev 12
   local binding:  label: 18
  lib entry: 10.10.2.0/24, rev 2
   local binding:  label: imp-null
  lib entry: 10.10.3.0/24, rev 8
   local binding:  label: 16
  lib entry: 10.10.4.0/24, rev 4
   local binding:  label: imp-null
```

```
        lib entry: 10.250.1.0/24, rev 16
         local binding:  label: 20
        lib entry: 10.250.2.0/24, rev 10
         local binding:  label: 17
        lib entry: 10.250.3.0/24, rev 14
         local binding:  label: 19
        lib entry: 10.250.4.0/24, rev 6
         local binding:  label: imp-null
    PE2#
```

We can see this in action with a few Wireshark captures.

Firstly, we can see the telnet traffic from R5 to R6 on PE1:

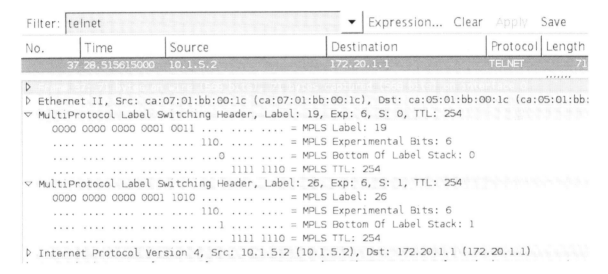

The traffic, which has a source of R5's GigabitEthernet interface, has two labels attached, 19 which is the inner tag and 26. The reply from R6 as PE1 sees it looks like this:

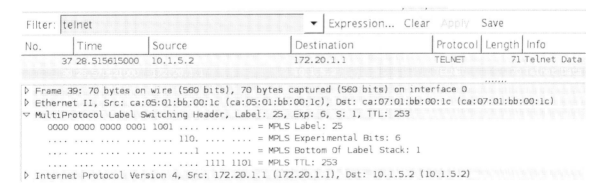

It has just label 25, which is PE2's outer tag.

If we look at the traffic from the opposite direction, we can see that the data comes from R6's loopback interface with two tags, the inner tag of 17 and tag 25 which is what R5 sees:

```
Filter: telnet                                           ▼  Expression... Clear Apply Save
No.         Time            Source              Destination          Protocol Ler
        51 39.923644000    10.1.5.2             172.20.1.1           TELNET
        53 39.965507000    172.20.1.1           10.1.5.2             TELNET
▷ Frame 53: 74 bytes on wire (592 bits), 74 bytes captured (592 bits) on interface 0
▷ Ethernet II, Src: ca:08:01:bb:00:1c (ca:08:01:bb:00:1c), Dst: ca:05:01:bb:00:38 (ca:05:0:
▽ MultiProtocol Label Switching Header, Label: 17, Exp: 6, S: 0, TTL: 254
     0000 0000 0000 0001 0001 .... .... .... = MPLS Label: 17
     .... .... .... .... .... 110. .... .... = MPLS Experimental Bits: 6
     .... .... .... .... .... ...0 .... .... = MPLS Bottom Of Label Stack: 0
     .... .... .... .... .... .... 1111 1110 = MPLS TTL: 254
▽ MultiProtocol Label Switching Header, Label: 25, Exp: 6, S: 1, TTL: 254
     0000 0000 0000 0001 1001 .... .... .... = MPLS Label: 25
     .... .... .... .... .... 110. .... .... = MPLS Experimental Bits: 6
     .... .... .... .... .... ...1 .... .... = MPLS Bottom Of Label Stack: 1
     .... .... .... .... .... .... 1111 1110 = MPLS TTL: 254
▷ Internet Protocol Version 4, Src: 172.20.1.1 (172.20.1.1), Dst: 10.1.5.2 (10.1.5.2)
```

The reply from R5 as PE2 sees it has just the one label; 26.

```
Filter: telnet                                           ▼  Expression... Clear Apply Sav
No.         Time            Source              Destination          Protocol Le
        51 39.923644000    10.1.5.2             172.20.1.1           TELNET
▷ Frame 51: 67 bytes on wire (536 bits), 67 bytes captured (536 bits) on interface 0
▷ Ethernet II, Src: ca:05:01:bb:00:38 (ca:05:01:bb:00:38), Dst: ca:08:01:bb:00:1c (ca:08:(
▽ MultiProtocol Label Switching Header, Label: 26, Exp: 6, S: 1, TTL: 253
     0000 0000 0000 0001 1010 .... .... .... = MPLS Label: 26
     .... .... .... .... .... 110. .... .... = MPLS Experimental Bits: 6
     .... .... .... .... .... ...1 .... .... = MPLS Bottom Of Label Stack: 1
     .... .... .... .... .... .... 1111 1101 = MPLS TTL: 253
▷ Internet Protocol Version 4, Src: 10.1.5.2 (10.1.5.2), Dst: 172.20.1.1 (172.20.1.1)
```

Through the above captures, we can see a series of tags being removed and swapped as they pass through the network. The set of labels that PE1 sends out are not the same as PE2 receives, or vice-versa. Recall from Chapter 4 that the routers within an MPLS network have different functions, Customer Edge (CE), Provider Edge (PE) and Provider

(P) routers, well the P router is also known as a Label Switch Router (LSR), and it is this router, P1 in our network, that is doing all of the swapping of the tags.

The packets that P1 receives from PE1 and PE2 that have two tags are sent on to the next PE router with just one tag, the outer tag, which denoted by having the Bottom of Label Stack bit set to 1. The first tag, the inner label (either 19 or 17 depending on our direction), is referred to as the VPN label. Now, while P1 may not know about the specific VRFs that it is being used as a transit for, it is aware of the labels associated with the BGP link between PE1 and PE2. We can list the labels that P1 is using and is being passed from PE1 and PE2 by using the command "sh mpls ldp bindings local". The output of this command is shown below.

```
P1#sh mpls ldp bindings local
  lib entry: 10.10.1.0/24, rev 2
    local binding:  label: imp-null
  lib entry: 10.10.2.0/24, rev 4
    local binding:  label: imp-null
  lib entry: 10.10.3.0/24, rev 8
    local binding:  label: 16
  lib entry: 10.10.4.0/24, rev 13
    local binding:  label: 18
  lib entry: 10.250.1.0/24, rev 6
    local binding:  label: imp-null
  lib entry: 10.250.2.0/24, rev 16
    local binding:  label: 20
  lib entry: 10.250.3.0/24, rev 10
    local binding:  label: 17
  lib entry: 10.250.4.0/24, rev 15
    local binding:  label: 19
P1#
```

If we look at the individual prefixes on P1, we can again confirm the label details we have seen on PE1 and PE2. If we look at the 10.250.4.0/24 and 10.250.3.0/24 prefixes on P1:

```
P1#sh mpls ldp bindings 10.250.4.0 24
  lib entry: 10.250.4.0/24, rev 15
    local binding:  label: 19
    remote binding: lsr: 10.250.4.1:0, label: imp-null
    remote binding: lsr: 10.250.3.1:0, label: 20
P1#sh mpls ldp bindings 10.250.3.0 24
  lib entry: 10.250.3.0/24, rev 10
    local binding:  label: 17
    remote binding: lsr: 10.250.3.1:0, label: imp-null
    remote binding: lsr: 10.250.4.1:0, label: 19
P1#
```

We have another method of confirming that the local label used by PE1 (10.250.3.1) for the first prefix is 20, and PE2 (10.250.4.1) used label 19 for the second prefix.

We can also see what P1 will do with the VPN labels as they pass through it by looking at the forwarding table.

```
P1#sh mpls forwarding-table
Local  Outgoing   Prefix           Bytes Label  Outgoing  Next Hop
Label  Label      or Tunnel Id     Switched     interface
16     Pop Label  10.10.3.0/24     0            Gi1/0     10.10.1.2
17     Pop Label  10.250.3.0/24    2974         Gi1/0     10.10.1.2
18     Pop Label  10.10.4.0/24     0            Gi2/0     10.10.2.2
19     Pop Label  10.250.4.0/24    3876         Gi2/0     10.10.2.2
20     17         10.250.2.0/24    0            Gi1/0     10.10.1.2
       17         10.250.2.0/24    0            Gi2/0     10.10.2.2
P1#
```

Here a packet with a label of 19, for BGP, which we know will have originated from PE1, will be passed to PE2 (Next Hop address 10.10.2.2) and will have that label removed. Under the Outgoing Label column, it lists the action of "Pop Label" which means to remove it, leaving just the outer label.

We can see this in action if we enable some debugging on PE1, using the command "debug mpls packet". Below is some of the output, Gi1/0 is the link to PE1 and Gi2/0 is the link to PE2, note that "rx" means a received packet and "tx":

```
P1#debug mpls packet
Packet debugging is on
P1#
*Apr 20 15:27:52.075: MPLS turbo: Gi1/0: rx: Len 68 Stack {19 6 254}
{26 6 254} - ipv4 data
*Apr 20 15:27:52.079: MPLS turbo: Gi2/0: tx: Len 64 Stack {26 6 253}
- ipv4 data
*Apr 20 15:27:52.143: MPLS turbo: Gi2/0: rx: Len 68 Stack {17 6 254}
{25 6 254} - ipv4 data
*Apr 20 15:27:52.143: MPLS turbo: Gi1/0: tx: Len 64 Stack {25 6 253}
- ipv4 data
*Apr 20 15:27:52.183: MPLS turbo: Gi1/0: rx: Len 68 Stack {19 6 254}
{26 6 254} - ipv4 data
*Apr 20 15:27:52.183: MPLS turbo: Gi2/0: tx: Len 64 Stack {26 6 253}
- ipv4 data
*Apr 20 15:27:52.195: MPLS turbo: Gi1/0: rx: Len 71 Stack {19 6 254}
{26 6 254} - ipv4 data
```

We can see here that P1 is popping off the first label (19 or 17) and is sending just the VRF label (26 or 25). If we do the same debugging on the two provider edge router we can see that they only receive the one label:

```
PE1#debug mpls packet
Packet debugging is on
PE1#
*Apr 20 15:30:33.535: MPLS turbo: Gi1/0: rx: Len 64 Stack {25 6 253}
- ipv4 data
*Apr 20 15:30:33.651: MPLS turbo: Gi1/0: rx: Len 70 Stack {25 6 253}
- ipv4 data
*Apr 20 15:30:33.667: MPLS turbo: Gi1/0: rx: Len 95 Stack {25 6 253}
- ipv4 data
*Apr 20 15:30:33.763: MPLS turbo: Gi1/0: rx: Len 64 Stack {25 6 253}
- ipv4 data

PE2#
*Apr 20 15:30:58.691: MPLS turbo: Gi1/0: rx: Len 64 Stack {26 6 253}
- ipv4 data
*Apr 20 15:30:58.815: MPLS turbo: Gi1/0: rx: Len 64 Stack {26 6 253}
- ipv4 data
*Apr 20 15:30:58.839: MPLS turbo: Gi1/0: rx: Len 67 Stack {26 6 253}
- ipv4 data
*Apr 20 15:30:58.863: MPLS turbo: Gi1/0: rx: Len 64 Stack {26 6 253}
- ipv4 data
```

A diagram of the label changes on a packet flow from R5 to R6 would look like this:

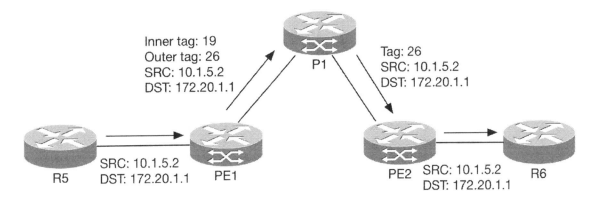

And the respective reply would look like this:

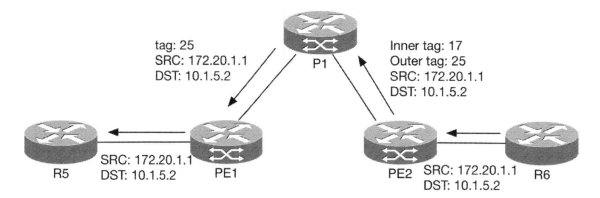

Hopefully, you should now have a very clear idea of what happens within an MPLS VPN cloud; though, there are still a few things that we need to cover.

Implicit Null

Within the ldp output examples we have seen previously, we see labels set as imp-null, rather than a number:

```
P1#sh mpls ldp bindings 10.250.4.0 24
  lib entry: 10.250.4.0/24, rev 15
  local binding:  label: 19
  remote binding: lsr: 10.250.4.1:0, label: imp-null
  remote binding: lsr: 10.250.3.1:0, label: 20
P1#sh mpls ldp bindings 10.250.3.0 24
  lib entry: 10.250.3.0/24, rev 10
  local binding:  label: 17
  remote binding: lsr: 10.250.3.1:0, label: imp-null
  remote binding: lsr: 10.250.4.1:0, label: 19
P1#
```

Implicit null is used where a prefix used within the MPLS cloud is generated locally. If we look at PE1, we can see that we use Gi1/0, 5/0 and Lo0 to connect to P1 and P2, as well as using Lo0 for the MP-BGP peer source. The associated lib entries (10.10.1.0/24, 10.10.3.0/24 and 10.250.3.0/24) all have their label set to imp-null:

```
PE1#sh mpls ldp bindings local
  lib entry: 10.10.1.0/24, rev 2
  local binding:  label: imp-null
  lib entry: 10.10.2.0/24, rev 8
  local binding:  label: 16
  lib entry: 10.10.3.0/24, rev 4
  local binding:  label: imp-null
```

```
    lib entry: 10.10.4.0/24, rev 12
     local binding:  label: 18
    lib entry: 10.250.1.0/24, rev 10
     local binding:  label: 17
    lib entry: 10.250.2.0/24, rev 14
     local binding:  label: 19
    lib entry: 10.250.3.0/24, rev 6
     local binding:  label: imp-null
    lib entry: 10.250.4.0/24, rev 16
     local binding:  label: 20
PE1#sh ip int bri | i up
GigabitEthernet1/0      10.10.1.2        YES NVRAM  up        up
GigabitEthernet2/0      10.1.1.1         YES NVRAM  up        up
GigabitEthernet3/0      10.1.3.1         YES NVRAM  up        up
GigabitEthernet4/0      10.1.5.1         YES NVRAM  up        up
GigabitEthernet5/0      10.10.3.1        YES NVRAM  up        up
Loopback0               10.250.3.1       YES NVRAM  up        up
PE1#
```

These are advertised as implicit null so that the router does not need to perform two lookups, one in the LFIB and then again in the RIB. We will return to this in a moment, when we discuss Penultimate Hop Popping.

TTL Propagation

If we look at the output from a traceroute between R5 and R6, we can see that our visibility into the cloud is actually pretty good:

```
R5#traceroute 172.20.1.1 source 192.168.1.1
Type escape sequence to abort.
Tracing the route to 172.20.1.1
VRF info: (vrf in name/id, vrf out name/id)
  1 10.1.5.1 24 msec 16 msec 4 msec
  2 10.10.3.2 [MPLS: Labels 19/26 Exp 0] 100 msec 84 msec 104 msec
  3 10.2.6.1 [MPLS: Label 26 Exp 0] 92 msec 76 msec 76 msec
  4 10.2.6.2 104 msec 96 msec *
R5#

R6#traceroute 192.168.1.1 source 172.20.1.1
Type escape sequence to abort.
Tracing the route to 192.168.1.1
VRF info: (vrf in name/id, vrf out name/id)
  1 10.2.6.1 20 msec 16 msec 24 msec
  2 10.10.4.2 [MPLS: Labels 17/26 Exp 0] 124 msec 124 msec 56 msec
  3 10.1.5.1 [MPLS: Label 26 Exp 0] 72 msec 56 msec 88 msec
```

```
    4 10.1.5.2 112 msec 64 msec *
R6#
```

However, many network providers prefer to "hide" their core routers from the end user. Can we make the results look any better? We can, and it's quite simple.

We can make it look like this:

```
R5#traceroute 172.20.1.1 source 192.168.1.1
Type escape sequence to abort.
Tracing the route to 172.20.1.1
VRF info: (vrf in name/id, vrf out name/id)
  1 10.1.5.1 12 msec 40 msec 24 msec
  2 10.2.6.1 [MPLS: Label 26 Exp 0] 64 msec 60 msec 48 msec
  3 10.2.6.2 96 msec 72 msec *
R5#

R6#traceroute 192.168.1.1 source 172.20.1.1
Type escape sequence to abort.
Tracing the route to 192.168.1.1
VRF info: (vrf in name/id, vrf out name/id)
  1 10.2.6.1 12 msec 20 msec 24 msec
  2 10.1.5.1 [MPLS: Label 26 Exp 0] 104 msec 72 msec 64 msec
  3 10.1.5.2 104 msec 68 msec *
R6#
```

And, we do this by entering the following commands:

```
PE1#conf t
PE1(config)#no mpls ip propagate-ttl forwarded
PE1(config)#

P1#conf t
P1(config)#no mpls ip propagate-ttl forwarded
P1(config)#

PE2#conf t
PE2(config)#no mpls ip propagate-ttl forwarded
PE2(config)#
```

With MPLS labels come another TTL field. When a packet enters a label-switched path (LSP), the TTL in the original IP packet will be copied into the MPLS TTL field. This MPLS TTL is decremented at each LSR it encounters, the TTL information in the IP header is untouched. At the last stage, the PE routers in our case, the label is popped off and the MPLS TTL is decremented by one again, before the current MPLS TTL value is applied to the IP header TTL. When we issued "debug mpls packet" on P1, we could see this occurring:

```
*Apr 20 15:27:52.075: MPLS turbo: Gi1/0: rx: Len 68 Stack {19 6 254}
{26 6 254} - ipv4 data
*Apr 20 15:27:52.079: MPLS turbo: Gi2/0: tx: Len 64 Stack {26 6 253}
- ipv4 data
```

The received packet comes in with an MPLS TTL of 254 and is transmitted with a TTL of 253. When we disable ttl propagation using the command "no mpls ip propagate-ttl forwarded", the MPLS TTL is calculated separately to the IP TTL, and the IP TTL remains constant through the LSP. None of the LSP hops are recorded in the traceroute from R5.

The same debug with ttl propagation disabled looks like this:

```
*Apr 20 15:37:52.143: MPLS turbo: Gi1/0: rx: Len 68 Stack {19 6 255}
{26 6 255} - ipv4 data
*Apr 20 15:37:52.143: MPLS turbo: Gi2/0: tx: Len 64 Stack {26 6 255}
- ipv4 data
```

Let's look at this through some Wireshark captures.

The packet leaves R5 towards PE1 with a IP TTL of 255:

The packet as it leaves PE1 on its way to P1 has two MPLS labels, both have a TTL of 255. The IP TTL is 254.

```
18 9.507142000    10.1.5.2           172.20.1.1        TELNET     71 Telnet Data ...
▷ Frame 18: 71 bytes on wire (568 bits), 71 bytes captured (568 bits) on interface 0
▷ Ethernet II, Src: ca:07:03:9c:00:1c (ca:07:03:9c:00:1c), Dst: ca:05:03:9c:00:1c (ca:05:03:9c:00:1c)
▷ MultiProtocol Label Switching Header, Label: 19, Exp: 6, S: 0, TTL: 255
▷ MultiProtocol Label Switching Header, Label: 26, Exp: 6, S: 1, TTL: 255
▽ Internet Protocol Version 4, Src: 10.1.5.2 (10.1.5.2), Dst: 172.20.1.1 (172.20.1.1)
    Version: 4
    Header length: 20 bytes
  ▷ Differentiated Services Field: 0xc0 (DSCP 0x30: Class Selector 6; ECN: 0x00: Not-ECT (Not ECN-Capable Transport))
    Total Length: 49
    Identification: 0x11b5 (4533)
  ▷ Flags: 0x00
    Fragment offset: 0
    Time to live: 254
    Protocol: TCP (6)
```

The packet as it leaves P1 on its way to PE2 has just one MPLS label, and its TTL remains at 255 and the IP TTL remains at 254.

```
14 8.174872000    10.1.5.2           172.20.1.1        TELNET     67 Telnet Data ...
▷ Frame 14: 67 bytes on wire (536 bits), 67 bytes captured (536 bits) on interface 0
▷ Ethernet II, Src: ca:05:03:9c:00:38 (ca:05:03:9c:00:38), Dst: ca:08:03:9c:00:1c (ca:08:03:9c:00:1c)
▷ MultiProtocol Label Switching Header, Label: 26, Exp: 6, S: 1, TTL: 255
▽ Internet Protocol Version 4, Src: 10.1.5.2 (10.1.5.2), Dst: 172.20.1.1 (172.20.1.1)
    Version: 4
    Header length: 20 bytes
  ▷ Differentiated Services Field: 0xc0 (DSCP 0x30: Class Selector 6; ECN: 0x00: Not-ECT (Not ECN-Capable Transport))
    Total Length: 49
    Identification: 0x93cb (37835)
  ▷ Flags: 0x00
    Fragment offset: 0
    Time to live: 254
    Protocol: TCP (6)
```

When the packet reaches R6, as expected no longer has an MPLS header but the IP TTL is now 253.

```
11 6.469127000    10.1.5.2           172.20.1.1        TELNET     55 Telnet Data ...
▷ Frame 11: 55 bytes on wire (440 bits), 55 bytes captured (440 bits) on interface 0
▷ Ethernet II, Src: ca:08:03:9c:00:70 (ca:08:03:9c:00:70), Dst: ca:04:03:9b:00:1c (ca:04:03:9b:00:1c)
▽ Internet Protocol Version 4, Src: 10.1.5.2 (10.1.5.2), Dst: 172.20.1.1 (172.20.1.1)
    Version: 4
    Header length: 20 bytes
  ▷ Differentiated Services Field: 0xc0 (DSCP 0x30: Class Selector 6; ECN: 0x00: Not-ECT (Not ECN-Capable Transport))
    Total Length: 41
    Identification: 0x7573 (30067)
  ▷ Flags: 0x00
    Fragment offset: 0
    Time to live: 253
    Protocol: TCP (6)
```

There are a couple of different options when we disable TTL propagation. The command "no mpls ip propagate-ttl" on its own prevents traceroute from seeing the internal network. Using the "forwarded" keyword prevents the traceroute from seeing the MPLS LSP hops, but only for packets forwarded from the customers network. If we use the keyword "local" instead of forwarded, the internal network is hidden from the traceroute seen by the provider's point of view.

We will see these different options in action when we look at troubleshooting MPLS, and we use the mpls traceroute commands.

Before we move on to look at what happens within the BGP side of our MPLS VPN, we need to discuss one last matter. Even though we have disabled ttl propagation, our traceroute result still had once MPLS label returned to us.

```
R5#traceroute 172.20.1.1 source 192.168.1.1
Type escape sequence to abort.
Tracing the route to 172.20.1.1
VRF info: (vrf in name/id, vrf out name/id)
  1 10.1.5.1 12 msec 40 msec 24 msec
  2 10.2.6.1 [MPLS: Label 26 Exp 0] 64 msec 60 msec 48 msec
  3 10.2.6.2 96 msec 72 msec *
R5#
```

So can we remove this completely? No, we can't and this is due to PHP, or Penultimate Hop Popping.

Penultimate Hop Popping

So far we have seen that, as we perform a telnet from R5 to R6, we have two tags added by PE1, and a tag removed by P1 before the packet finally reaches R6.

If P1 left both tags on the packet, then the PE routers would have to do two lookups in the LFIB. This would mean a greater workload on that router, which can cause spikes in CPU load. Instead, MPLS uses Penultimate Hop Popping (PHP). With PHP, the last but one router in an LSP pops off the outer label so the PE routers only receive the packet with the VPN label in it -- the VRF specific label. In turn, the PE routers only need to do one lookup, and the workload is distributed evenly. PHP is tied to implicit null. If a label is defined as implicit-null, this informs the neighboring router to perform PHP.

We can see this in action by doing a traceroute from R5 to R6.

Recall from the previous section, on TTL propagation, that our original traceroute looked like this:

```
R5#traceroute 172.20.1.1 source 192.168.1.1
Type escape sequence to abort.
```

```
Tracing the route to 172.20.1.1
VRF info: (vrf in name/id, vrf out name/id)
  1 10.1.5.1 24 msec 16 msec 4 msec
  2 10.10.3.2 [MPLS: Labels 19/26 Exp 0] 100 msec 84 msec 104 msec
  3 10.2.6.1 [MPLS: Label 26 Exp 0] 92 msec 76 msec 76 msec
  4 10.2.6.2 104 msec 96 msec *
R5#
```

The labels referred to come from P1's forwarding table (19), and also from PE2's forwarding table (26):

```
P1#sh mpls forwarding-table
Local  Outgoing   Prefix           Bytes Label  Outgoing   Next Hop
Label  Label      or Tunnel Id     Switched     interface
16     Pop Label  10.10.4.0/24     0            Gi2/0      10.10.2.2
17     Pop Label  10.250.4.0/24    4447         Gi2/0      10.10.2.2
18     Pop Label  10.10.3.0/24     0            Gi1/0      10.10.1.2
19     Pop Label  10.250.3.0/24    4374         Gi1/0      10.10.1.2
20     17         10.250.2.0/24    0            Gi1/0      10.10.1.2
       17         10.250.2.0/24    0            Gi2/0      10.10.2.2
P1#

PE2#sh mpls forwarding-table labels 26
Local  Outgoing   Prefix            Bytes Label  Outgoing   Next Hop
Label  Label      or Tunnel Id      Switched     interface
26     No Label   172.20.1.0/24[V]  378          Gi4/0      10.2.6.2
PE2#
```

With TTL propagation disabled, the traceroute just has label 26 from PE2:

```
R5#trace 172.20.1.1
Type escape sequence to abort.
Tracing the route to 172.20.1.1
VRF info: (vrf in name/id, vrf out name/id)
  1 10.1.5.1 40 msec 24 msec 28 msec
  2 10.2.6.1 [MPLS: Label 26 Exp 0] 88 msec 92 msec 72 msec
  3 10.2.6.2 116 msec 84 msec *
R5#
```

If we do some debugging on P1, we can see this is action:

```
P1#
*Apr 26 13:19:52.487: MPLS turbo: Gi2/0: rx: Len 78 Stack {19 6 255}
{26 6 255} - ipv4 data
*Apr 26 13:19:52.487: MPLS turbo: Gi1/0: tx: Len 74 Stack {26 6 255}
- ipv4 data
```

P1#

P1 receives a packet with both labels 19 and 26, but only passes label 26 onwards, to PE1. PE1 does not have a corresponding action for label 26, therefore, is unable to remove it:

```
PE1#sh mpls forwarding-table
Local  Outgoing    Prefix          Bytes Label  Outgoing    Next Hop
Label  Label       or Tunnel Id    Switched     interface
16     Pop Label   10.10.4.0/24    0            Gi5/0       10.10.3.2
17     Pop Label   10.250.2.0/24   0            Gi5/0       10.10.3.2
18     Pop Label   10.10.2.0/24    0            Gi1/0       10.10.1.1
19     Pop Label   10.250.1.0/24   0            Gi1/0       10.10.1.1
20     17          10.250.4.0/24   0            Gi1/0       10.10.1.1
       19          10.250.4.0/24   0            Gi5/0       10.10.3.2
21     No Label    10.1.1.0/24[V]  0            aggregate/RED
22     No Label    192.168.1.0/24[V]  \
                                   0            Gi2/0       10.1.1.2
23     No Label    10.1.3.0/24[V]  0            aggregate/WHITE
24     No Label    192.168.1.0/24[V]  \
                                   0            Gi3/0       10.1.3.2
25     No Label    10.1.5.0/24[V]  1372         aggregate/BLUE
27     No Label    192.168.1.0/24[V]  \
                                   686          Gi4/0       10.1.5.2
PE1#
```

Without the label in its LFIB, PE1 is unable to remove it. This is why R5 can see that particular label on the
hop during the traceroute sequence. This does mean, though, that PE1 does not have to do two lookups; one for label 19, the other for label 26.

Earlier we discussed implicit-null, and now that we have covered PHP we can look at explicit null.

Explicit Null

With the default of implicit null, we have seen that through PHP the last but one router (P1) sends just the inner label to the egress router (PE2 if the packet is originating from R5 towards R6). Within the label header is the EXP field, which sits between the label and the Bottom of Stack flag. If the network is configured for QoS, based on the EXP bits, then any QoS settings will be lost between P1 and PE2.

The opposite of implicit null is explicit null. We enable explicit null by specifying it as part of the label distribution protocol:

```
PE2#conf t
PE2(config)#mpls ldp explicit-null
```

Explicit null changes the way the MPLS packets handle QoS settings, and the outer label is not popped, instead the label value is set to 0, with all other fields, including the EXP bits remaining untouched. The QoS settings will therefore be preserved.

Explicit null should be configured manually in last hop router. So, if we set it on just PE2, we can see the effect on R5 with a traceroute but not on R6. Firstly, let's remind ourselves of the output with implicit null:

```
R5#trace 172.20.1.1
Type escape sequence to abort.
Tracing the route to 172.20.1.1
VRF info: (vrf in name/id, vrf out name/id)
  1 10.1.5.1 28 msec 28 msec 24 msec
  2 10.2.6.1 [MPLS: Label 26 Exp 0] 88 msec 88 msec 68 msec
  3 10.2.6.2 100 msec 116 msec *
R5#
```

And with explicit null enabled on PE2 we can see that our labels now show as "0/26":

```
R5#trace 172.20.1.1
Type escape sequence to abort.
Tracing the route to 172.20.1.1
VRF info: (vrf in name/id, vrf out name/id)
  1 10.1.5.1 20 msec 16 msec 32 msec
  2 10.2.6.1 [MPLS: Labels 0/26 Exp 0] 60 msec 56 msec 92 msec
  3 10.2.6.2 136 msec 108 msec *
R5#
```

Without enabling it on PE1 a traceroute from R6 to R5's loopback looks like this:

```
R6#trace 192.168.1.1
Type escape sequence to abort.
Tracing the route to 192.168.1.1
VRF info: (vrf in name/id, vrf out name/id)
  1 10.2.6.1 20 msec 20 msec 4 msec
  2 10.1.5.1 [MPLS: Label 26 Exp 0] 76 msec 104 msec 104 msec
  3 10.1.5.2 88 msec 112 msec *
R6#
```

Once we enable explicit null on PE1:

```
PE1#conf t
PE1(config)#mpls ldp explicit-null
PE1(config)#
```

R6 will also see any QoS settings retained:

```
R6#trace 192.168.1.1
Type escape sequence to abort.
Tracing the route to 192.168.1.1
VRF info: (vrf in name/id, vrf out name/id)
  1 10.2.6.1 4 msec 24 msec 4 msec
  2 10.1.5.1 [MPLS: Labels 0/26 Exp 0] 80 msec 76 msec 80 msec
  3 10.1.5.2 104 msec 100 msec *
R6#
```

We can do a lot to influence how our traffic is moved, or viewed as it moved, through our core, but before we look at influencing our traffic in the core, let's look at the core itself.

7. Inside the Service Provider Network

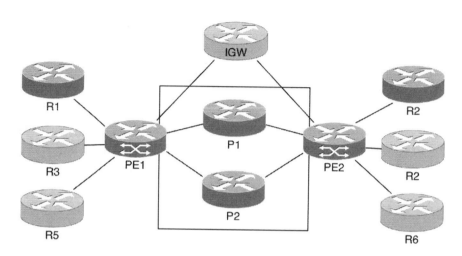

Hopefully, you have read my first book in this series, <u>BGP for Cisco Networks</u>, in that volume, I wrote about Extended Communities for BGP. A Community is a BGP attribute, used to group routes. It does not directly influence the BGP decision process, but is commonly used with this in mind. We can use a route-map to set values, such as the community of 200:300. Later on, we can use community-lists to match those settings and make decisions based on the values we target (i.e. matching a community of 200:300 and setting the local-preference to 150). They are very useful and powerful in BGP routing.

In 2006, the extended community attribute was added under RFC 4360, allowing it to be used within MPLS to hold the route target and the route origin communities.

There was a bit of a catch-22 when discussing the extended communities. Talking about it in any great depth in my previous book would have required an understanding of MPLS, and talking about it here requires some understanding of BGP. Hopefully, this is the right way round!

To recap our MPLS network, we have two provider edge routers, PE1 and PE2. These are peered with each other through BGP, or more specifically MP-BGP, which stands for Multi-Protocol BGP. This is also referred to as M-BGP.

Our customer traffic, which all has overlapping IP address schemes, is separated into different VRFs and carried across our BGP core. From a BGP point of view PE1 and PE2 are, relatively, unaware of how many routers exist between them. Although it is only one router, it could be 10, or 20, or 200. P1, which connects PE1 and PE2 together through EIGRP, is similarly unaware of the VRFs used by PE1 and PE2 to carry the customer data across.

The setup of BGP on PE1 and PE2 is worth explaining again. The following examples are taken from PE1. We started with a standard BGP peering, specifying the neighbor's IP address, its remote-as number, and our update-source:

```
router bgp 100
 bgp log-neighbor-changes
 neighbor 10.250.4.1 remote-as 100
 neighbor 10.250.4.1 update-source Loopback0
```

Next, we created an address-family with a type of VPNV4 and added our neighbor to that using the activate keyword. The IOS automatically added the line enabling extended communities to be sent:

```
address-family vpnv4
  neighbor 10.250.4.1 activate
  neighbor 10.250.4.1 send-community extended
exit-address-family
```

Next, we created address families, this time with a type of IPv4 VRF. We gave each one a name, corresponding to the VRFs for our customers. Within these address families, we redistributed from OSPF, again matching the OSPF process to the particular customer:

```
address-family ipv4 vrf BLUE
  redistribute ospf 3
exit-address-family
!
address-family ipv4 vrf RED
  redistribute ospf 1
exit-address-family
!
address-family ipv4 vrf WHITE
  redistribute ospf 2
exit-address-family
```

With this in place, we are able to look at some of the MPLS specific BGP functions.

If we try to look at the BGP routes on PE1 without specifying any vrf, we do not get any results:

```
PE1#sh ip bgp
PE1#
```

The peering is up and stable:

```
BGP neighbor is 10.250.4.1,  remote AS 100, internal link
  BGP version 4, remote router ID 10.250.4.1
  BGP state = Established, up for 02:21:03
  Last read 00:00:42, last write 00:00:44, hold time is 180,
keepalive interval is 60 seconds
  Neighbor sessions:
    1 active, is not multisession capable (disabled)
  Neighbor capabilities:
    Route refresh: advertised and received(new)
    Four-octets ASN Capability: advertised and received
    Address family IPv4 Unicast: advertised and received
    Address family VPNv4 Unicast: advertised and received
```

But, we are not advertising any of our own routes into BGP. We are, however, advertising our customers' routes, and we can see this by adding their specific information to the "sh ip bgp" command:

```
PE1#sh ip bgp vpnv4 vrf RED | beg Network
   Network          Next Hop            Metric LocPrf Weight Path
Route Distinguisher: 100:1 (default for vrf RED)
 *>  10.1.1.0/24     0.0.0.0                  0            32768 ?
 *>i10.2.2.0/24     10.250.4.1               0    100       0 ?
 *>i172.20.1.0/24   10.250.4.1               2    100       0 ?
 *>  192.168.1.0    10.1.1.2                 2            32768 ?
PE1#
```

Here, we can see that BGP is aware of the RD (Route Distinguisher) of 100:1. We set the first part of the RD to match our BGP AS and the second part to match the OSPF process specific to vrf RED.

If we look at greater depth at a particular prefix, we can see some very interesting information about how BGP is treating the VRFs:

```
PE1#sh ip bgp vpnv4 vrf RED 172.20.1.0/24
BGP routing table entry for 100:1:172.20.1.0/24, version 15
Paths: (1 available, best #1, table RED)
  Not advertised to any peer
```

```
    Local
        10.250.4.1 (metric 131072) from 10.250.4.1 (10.250.4.1)
          Origin incomplete, metric 2, localpref 100, valid, internal, best
          Extended Community: RT:100:1 OSPF DOMAIN ID:0x0005:0x000000010200
            OSPF RT:0.0.0.0:2:0 OSPF ROUTER ID:10.250.4.1:0
          mpls labels in/out nolabel/22
    PE1#
```

We can see that the routing table entry is denoted by the route distinguisher (100:1). The first line of returned data shows us "BGP routing table entry for 100:1:172.20.1.0/24", and each VRF has their own BGP routing table, as the second line shows "table RED".

On the seventh line, we get to see the extended community attribute: "Extended Community: RT:100:1 OSPF DOMAIN ID:0x0005:0x000000010200", where we have the route target (100:1) and the OSPF domain ID. This matches the following output from OSPF:

```
    PE2#sh ip ospf 1
     Routing Process "ospf 1" with ID 10.250.4.1
       Domain ID type 0x0005, value 0.0.0.1
     Start time: 00:00:39.728, Time elapsed: 00:18:02.360
     Supports only single TOS(TOS0) routes
     Supports opaque LSA
     Supports Link-local Signaling (LLS)
     Supports area transit capability
     Supports NSSA (compatible with RFC 1587)
     Connected to MPLS VPN Superbackbone, VRF RED
```

As per the RFC (4577), which explains how OSPF and BGP work together in a PE-CE environment, the domain identifier type is denoted as 0005, which is the Cisco default. IOS then encodes the value of 000000010200 onto the domain ID, which just means that it is in OSPF process 1. We can change the domain ID if we want to, as follows:

```
    R2#conf t
    R2(config)#router ospf 1
    R2(config-router)#domain-id 2.2.2.2
    R2(config-router)#exit
    R2(config)#

    PE2#conf t
    PE2(config)#router ospf 1 vrf RED
    PE2(config-router)#domain-id 2.2.2.2
    PE2(config-router)#
```

```
PE1#conf t
PE1(config)#router ospf 1 vrf RED
PE1(config-router)#domain-id 2.2.2.2
PE1(config-router)#

R1#conf t
R1(config)#router ospf 1
R1(config-router)#domain-id 2.2.2.2
R1(config-router)#
```

And now, we can see that this is shown in the OSPF process details, and within our "superbackbone":

```
PE2#sh ip ospf 1
 Routing Process "ospf 1" with ID 10.250.4.1
   Domain ID type 0x0005, value 2.2.2.2
PE2#sh ip bgp vpnv4 vrf RED 172.20.1.0/24 | i Extended
     Extended Community: RT:100:1 OSPF DOMAIN
ID:0x0005:0x020202020200
PE2#
```

Similarly, VRFs WHITE (OSPF process 2) and BLUE (OSPF process 3) have domain-ids that reflect their own process ID:

```
PE2#sh ip ospf 2 | i Domain
   Domain ID type 0x0005, value 0.0.0.2
PE2#sh ip bgp vpnv4 vrf WHITE 172.20.1.0/24 | i Extended
     Extended Community: RT:100:2 OSPF DOMAIN
ID:0x0005:0x000000020200
PE2#sh ip ospf 3 | i Domain
   Domain ID type 0x0005, value 0.0.0.3
PE2#sh ip bgp vpnv4 vrf BLUE 172.20.1.0/24 | i Extended
     Extended Community: RT:100:3 OSPF DOMAIN
ID:0x0005:0x000000030200
PE2#
```

Returning to the output we were previously discussing, on the eighth line (OSPF RT:0.0.0.0:2:0 OSPF ROUTER ID:10.250.4.1:0), we can see the OSPF route type ("OSPF RT:0.0.0.0:2:0"), along with the OSPF router ID ("10.250.4.1:0"), which corresponds to PE2's OSPF router ID for the VRF RED. The route type is broken down into three components: the 32-bit area number (showing us we are using area 0), the route-type, and any options. We can see a "2" as our route-type, though we are advertising type 1 LSAs. We will look at this in greater depth in the next chapter.

The last line ("mpls labels in/out nolabel/22") shows which VPN label the PE will attach to the RED company's VRF.

We can confirm this by checking PE2's routing table:

```
PE2#sh mpls forwarding-table
Local  Outgoing Prefix              Bytes Label  Outgoing     Next Hop
Label  Label    or Tunnel Id        Switched     interface
<truncated>
21     No Label 10.2.2.0/24[V]      0            aggregate/RED
22     No Label 172.20.1.0/24[V]    0            Gi2/0        10.2.2.2
<truncated>
```

We will look at the some different examples of how a different IGP can change the vpnv4 BGP details in the next chapter, where we will look at different PE-CE routing protocols.

7.1 The BGP-free core

The term BGP-free core is often spoken about when talking about MPLS networks. So, what is a *BGP-free core*? Well, we are using one here. We use BGP on the edges of our network, at the PE devices. However, instead of running BGP within the network, we have opted to use an IGP between our PE and P routers.

Within a BGP AS, we would require a full mesh between the routers. Also, we could encounter the rule of synchronization, which would necessitate having an IGP along with BGP to get all the routers to share the routes that they need. Therefore, it makes a lot of sense not to run BGP within the MPLS "cloud". Running multiple protocols on routers can be a drain on processing power, as well as taking up valuable memory.

We should, however, look at a couple of important aspects of a BGP core. We will step away from our main topology for a moment to look at these.

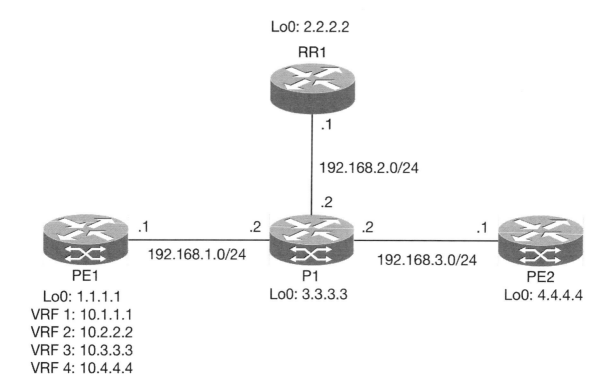

Our configurations are as follows:

RR1:

```
RR1(config)#int lo0
RR1(config-if)#ip add 2.2.2.2 255.255.255.255
RR1(config-if)#int gi 1/0
RR1(config-if)#ip add 192.168.2.1 255.255.255.0
RR1(config-if)#no shut
RR1(config-if)#router eigrp 100
RR1(config-router)#eigrp router-id 2.2.2.2
RR1(config-router)#netw 192.168.2.0 0.0.0.255
RR1(config-router)#netw 2.2.2.2 0.0.0.0
RR1(config-router)#router bgp 100
RR1(config-router)#neigh 1.1.1.1 remote-as 100
RR1(config-router)#neigh 1.1.1.1 update-source lo0
RR1(config-router)#neigh 4.4.4.4 remote-as 100
RR1(config-router)#neigh 4.4.4.4 update-source lo0
RR1(config-router)#address-family vpnv4
RR1(config-router-af)#neigh 1.1.1.1 activate
RR1(config-router-af)#neigh 1.1.1.1 send-community bo
RR1(config-router-af)#neigh 1.1.1.1 route-reflector-client
```

```
RR1(config-router-af)#neigh 4.4.4.4 activate
RR1(config-router-af)#neigh 4.4.4.4 send-community bo
RR1(config-router-af)#neigh 4.4.4.4 route-reflector-client
RR1(config-router-af)#end
```

PE1:

```
PE1(config)#int lo0
PE1(config-if)#ip add 1.1.1.1 255.255.255.255
PE1(config-if)#int gi 1/0
PE1(config-if)#ip add 192.168.1.1 255.255.255.0
PE1(config-if)#mpls ip
PE1(config-if)#no shut
PE1(config-if)#router eigrp 100
PE1(config-router)#eigrp router-id 1.1.1.1
PE1(config-router)#netw 192.168.1.0 0.0.0.255
PE1(config-router)#netw 1.1.1.1 0.0.0.0
PE1(config-router)#mpls ldp router-id lo0 force
PE1(config)#router bgp 100
PE1(config-router)#neigh 2.2.2.2 remote-as 100
PE1(config-router)#neigh 2.2.2.2 update-source lo0
PE1(config-router)#address-family vpnv4
PE1(config-router-af)#neigh 2.2.2.2 activate
PE1(config-router-af)#neigh 2.2.2.2 send-community bo
```

P1:

```
P1(config)#int lo0
P1(config-if)#ip add 3.3.3.3 255.255.255.255
P1(config-if)#int gi 2/0
P1(config-if)#desc Link to PE1
P1(config-if)#ip add 192.168.1.2 255.255.255.0
P1(config-if)#mpls ip
P1(config-if)#no shut
P1(config-if)#int gi 1/0
P1(config-if)#desc link to RR1
P1(config-if)#ip add 192.168.2.2 255.255.255.0
P1(config-if)#no shut
P1(config-if)#int gi 3/0
P1(config-if)#ip add 192.168.3.2 255.255.255.0
P1(config-if)#desc Link to PE2
P1(config-if)#no shut
P1(config-if)#mpls ip
P1(config-if)#router eigrp 100
P1(config-router)#eigrp router-id 3.3.3.3
P1(config-router)#netw 192.168.1.0 0.0.0.255
P1(config-router)#netw 192.168.2.0 0.0.0.255
```

```
P1(config-router)#netw 192.168.3.0 0.0.0.255
P1(config-router)#netw 3.3.3.3 0.0.0.0
P1(config-router)#mpls ldp router-id lo0 force
```

PE2:

```
PE2(config)#int lo0
PE2(config-if)#ip add 4.4.4.4 255.255.255.255
PE2(config-if)#int gi 1/0
PE2(config-if)#ip add 192.168.3.1 255.255.255.0
PE2(config-if)#no shut
PE2(config-if)#mpls ip
PE2(config-if)#router eigrp 100
PE2(config-router)#eigrp router-id 4.4.4.4
PE2(config-router)#netw 192.168.3.0 0.0.0.255
PE2(config-router)#netw 4.4.4.4 0.0.0.0
PE2(config-router)#mpls ldp router-id lo0 force
PE2(config)#router bgp 100
PE2(config-router)#neigh 2.2.2.2 remote-as 100
PE2(config-router)#neigh 2.2.2.2 update-source lo0
PE2(config-router)#address-family vpnv4
PE2(config-router-af)#neigh 2.2.2.2 activate
PE2(config-router-af)#neigh 2.2.2.2 send-community bo
PE2(config-router-af)#exit
PE2(config-router)#exit
```

On PE1 and PE2, we will add a small handful of VRFs:

```
PE1(config-router-af)#ip vrf 1
PE1(config-vrf)#rd 1:1
PE1(config-vrf)#route-target bo 1:1
PE1(config-vrf)#exit
PE1(config)#ip vrf 2
PE1(config-vrf)#rd 2:2
PE1(config-vrf)#route-target bo 2:2
PE1(config-vrf)#exit
PE1(config)#ip vrf 3
PE1(config-vrf)#rd 3:3
PE1(config-vrf)#route-target bo 3:3
PE1(config)#int lo1
PE1(config-if)#ip vrf for 1
PE1(config-if)#ip add 10.1.1.1 255.255.255.255
PE1(config-if)#int lo2
PE1(config-if)#ip vrf for 2
PE1(config-if)#ip add 10.2.2.2 255.255.255.255
PE1(config-if)#int lo3
```

```
PE1(config-if)#ip vrf for 3
PE1(config-if)#ip add 10.3.3.3 255.255.255.255

PE2(config)#ip vrf 1
PE2(config-vrf)#rd 1:1
PE2(config-vrf)#route-tar bo 1:1
PE2(config-vrf)#ip vrf 2
PE2(config-vrf)#rd 2:2
PE2(config-vrf)#route-tar bo 2:2
PE2(config-vrf)#ip vrf 3
PE2(config-vrf)#rd 3:3
PE2(config-vrf)#route-tar bo 3:3
PE2(config-vrf)#end
```

Next, we add these to BGP:

```
PE1(config-if)#router bgp 100
PE1(config-router)#address-family ipv4 vrf 1
PE1(config-router-af)#network 10.1.1.1 mask 255.255.255.255
PE1(config-router-af)#exit
PE1(config-router)#address-family ipv4 vrf 2
PE1(config-router-af)#network 10.2.2.2 mask 255.255.255.255
PE1(config-router-af)#exit
PE1(config-router)#address-family ipv4 vrf 3
PE1(config-router-af)#network 10.3.3.3 mask 255.255.255.255
PE1(config-router-af)#exit
PE1(config-router)#exit
```

RR1 is advertising three prefixes to PE2:

```
RR1#sh bgp vpnv4 uni all neigh 4.4.4.4 advertised-routes | i Total
Total number of prefixes 3
RR1#

PE2#sh ip bgp vpnv4 all | beg Net
   Network         Next Hop       Metric LocPrf Weight Path
Route Distinguisher: 1:1 (default for vrf 1)
*>i 10.1.1.1/32    1.1.1.1             0    100      0 i
Route Distinguisher: 2:2 (default for vrf 2)
*>i 10.2.2.2/32    1.1.1.1             0    100      0 i
Route Distinguisher: 3:3 (default for vrf 3)
*>i 10.3.3.3/32    1.1.1.1             0    100      0 i
PE2#
```

Now, we will add another to PE1, but not to PE2, and advertise it in BGP:

```
PE1(config)#ip vrf 4
PE1(config-vrf)#rd 4:4
PE1(config-vrf)#route-target bo 4:4
PE1(config-vrf)#int lo4
PE1(config-if)#ip vrf for 4
PE1(config-if)#ip add 10.4.4.4 255.255.255.255
PE1(config-if)#router bgp 100
PE1(config-router)#address-family ipv4 vrf 4
PE1(config-router-af)#netw 10.4.4.4 mask 255.255.255.255
PE1(config-router-af)#
```

RR1 is now advertising four prefixes:

```
RR1#sh bgp vpnv4 uni all neigh 4.4.4.4 advertised-routes | i Total
Total number of prefixes 4
RR1#
```

However, PE2 is unaware of this RT and therefore rejects the route. This is called automatic route filtering. We can see the following in the debug output:

```
PE2#debug bgp all updates
BGP updates debugging is on for all address families
PE2#
*Sep 24 19:41:31.627: BGP(4): 2.2.2.2 rcvd UPDATE w/ attr: nexthop
1.1.1.1, origin i, localpref 100, metric 0, originator 1.1.1.1,
clusterlist 2.2.2.2, extended community RT:4:4
*Sep 24 19:41:31.639: BGP(4): 2.2.2.2 rcvd 4:4:10.4.4.4/32, label 24 -
- DENIED due to: extended community not supported;
PE2#
```

This is, for the most part, fine and will not create that much of an issue on PE2. The issue comes though, if we add a large number of VRFs to PE1 and advertise them through BGP. This can lead to greater work on PE2

There is a neat way around this. We can create another address family on RR1 and PE1, called the "rtfilter." The rtfilter allows the PE device to advertise a list of RTs that it wishes to import, called the route target constraint. The route-reflector then creates an outbound filter, to only send the routes belonging to the requested RTs:

```
RR1#conf t
RR1(config)#router bgp 100
RR1(config-router)#address-family rtfilter unicast
RR1(config-router-af)#neig 4.4.4.4 activate
```

```
RR1(config-router-af)#neig 4.4.4.4 route-reflector-client
RR1(config-router-af)#
RR1(config-router-af)#end

PE2#conf t
PE2(config)#router bgp 100
PE2(config-router)#address-family rtfilter unicast
PE2(config-router-af)#neigh 2.2.2.2 activate
PE2(config-router-af)#
```

Even though we are still advertising four routes from PE1, RR1 only advertises the ones requested by PE2.

```
RR1#sh bgp vpnv4 uni all neigh 4.4.4.4 advertised-routes | i Total
Total number of prefixes 3
RR1#
```

PE2 no longer needs to spend precious CPU cycles ignoring routes.

The final part of using BGP within the core, specifically; using a route-reflector within the core, is probably the most obvious one. If we shut down Gi1/0 on RR1 (simulating a failure of that router), after a short period, PE1 and PE2 will lose the VPNv4 routes that from the other PE device that are passed through that particular route-reflector. Best practice suggests to have more than one route-reflector.

8. Customer to Provider Routing

In our topology so far, we have used OSPF for our CE-PE routing protocol, but we are not limited to just this one protocol. From the viewpoint of the CE router, we are not doing anything unusual. We have no VRFs, and it is not configured for MPLS. The CE router can do anything we want it to. This includes RIP, EIGRP, IS-IS, static routing, and BGP. We will now set these up on our CE routers. They do not have to match at either side; RED's R1 router can run RIP, with R2 running EIGRP if we so wished. Before we start configuring new routers we'll, finish off some OSPF features first though.

8.1 CE-PE routing with OSPF

We have used OSPF as our IGP so far; so, it makes sense to start this chapter with a few last OSPF topics before we move on.

OSPF Sham-links

Sham-links are included in the expanded blueprint (see Alternative Syllabi), hence it's incluclsion here.

Consider this change in our topology: the BLUE company decides to add a backup route between their two sites. It is not as fast as the MPLS line, but it is good for some redundancy.

The topology now looks like this:

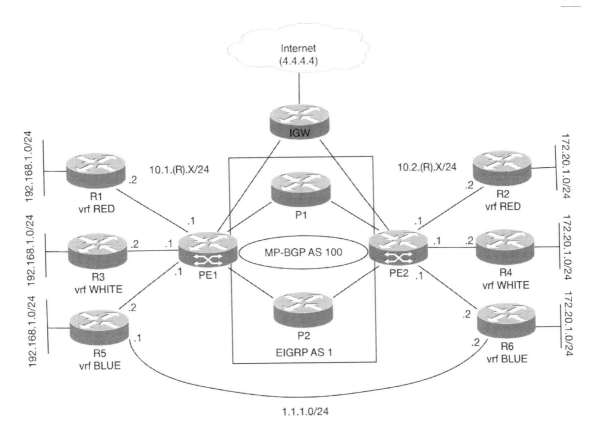

Our routing table for R5 looks like this at the moment:

```
R5#sh ip route | beg Gate
Gateway of last resort is not set

        10.0.0.0/8 is variably subnetted, 3 subnets, 2 masks
C          10.1.5.0/24 is directly connected, GigabitEthernet1/0
L          10.1.5.2/32 is directly connected, GigabitEthernet1/0
O IA       10.2.6.0/24 [110/2] via 10.1.5.1, 00:15:03, Gi1/0
        172.20.0.0/24 is subnetted, 1 subnets
O IA       172.20.1.0 [110/3] via 10.1.5.1, 00:15:03, Gi1/0
        192.168.1.0/24 is variably subnetted, 2 subnets, 2 masks
C          192.168.1.0/24 is directly connected, Loopback0
L          192.168.1.1/32 is directly connected, Loopback0
R5#
```

R5 and R6 are configured as follows:

```
R5#conf t
R5(config)#int gi2/0
```

```
R5(config-if)#ip add 1.1.1.1 255.255.255.0
R5(config-if)#no shut
R5(config-if)#ip ospf 3 area 0

R6#conf t
R6(config)#int gi2/0
R6(config-if)#ip add 1.1.1.2 255.255.255.0
R6(config-if)#no shut
R6(config-if)#ip ospf 3 area 0
```

And now R5's routing table looks like this:

```
R5#sh ip route | beg Gate
Gateway of last resort is not set

      1.0.0.0/8 is variably subnetted, 2 subnets, 2 masks
C        1.1.1.0/24 is directly connected, GigabitEthernet2/0
L        1.1.1.1/32 is directly connected, GigabitEthernet2/0
      10.0.0.0/8 is variably subnetted, 3 subnets, 2 masks
C        10.1.5.0/24 is directly connected, GigabitEthernet1/0
L        10.1.5.2/32 is directly connected, GigabitEthernet1/0
O        10.2.6.0/24 [110/2] via 1.1.1.2, 00:00:53, Gi2/0
      172.20.0.0/24 is subnetted, 1 subnets
O        172.20.1.0 [110/2] via 1.1.1.2, 00:00:53, Gi2/0
      192.168.1.0/24 is variably subnetted, 2 subnets, 2 masks
C        192.168.1.0/24 is directly connected, Loopback0
L        192.168.1.1/32 is directly connected, Loopback0
R5#
```

R5 now prefers the backup link for R6's connected networks. This does make a lot of sense, so the behavior is definitely expected. The routes through the MPLS cloud are seen as O IA meaning OSPF inter-area, which are less preferred than the intra-area routes that the new link offers:

```
R5#sh ip route 172.20.1.0
Routing entry for 172.20.1.0/24
  Known via "ospf 3", distance 110, metric 2, type intra area
  Last update from 1.1.1.2 on GigabitEthernet2/0, 00:11:46 ago
  Routing Descriptor Blocks:
  * 1.1.1.2, from 172.20.1.1, 00:11:46 ago, via GigabitEthernet2/0
      Route metric is 2, traffic share count is 1
R5#
```

The issue here is that the link is designed to be a back-up link, rather than the default. Because of the preference for intra-area routes over inter-area routes, raising the OSPF cost on the Gi 2/0 interfaces will have no effect:

```
R5#conf t
R5(config)#int gi 2/0
R5(config-if)#ip ospf cost 65535
R5(config-if)#exit
R5(config)#exit
R5#sh ip route ospf | beg Gate
Gateway of last resort is not set

      10.0.0.0/8 is variably subnetted, 3 subnets, 2 masks
O        10.2.6.0/24 [110/65536] via 1.1.1.2, 00:01:24, Gi2/0
      172.20.0.0/24 is subnetted, 1 subnets
O        172.20.1.0 [110/65536] via 1.1.1.2, 00:01:24, Gi2/0
R5#

R6#conf t
R6(config)#int gi 2/0
R6(config-if)#ip ospf cost 65535
R6(config-if)#exit
R6(config)#exit
R6#sh ip route ospf | beg Gate
Gateway of last resort is not set

      10.0.0.0/8 is variably subnetted, 3 subnets, 2 masks
O        10.1.5.0/24 [110/65536] via 1.1.1.1, 00:00:30, Gi2/0
O     192.168.1.0/24 [110/65536] via 1.1.1.1, 00:00:30, Gi2/0
R6#
```

Although the cost has increased from 2 to the largest possible of 65535, the direct route over the backup route is still preferred. We must instead use a sham link.

A sham link acts as an intra-area connection between our PE routers, effectively hiding the BGP process inside our MPLS core. There are a couple of requirements for a sham link, which include dedicated loopback interfaces that must be advertised with /32 addresses, that are reachable by the other PE router, and that these loopback interfaces must be added to the particular VRF for the OSPF process.

First, we create the loopback interfaces, numbering them with the respective router's number. If you add the ip address before setting the ip vrf forwarding command, remember to set the IP address again as it will be removed (as shown on PE2):

```
PE1#conf t
PE1(config)#int lo5
PE1(config-if)#ip vrf forwarding BLUE
PE1(config-if)#ip add 2.2.2.5 255.255.255.255
```

```
    PE1(config-if)#exit

    PE2#conf t
    PE2(config)#int lo6
    PE2(config-if)#ip add 2.2.2.6 255.255.255.255
    PE2(config-if)#ip vrf forwarding BLUE
    % Interface Loopback6 IPv4 disabled and address(es) removed due to
    disabling VRF BLUE
    PE2(config-if)#ip add 2.2.2.6 255.255.255.255
    PE2(config-if)#exit
```

Since the loopbacks need to be reachable from the other PE router, they must be advertised within BGP:

```
    PE1(config)#router bgp 100
    PE1(config-router)#address-family ipv4 vrf BLUE
    PE1(config-router-af)#network 2.2.2.5 mask 255.255.255.255
    PE1(config-router-af)#

    PE2(config)#router bgp 100
    PE2(config-router)#address-family ipv4 vrf BLUE
    PE2(config-router-af)#network 2.2.2.6 mask 255.255.255.255
    PE2(config-router-af)#
```

We can see the loopback within the routing table for vrf BLUE, and we have reachability:

```
    PE2#sh ip route vrf BLUE | beg Gate
    Gateway of last resort is not set

          1.0.0.0/24 is subnetted, 1 subnets
    O        1.1.1.0 [110/65536] via 10.2.6.2, 00:28:59, Gi4/0
          2.0.0.0/32 is subnetted, 2 subnets
    B        2.2.2.5 [200/0] via 10.250.3.1, 00:01:41
    C        2.2.2.6 is directly connected, Loopback6
          10.0.0.0/8 is variably subnetted, 3 subnets, 2 masks
    O        10.1.5.0/24 [110/65537] via 10.2.6.2, 00:28:59, Gi4/0
    C        10.2.6.0/24 is directly connected, GigabitEthernet4/0
    L        10.2.6.1/32 is directly connected, GigabitEthernet4/0
          172.20.0.0/24 is subnetted, 1 subnets
    O        172.20.1.0 [110/2] via 10.2.6.2, 01:42:12, Gi4/0
    O     192.168.1.0/24 [110/65537] via 10.2.6.2, 00:28:59, Gi4/0
    PE2#ping vrf BLUE 2.2.2.5 so lo6
    Type escape sequence to abort.
    Sending 5, 100-byte ICMP Echos to 2.2.2.5, timeout is 2 seconds:
    Packet sent with a source address of 2.2.2.6
    !!!!!
```

```
Success rate is 100 percent (5/5)
PE2#
```

Our remaining task is to configure the sham-links within the OSPF process for vrf BLUE:

```
PE1(config)#router ospf 3 vrf BLUE
PE1(config-router)#area 0 sham-link 2.2.2.5 2.2.2.6
PE1(config-router)#

PE2(config)#router ospf 3 vrf BLUE
PE2(config-router)#area 0 sham-link 2.2.2.6 2.2.2.5
PE2(config-router)#
*May  8 11:53:34.215: %OSPF-5-ADJCHG: Process 3, Nbr 10.250.3.5 on
OSPF_SL0 from LOADING to FULL, Loading Done
PE2(config-router)#
```

We can see that we have a new adjacency formed, which we can confirm by looking at the OSPF neighbors from one of the PE routers. We can use the "sh ip ospf sham-links" command as well:

```
PE1#sh ip ospf neigh

Neighbor ID     Pri   State        Dead Time   Address     Interface
10.250.4.4       0    FULL/  -        -        2.2.2.6     OSPF_SL0
192.168.1.1      1    FULL/DR      00:00:31    10.1.5.2    Gi4/0
192.168.1.1      1    FULL/DR      00:00:36    10.1.3.2    Gi3/0
192.168.1.1      1    FULL/DR      00:00:31    10.1.1.2    Gi2/0
PE1#sh ip ospf sham-links
Sham Link OSPF_SL0 to address 2.2.2.6 is up
Area 0 source address 2.2.2.5
  Run as demand circuit
  DoNotAge LSA allowed. Cost of using 1 State POINT_TO_POINT,
  Timer intervals configured, Hello 10, Dead 40, Wait 40,
    Hello due in 00:00:05
    Adjacency State FULL (Hello suppressed)
    Index 2/2, retransmission queue length 0, number of
retransmission 0
    First 0x0(0)/0x0(0) Next 0x0(0)/0x0(0)
    Last retransmission scan length is 0, maximum is 0
    Last retransmission scan time is 0 msec, maximum is 0 msec
PE1#
```

Our routing tables on R5 and R6 have also updated, now preferring the route through the MPLS network:

```
R5#sh ip route ospf | beg Gate
```

```
Gateway of last resort is not set

         2.0.0.0/32 is subnetted, 2 subnets
O E2     2.2.2.5 [110/1] via 10.1.5.1, 00:06:06, GigabitEthernet1/0
O E2     2.2.2.6 [110/1] via 10.1.5.1, 00:05:18, GigabitEthernet1/0
         10.0.0.0/8 is variably subnetted, 3 subnets, 2 masks
O           10.2.6.0/24 [110/3] via 10.1.5.1, 00:01:15, Gi1/0
         172.20.0.0/24 is subnetted, 1 subnets
O           172.20.1.0 [110/4] via 10.1.5.1, 00:01:15, Gi1/0
R5#

R6#sh ip route ospf | beg Gate
Gateway of last resort is not set

         2.0.0.0/32 is subnetted, 2 subnets
O E2     2.2.2.5 [110/1] via 10.2.6.1, 00:07:06, GigabitEthernet1/0
O E2     2.2.2.6 [110/1] via 10.2.6.1, 00:06:18, GigabitEthernet1/0
         10.0.0.0/8 is variably subnetted, 3 subnets, 2 masks
O           10.1.5.0/24 [110/3] via 10.2.6.1, 00:02:15, Gi1/0
O        192.168.1.0/24 [110/4] via 10.2.6.1, 00:02:15, Gi1/0
R6#
```

If we shut down the Gi1/0 interface on R6, we should see the backup line becoming the preferred route:

```
R6#conf t
R6(config)#int gi 1/0
R6(config-if)#shut
R6(config-if)#exit
*May  10 11:57:10.039: %OSPF-5-ADJCHG: Process 3, Nbr 10.250.4.4 on
GigabitEthernet1/0 from FULL to DOWN, Neighbor Down: Interface down
or detached
R6(config)#exit
R6#
*May  10 11:57:12.015: %LINK-5-CHANGED: Interface GigabitEthernet1/0,
changed state to administratively down
*May  10 11:57:13.015: %LINEPROTO-5-UPDOWN: Line protocol on
Interface GigabitEthernet1/0, changed state to down
*May  10 11:57:13.095: %SYS-5-CONFIG_I: Configured from console by
console
R6#sh ip route ospf | beg Gate
Gateway of last resort is not set

         2.0.0.0/32 is subnetted, 2 subnets
O E2     2.2.2.5 [110/1] via 1.1.1.1, 00:00:02, GigabitEthernet2/0
O E2     2.2.2.6 [110/1] via 1.1.1.1, 00:00:02, GigabitEthernet2/0
         10.0.0.0/24 is subnetted, 1 subnets
```

```
O          10.1.5.0 [110/65536] via 1.1.1.1, 00:00:02, Gi2/0
O          192.168.1.0/24 [110/65536] via 1.1.1.1, 00:00:02, Gi2/0
R6#
```

This is working exactly how we would like it to, and if we bring the interface back up again, we can see the routes preferring the MPLS network again:

```
R6#conf t
R6(config)#int gi1/0
R6(config-if)#no shut
R6(config-if)#
*May 10 11:59:04.051: %LINK-3-UPDOWN: Interface GigabitEthernet1/0, changed state to up
*May 10 11:59:05.051: %LINEPROTO-5-UPDOWN: Line protocol on Interface GigabitEthernet1/0, changed state to up
*May 10 11:59:09.803: %OSPF-5-ADJCHG: Process 3, Nbr 10.250.4.4 on GigabitEthernet1/0 from LOADING to FULL, Loading Done
R6(config-if)#do sh ip route ospf | beg Gate
Gateway of last resort is not set

      2.0.0.0/32 is subnetted, 2 subnets
O E2     2.2.2.5 [110/1] via 10.2.6.1, 00:00:40, GigabitEthernet1/0
O E2     2.2.2.6 [110/1] via 10.2.6.1, 00:00:40, GigabitEthernet1/0
      10.0.0.0/8 is variably subnetted, 3 subnets, 2 masks
O        10.1.5.0/24 [110/3] via 10.2.6.1, 00:00:40, Gi1/0
O        192.168.1.0/24 [110/4] via 10.2.6.1, 00:00:40, Gi1/0
R6(config-if)#
```

Instead of having the largest cost possible for the backup link, we could have a lower cost and also specify a cost on our sham-link. For example, we could specify a cost of 10:

```
PE1(config)#router ospf 3 vrf BLUE
PE1(config-router)#area 0 sham-link 2.2.2.5 2.2.2.6 cost 10
```

This would allow us to control the costs to a degree and have greater control over our routing. Now that we have two links between R5 and R6 and are effectively advertising our routes through both links, what is there to prevent routing loops? It is very feasible that routes advertised through the sham-link to one router could be advertised back through the MPLS network. Well, thankfully OSPF has its own inbuilt mechanism to prevent routing loops. If that was not enough, we have another when we start to redistribute between OSPF and BGP. This is with the down bit, or DN Bit. We will look at this a bit later when we look at VRF-lite.

That pretty much wraps up OSPF for the moment. Let's move on to something a little simpler and look at RIP. We will then go back to the slightly more complex and look at EIGRP and BGP.

8.2 CE-PE Routing with RIP

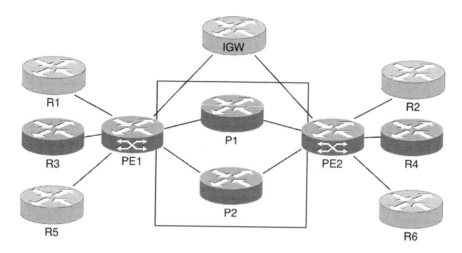

We will set up R4 to use RIP to communicate with R3. As far as routing protocols go, RIP is fairly easy to master. It does have ts own little quirks, but it is certainly less complex than, say OSPF, or EIGRP.

As this is the first time we have set up a different protocol to work with our MPLS backbone, let's just have a quick refresher of the current set up of PE2 and R4 for VRF WHITE:

On PE2, we have a VRF defined, which sets our route distinguisher and the route targets that we want to import and export. This will not need to be changed.

```
ip vrf WHITE
 rd 100:2
 route-target export 100:2
 route-target import 100:2
```

We have an interface to connect us to our customer, which specifies that it will be forwarding traffic for VRF WHITE and that it uses OSPF.

```
interface GigabitEthernet3/0
 ip vrf forwarding WHITE
 ip address 10.2.4.1 255.255.255.0
```

```
 ip ospf 2 area 0
 negotiation auto
```

We have a VRF-specific OSPF routing process; this will also redistribute from our BGP process into OSPF:

```
router ospf 2 vrf WHITE
 router-id 10.250.4.3
 redistribute bgp 100 subnets
```

Lastly, we have an address family within our BGP routing process that will redistribute our OSPF process into BGP:

```
router bgp 100
 address-family ipv4 vrf WHITE
  redistribute ospf 2
 exit-address-family
```

The setup on R4 is less complex. It is not MPLS aware, nor does it need to be. It only knows about OSPF:

```
interface Loopback0
 ip address 172.20.1.1 255.255.255.0
 ip ospf network point-to-point
 ip ospf 2 area 0
!
interface GigabitEthernet1/0
 ip address 10.2.4.2 255.255.255.0
 ip ospf 2 area 0
 negotiation auto
!
router ospf 2
```

We will begin by removing the current OSPF connection between R4 and PE2, and replacing it with a RIP one. We can remove the majority of it with just one command (no router ospf 2):

```
R4#conf t
R4(config)#no router ospf 2
R4(config)#
*May  10 13:31:55.515: %OSPF-5-ADJCHG: Process 2, Nbr 10.250.4.3 on
GigabitEthernet1/0 from FULL to DOWN, Neighbor Down: Interface down
or detached
R4(config)#
```

Now we can see that most of the configuration has been removed for us:

```
R4(config)#do sh run int lo0
Building configuration...

Current configuration : 96 bytes
!
interface Loopback0
 ip address 172.20.1.1 255.255.255.0
 ip ospf network point-to-point
end

R4(config)#do sh run int gi1/0
Building configuration...

Current configuration : 89 bytes
!
interface GigabitEthernet1/0
 ip address 10.2.4.2 255.255.255.0
 negotiation auto
end
```

We can remove the remaining OSPF command on lo0, or we could leave it in, as it won't cause us any problems within our topology:

```
R4(config)#int lo0
R4(config-if)#no ip ospf network point-to-point
R4(config-if)#exit
```

Now, we can start setting up our RIP process:

```
R4(config)#router rip
R4(config-router)#version 2
R4(config-router)#no auto-summary
R4(config-router)#network 172.20.1.0
R4(config-router)#network 10.2.4.0
R4(config-router)#
```

Similarly, we can do the same on PE2:

```
PE2#conf t
PE2(config)#no router ospf 2 vrf WHITE
```

The OSPF configuration is now removed from the connecting interface:

```
PE2(config)#do sh run int gi3/0
Building configuration...

Current configuration : 114 bytes
!
interface GigabitEthernet3/0
 ip vrf forwarding WHITE
 ip address 10.2.4.1 255.255.255.0
 negotiation auto
end
```

The redistribution command has also been removed from the BGP address family:

```
PE2#sh run | beg address-family
address-family vpnv4
  neighbor 10.250.3.1 activate
  neighbor 10.250.3.1 send-community extended
 exit-address-family
 !
 address-family ipv4 vrf BLUE
  network 2.2.2.6 mask 255.255.255.255
  redistribute ospf 3
 exit-address-family
 !
 address-family ipv4 vrf RED
  redistribute ospf 1
 exit-address-family
 !
 address-family ipv4 vrf WHITE
 exit-address-family
```

We can now configure RIP on PE2, which, thankfully, supports address families. We also need to remember to redistribute BGP into our RIP network:

```
PE2#conf t
PE2(config)#router rip
PE2(config-router)#version 2
PE2(config-router)#no auto-summary
PE2(config-router)#address-family ipv4 vrf WHITE
PE2(config-router-af)#version 2
PE2(config-router-af)#no auto-summary
PE2(config-router-af)#network 10.2.4.0
PE2(config-router-af)#redistribute bgp 100 metric 1
PE2(config-router-af)#exit-address-family
PE2(config-router)#
```

We need to redistribute RIP onto our BGP process:

```
PE2(config)#router bgp 100
PE2(config-router)#address-family ipv4 vrf WHITE
PE2(config-router-af)#redistribute rip
PE2(config-router-af)#
```

That is all the reconfiguration that we need to do. We can check the routing table on R4 and R3 to make sure that the two can still talk:

```
R4#sh ip route rip | beg Gate
Gateway of last resort is not set

      10.0.0.0/8 is variably subnetted, 3 subnets, 2 masks
R        10.1.3.0/24 [120/1] via 10.2.4.1, 00:00:06, Gi1/0
R        192.168.1.0/24 [120/1] via 10.2.4.1, 00:00:06, Gi1/0
R4#ping 192.168.1.1
Type escape sequence to abort.
Sending 5, 100-byte ICMP Echos to 192.168.1.1, timeout is 2 seconds:
!!!!!
Success rate is 100 percent (5/5)
R4#

R3#sh ip route ospf | beg Gate
Gateway of last resort is not set

      10.0.0.0/8 is variably subnetted, 3 subnets, 2 masks
O E2     10.2.4.0/24 [110/1] via 10.1.3.1, 00:02:14, Gi1/0
      172.20.0.0/24 is subnetted, 1 subnets
O E2     172.20.1.0 [110/1] via 10.1.3.1, 00:02:14, Gi1/0
R3#ping 172.20.1.1
Type escape sequence to abort.
Sending 5, 100-byte ICMP Echos to 172.20.1.1, timeout is 2 seconds:
!!!!!
Success rate is 100 percent (5/5)
R3#telnet 172.20.1.1
Trying 172.20.1.1 ... Open


User Access Verification

Password:
R4>exit

[Connection to 172.20.1.1 closed by foreign host]
R3#
```

And there we have using RIP as our CE-PE routing protocol.

8.3 CE-PE Routing with EIGRP

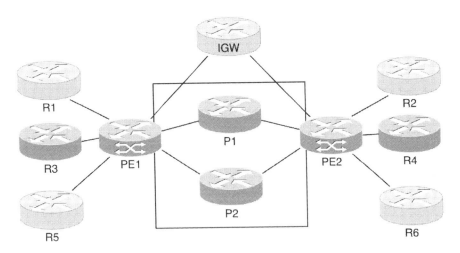

We will now turn our attention to R3, and set this to use EIGRP to peer with PE1.

The process is very similar to how we have just set R4 and PE2 up to use RIP.

```
R3(config)#no router ospf 2
R3(config)#
*May  10 14:47:45.610: %OSPF-5-ADJCHG: Process 2, Nbr 10.250.3.3 on
GigabitEthernet1/0 from FULL to DOWN, Neighbor Down: Interface down
or detached
R3(config)#int lo0
R3(config-if)#no ip ospf network point-to-point
R3(config-if)#router eigrp 3
R3(config-router)#network 192.168.1.0 0.0.0.255
R3(config-router)#network 10.1.3.0 0.0.0.255


PE1(config)#no router ospf 2 vrf WHITE
PE1(config)#router eigrp 3
PE1(config-router)#address-family ipv4 vrf WHITE
PE1(config-router-af)#network 10.1.3.0 0.0.0.255
PE1(config-router-af)#redistribute bgp 100 metric 1000 10 100 1 1500
PE1(config-router-af)#exit
%Warning: EIGRP Autonomous-System number must be provided
```

If you see the warning above, it can be a little confusing. If you use the context sensitive help (the question mark to you and me), there does not appear to be an option for setting a separate EIGRP AS within an address family:

```
PE1(config-router)#address-family ipv4 vrf WHITE
PE1(config-router-af)#?
Address Family configuration commands:
  auto-summary           Enable automatic network number summarization
  bfd                    BFD configuration commands
  default                Set a command to its defaults
  default-information    Control distribution of default information
  default-metric         Set metric of redistributed routes
  distance               Define an administrative distance
  distribute-list        Filter entries in eigrp updates
  eigrp                  EIGRP specific commands
  exit-address-family    Exit Address Family configuration mode
  help                   Description of the interactive help system
  maximum-paths          Forward packets over multiple paths
  maximum-prefix         Maximum number of prefixes acceptable in
aggregate
  metric                 Modify metrics and parameters for
advertisement
  neighbor               Specify a neighbor router
  network                Enable routing on an IP network
  no                     Negate a command or set its defaults
  offset-list            Add or subtract offset from EIGRP metrics
  passive-interface      Suppress routing updates on an interface
  redistribute           Redistribute IPv4 routes from another routing
protocol
  shutdown               Shutdown address family
  summary-metric         Specify summary to apply metric/filtering
  timers                 Adjust routing timers
```

Strangely though, it is there:

```
PE1(config-router-af)#autonomous-system 3
PE1(config-router-af)#
*May  10 15:02:15.078: %DUAL-5-NBRCHANGE: EIGRP-IPv4 3: Neighbor
10.1.3.2 (GigabitEthernet3/0) is up: new adjacency
PE1(config-router-af)#
```

Thankfully, the warning displayed tells us what we need to configure. We can have different AS numbers for each VRF and a separate one for our main EIGRP routing process this way. We will see a different implementation of this when we look at EIGRP "named mode" later on. This ability to separate EIGRP processes makes perfect sense, as a VRF is independent of the global routing table, and has its own routing table. It should also have its own separate AS number, similar to the OSPF process. We will see this also with the BGP AS number when we explore using BGP as our CE-PE routing protocol.

We can, however, see the requirement for the EIGRP AS when we create the address family within EIGRP:

```
PE1(config)#router eigrp 3
PE1(config-router)#address-family ipv4 vrf WHITE ?
  autonomous-system  Specify Address-Family Autonomous System Number
  <cr>

PE1(config-router)#address-family ipv4 vrf WHITE autonomous-system 3
PE1(config-router-af)#exit
PE1(config-router)#exit
PE1(config)#exit
PE1#
```

Depending on which method we choose, our configuration will reflect the different styles. Our first method will show, as per this truncated output, the autonomous system on a separate line.

```
router eigrp 3
 !
 address-family ipv4 vrf WHITE
  autonomous-system 3
 exit-address-family
 !
```

If we create the address family with the autonomous system specified on the same line, then, this is shown as follows:

```
router eigrp 3
 !
 address-family ipv4 vrf WHITE autonomous-system 3
 exit-address-family
 !
```

If we mix both the options, we get the following:

```
router eigrp 3
 !
 address-family ipv4 vrf WHITE autonomous-system 3
  autonomous-system 3
```

```
    exit-address-family
    !
```

We cannot, for obvious reasons, have a different AS specified within the address family:

```
    PE1(config)#router eigrp 3
    PE1(config-router)#address-family ipv4 vrf WHITE
    PE1(config-router-af)#autonomous-system 4
    Changing from AS(3) to AS(4) is not allowed
    PE1(config-router-af)#
```

By specifying the AS, we can see the adjacency come up.

We still need to complete the last remaining task, which is to redistribute EIGRP into BGP:

```
    PE1(config)#router bgp 100
    PE1(config-router)#address-family ipv4 vrf WHITE
    PE1(config-router-af)#redistribute eigrp 3 metric 1
```

Now, R3 can see the routes that were advertised by R4's RIP process in its own routing table as EIGRP learned routes:

```
    R3#sh ip route eigrp | beg Gate
    Gateway of last resort is not set

         10.0.0.0/8 is variably subnetted, 3 subnets, 2 masks
    D EX    10.2.4.0/24 [170/2562816] via 10.1.3.1, 00:08:26, Gi1/0
         172.20.0.0/24 is subnetted, 1 subnets
    D EX    172.20.1.0 [170/2562816] via 10.1.3.1, 00:08:26, Gi1/0
    R3#ping 172.20.1.1
    Type escape sequence to abort.
    Sending 5, 100-byte ICMP Echos to 172.20.1.1, timeout is 2 seconds:
    !!!!!
    Success rate is 100 percent (5/5)
    R3#
```

Now, we will have a look at using BGP as our CE-PE protocol.

8.4 CE-PE Routing with BGP

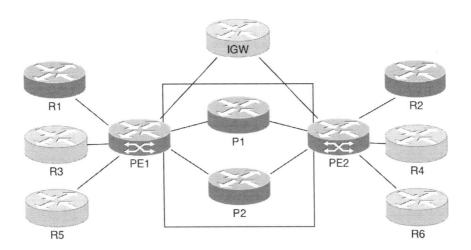

We will continue back up the topology and set R1 and R2 to use BGP. Similar to the previous couple of examples, we start by removing the OSPF configuration from both routers:

```
R1#conf t
R1(config)#no router ospf 1
R1(config)#int lo0
R1(config-if)#no ip ospf network point-to-point
R1(config-if)#

R2#conf t
R2(config)#no router ospf 1
R2(config)#int lo0
R2(config-if)#no ip ospf network point-to-point
R2(config-if)#
```

Then, we can create the BGP processes starting with our CE routers. We will be using AS 65001 for our purposes, advertise our networks and form an eBGP relationship with the respective PE routers:

```
R1(config)#router bgp 65001
R1(config-router)#network 10.1.1.0 mask 255.255.255.0
R1(config-router)#network 192.168.1.0 mask 255.255.255.0
R1(config-router)#neighbor 10.1.1.1 remote-as 100

R2(config-if)#router bgp 65001
R2(config-router)#network 172.20.1.0 mask 255.255.255.0
```

```
R2(config-router)#network 10.2.2.0 mask 255.255.255.0
R2(config-router)#neigh 10.2.2.1 remote-as 100
```

Next, we can remove the OSPF specific entries on PE1 and PE2 for vrf RED:

```
PE1#conf t
PE1(config)#int gi2/0
PE1(config-if)#no ip ospf 1 area 0
PE1(config-if)#no router ospf 1 vrf RED
PE1(config)#router bgp 100
PE1(config-router)#address-family ipv4 vrf RED
PE1(config-router-af)#no redistribute ospf 1
PE1(config-router-af)#

PE2#conf t
PE2(config)#int gi2/0
PE2(config-if)#no ip ospf 1 area 0
PE2(config-if)#no router ospf 1 vrf RED
PE2(config)#router bgp 100
PE2(config-router)#address-family ipv4 vrf RED
PE2(config-router-af)#no redistribute ospf 1
PE2(config-router-af)#
```

Still within the BGP 100 process, and more specifically within the IPv4 address family for VRF RED, we create our neighbor peering to R1 and R2:

```
PE1(config-router-af)#neighbor 10.1.1.2 remote-as 65001
PE1(config-router-af)#neighbor 10.1.1.2 activate

PE2(config-router-af)#neighbor 10.2.2.2 remote-as 65001
PE2(config-router-af)#neighbor 10.2.2.2 activate
```

The "activate" command is not strictly required. Address exchange is automatically enabled for IPv4 address families. For all other address families it is disabled. If manual activation under an address family becomes second nature to you then it is less likely to cause potential issues later on.

At this stage, we should see our peers activate and our neighbor relationships form:

```
R1(config-router)#
*May 17 12:47:29.275: %BGP-5-ADJCHANGE: neighbor 10.1.1.1 Up

PE1(config-router-af)#
*May 17 12:47:28.943: %BGP-5-ADJCHANGE: neighbor 10.1.1.2 vpn vrf RED Up
```

```
R2(config-router)#
*May 17 12:47:45.703: %BGP-5-ADJCHANGE: neighbor 10.2.2.1 Up

PE2(config-router-af)#
*May 17 12:47:45.691: %BGP-5-ADJCHANGE: neighbor 10.2.2.2 vpn vrf RED
Up
```

All looks promising so far, but there is an inherent issue in our CE set up on R1 and R2. If we look at their routing tables, we can see that they have no knowledge of their partner's routes, just their own:

```
R1#sh ip bgp | beg Network
   Network          Next Hop            Metric LocPrf Weight Path
*> 10.1.1.0/24      0.0.0.0                  0         32768 i
*> 192.168.1.0      0.0.0.0                  0         32768 i
R1#

R2#sh ip bgp | beg Network
   Network          Next Hop            Metric LocPrf Weight Path
*> 10.2.2.0/24      0.0.0.0                  0         32768 i
*> 172.20.1.0/24    0.0.0.0                  0         32768 i
R2#
```

What is happening here? If we have a look at PE1 and PE2, we can see that they are in fact sending everything that they should be:

```
PE1#sh ip bgp vpnv4 vrf RED | beg Network
   Network          Next Hop            Metric LocPrf Weight Path
Route Distinguisher: 100:1 (default for vrf RED)
 r> 10.1.1.0/24     10.1.1.2                 0             0 65001 i
*>i10.2.2.0/24      10.250.4.1               0   100       0 65001 i
*>i172.20.1.0/24    10.250.4.1               0   100       0 65001 i
*> 192.168.1.0      10.1.1.2                 0             0 65001 i
PE1#

PE2#sh ip bgp vpnv4 vrf RED | beg Network
   Network          Next Hop            Metric LocPrf Weight Path
Route Distinguisher: 100:1 (default for vrf RED)
*>i10.1.1.0/24      10.250.3.1               0   100       0 65001 i
 r> 10.2.2.0/24     10.2.2.2                 0             0 65001 i
*> 172.20.1.0/24    10.2.2.2                 0             0 65001 i
*>i192.168.1.0      10.250.3.1               0   100       0 65001 i
PE2#
```

if you have read my first book, you will know that due to loop prevention BGP will drop a route that contains its own AS number. Thankfully, there are a couple of options around this.

The first option takes place on the PE routers, and this is called "as-override". This option takes the AS path and replaces it with its own:

```
PE1#conf t
PE1(config)#router bgp 100
PE1(config-router)#address-family ipv4 vrf RED
PE1(config-router-af)#neigh 10.1.1.2 as-override

PE2#conf t
PE2(config)#router bgp 100
PE2(config-router)#address-family ipv4 vrf RED
PE2(config-router-af)#neigh 10.2.2.2 as-override
PE2(config-router-af)#
```

And, lo and behold, R1 and R2 can now see the routes, and, more importantly, have reachability.

```
R1#sh ip bgp | beg Network
   Network          Next Hop         Metric LocPrf Weight Path
*> 10.1.1.0/24      0.0.0.0              0         32768 i
*> 10.2.2.0/24      10.1.1.1                           0 100 100 i
*> 172.20.1.0/24    10.1.1.1                           0 100 100 i
*> 192.168.1.0      0.0.0.0              0         32768 i
R1#

R2#sh ip bgp | beg Network
   Network          Next Hop         Metric LocPrf Weight Path
*> 10.1.1.0/24      10.2.2.1                           0 100 100 i
*> 10.2.2.0/24      0.0.0.0              0         32768 i
*> 172.20.1.0/24    0.0.0.0              0         32768 i
*> 192.168.1.0      10.2.2.1                           0 100 100 i
R2#

R1#ping 172.20.1.1 so lo0
Type escape sequence to abort.
Sending 5, 100-byte ICMP Echos to 172.20.1.1, timeout is 2 seconds:
Packet sent with a source address of 192.168.1.1
!!!!!
Success rate is 100 percent (5/5)
R1#ping 172.20.1.1
Type escape sequence to abort.
Sending 5, 100-byte ICMP Echos to 172.20.1.1, timeout is 2 seconds:
```

```
!!!!!
Success rate is 100 percent (5/5)
R1#

R2#ping 192.168.1.1
Type escape sequence to abort.
Sending 5, 100-byte ICMP Echos to 192.168.1.1, timeout is 2 seconds:
!!!!!
Success rate is 100 percent (5/5)
R2#
```

The second option is to put the onus back on the customer equipment. This option is to allow our own AS in, using the neighbor command "allowas-in". We will remove the as-override commands from our PE routers in order to not confuse matters:

```
PE1(config)#router bgp 100
PE1(config-router)#address-family ipv4 vrf RED
PE1(config-router-af)#no neigh 10.1.1.2 as-override

PE2(config)#router bgp 100
PE2(config-router)#address-family ipv4 vrf RED
PE2(config-router-af)#no neigh 10.2.2.2 as-override
```

As expected, with this change R1 and R2 are now missing the routes again:

```
R1#sh ip bgp | beg Network
   Network          Next Hop         Metric LocPrf Weight Path
*> 10.1.1.0/24      0.0.0.0               0         32768 i
*> 192.168.1.0      0.0.0.0               0         32768 i
R1#

R2#sh ip bgp | beg Network
   Network          Next Hop         Metric LocPrf Weight Path
*> 10.2.2.0/24      0.0.0.0               0         32768 i
*> 172.20.1.0/24    0.0.0.0               0         32768 i
R2#
```

Allowas-in is set per neighbor. It has an optional variable of the number of occurrences of our own AS we wish to accept, so we can still retain a level of loop prevention:

```
R1(config)#router bgp 65001
R1(config-router)#neigh 10.1.1.1 allowas-in 1

R2(config)#router bgp 65001
R2(config-router)#neigh 10.2.2.1 allowas-in 1
```

We have the routes back now, and they show the correct AS path as we would hope for.

```
R1#sh ip bgp | beg Network
   Network          Next Hop         Metric LocPrf Weight Path
*> 10.1.1.0/24      0.0.0.0               0         32768 i
*> 10.2.2.0/24      10.1.1.1                            0 100 65001 i
*> 172.20.1.0/24    10.1.1.1                            0 100 65001 i
*> 192.168.1.0      0.0.0.0               0         32768 i
R1#

R2#sh ip bgp | beg Network
   Network          Next Hop         Metric LocPrf Weight Path
*> 10.1.1.0/24      10.2.2.1                            0 100 65001 i
*> 10.2.2.0/24      0.0.0.0               0         32768 i
*> 172.20.1.0/24    0.0.0.0               0         32768 i
*> 192.168.1.0      10.2.2.1                            0 100 65001 i
R2#
```

If we had used AS 65001 on R1 and 65002 on R2, we would not have had this issue. Then gain, it wouldn't be as interesting if it were too easy! That said; let's just check out our reachability before we do move on to something that is easy.

```
R1#ping 172.20.1.1
Type escape sequence to abort.
Sending 5, 100-byte ICMP Echos to 172.20.1.1, timeout is 2 seconds:
!!!!!
Success rate is 100 percent (5/5)
R1#

R2#ping 192.168.1.1
Type escape sequence to abort.
Sending 5, 100-byte ICMP Echos to 192.168.1.1, timeout is 2 seconds:
!!!!!
Success rate is 100 percent (5/5)
R2#
```

All good! Now, it's time to look at static routing.

8.5 CE-PE Routing with static routing

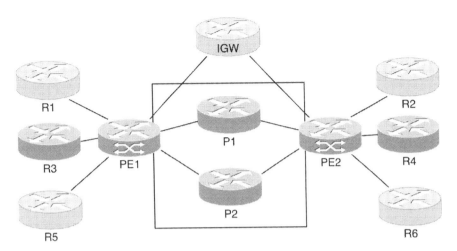

You are probably more than aware that static routing is pretty much verboten on the CCIE exam, but I am including CE-PE static routing here for completeness.

We'll use R4 for this example, again, starting by removing our IGP configuration:

```
R4#conf t
R4(config)#no router rip
```

We, then, add a default route to R4 to send all traffic to PE2:

```
R4(config)#ip route 0.0.0.0 0.0.0.0 10.2.4.1
R4(config)#
```

R4's routing table is now quite simple:

```
R4#sh ip route | beg Gate
Gateway of last resort is 10.2.4.1 to network 0.0.0.0

S*     0.0.0.0/0 [1/0] via 10.2.4.1
       10.0.0.0/8 is variably subnetted, 2 subnets, 2 masks
C         10.2.4.0/24 is directly connected, GigabitEthernet1/0
L         10.2.4.2/32 is directly connected, GigabitEthernet1/0
       172.20.0.0/16 is variably subnetted, 2 subnets, 2 masks
C         172.20.1.0/24 is directly connected, Loopback0
L         172.20.1.1/32 is directly connected, Loopback0
R4#
```

On PE2, we start by removing the RIP configuration:

```
PE2#conf t
PE2(config)#no router rip
PE2(config)#router bgp 100
PE2(config-router)#address-family ipv4 vrf WHITE
PE2(config-router-af)#no redistribute rip
PE2(config-router-af)#
```

Then, we simply add a single command to our BGP configuration, like we have done in the past; but this time, we are distributing static routes:

```
PE2(config-router-af)#redistribute static
PE2(config-router-af)#exit
PE2(config-router)#exit
```

Next, we need to give the router something to actually redistribute, so we set up a route under the specific VRF towards R4. Remember that we already have PE1 redistributing from EIGRP into BGP, so our static route is in the outbound (outbound from the MPLS cloud) direction towards R4.

```
PE2(config)#ip route vrf WHITE 172.20.1.0 255.255.255.0 10.2.4.2
```

We can check the routing table on R3, and we should be able to see that it is learning of R4's loopback interface network through EIGRP:

```
R3#sh ip route | beg Gate
Gateway of last resort is not set

      10.0.0.0/8 is variably subnetted, 2 subnets, 2 masks
C        10.1.3.0/24 is directly connected, GigabitEthernet1/0
L        10.1.3.2/32 is directly connected, GigabitEthernet1/0
      172.20.0.0/24 is subnetted, 1 subnets
D EX     172.20.1.0 [170/2562816] via 10.1.3.1, 00:01:38, Gi1/0
      192.168.1.0/24 is variably subnetted, 2 subnets, 2 masks
C        192.168.1.0/24 is directly connected, Loopback0
L        192.168.1.1/32 is directly connected, Loopback0
R3#
```

From R4, we should be able to ping R3's loopback interface from our own loopback interface:

```
R4#ping 192.168.1.1 so lo0
Type escape sequence to abort.
Sending 5, 100-byte ICMP Echos to 192.168.1.1, timeout is 2 seconds:
```

```
    Packet sent with a source address of 172.20.1.1
    !!!!!
    Success rate is 100 percent (5/5)
    R4#
```

This is successful, but a ping without specifying a source fails.

```
    R4#ping 192.168.1.1
    Type escape sequence to abort.
    Sending 5, 100-byte ICMP Echos to 192.168.1.1, timeout is 2 seconds:
    .....
    Success rate is 0 percent (0/5)
    R4#
```

This is because the ping will be sourced by the nearest interface to the destination. Because we have one default route, the ping will be sourced from the interface connecting us to the default route's IP address - which will be our physical interface.

It would make no sense to add another static route on PE2 that contains the connected network that it already knows about from its own routing table. In fact, it just does not work:

```
    PE2(config)#ip route vrf WHITE 10.2.4.0 255.255.255.0 10.2.4.2
    PE2(config)#exit
    PE2#sh ip route vrf WHITE | beg Gateway
    Gateway of last resort is not set

          10.0.0.0/8 is variably subnetted, 3 subnets, 2 masks
    B        10.1.3.0/24 [200/0] via 10.250.3.1, 00:30:21
    C        10.2.4.0/24 is directly connected, GigabitEthernet3/0
    L        10.2.4.1/32 is directly connected, GigabitEthernet3/0
          172.20.0.0/24 is subnetted, 1 subnets
    S        172.20.1.0 [1/0] via 10.2.4.2
    B     192.168.1.0/24 [200/1] via 10.250.3.1, 00:30:21
    PE2#
```

Whereas the static route to 172.20.1.0/24 appears as a static route in the routing table, the fact that PE2 is already connected to the 10.2.4.0/24 network means that it will not add this network to its own routing table again. Therefore we cannot use "redistribute static" to achieve this. We can instead leverage another of BGP's redistribution commands to fix this, this time by redistributing our connected networks:

```
    PE2(config)#router bgp 100
    PE2(config-router)#address-family ipv4 vrf WHITE
    PE2(config-router-af)#redistribute connected
```

With this in place R3, now knows of the 10.2.4.0/24 network, and a ping from R4 without specifying the loopback interface succeeds:

```
R3#sh ip route | beg Gate
Gateway of last resort is not set

      10.0.0.0/8 is variably subnetted, 3 subnets, 2 masks
C        10.1.3.0/24 is directly connected, GigabitEthernet1/0
L        10.1.3.2/32 is directly connected, GigabitEthernet1/0
D EX     10.2.4.0/24 [170/2562816] via 10.1.3.1, 00:00:11, Gi1/0
      172.20.0.0/24 is subnetted, 1 subnets
D EX     172.20.1.0 [170/2562816] via 10.1.3.1, 00:02:35, Gi1/0
      192.168.1.0/24 is variably subnetted, 2 subnets, 2 masks
C        192.168.1.0/24 is directly connected, Loopback0
L        192.168.1.1/32 is directly connected, Loopback0
R3#

R4#ping 192.168.1.1
Type escape sequence to abort.
Sending 5, 100-byte ICMP Echos to 192.168.1.1, timeout is 2 seconds:
!!!!!
Success rate is 100 percent (5/5)
R4#

R3#ping 172.20.1.1
Type escape sequence to abort.
Sending 5, 100-byte ICMP Echos to 172.20.1.1, timeout is 2 seconds:
!!!!!
Success rate is 100 percent (5/5)
R3#
```

Next, we'll remove our static routing and use IS-IS as an IGP for the White company.

8.6 CE-PE Routing with IS-IS

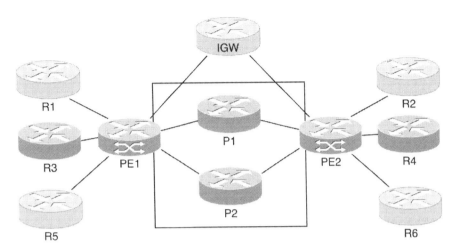

IS-IS Is only featured on the written exam. However, since static routing is pretty much a big no-no in the exam, we'll quickly run through it. We'll change R4, which currently uses static routes, back to use a dynamic routing protocol –namely, ISIS.

ISIS has many similarities to OSPF. It uses levels, which are similar to the stub or nssa areas in OSPF. Levels can be level 1, 1-2 or 2. By default, Cisco routers will use type 1-2, which can form an adjacency with a level 1 or a level 2. Level 1's cannot form an adjacency with a level 2, but will form with another level 1, or a level 1-2 router.

I will not go into the nuts and bolts of IS-IS now but, instead, will save that for the IGP volume. If you do want to have a more in depth look at IS-IS, please visit my blog page on it here: http://www.802101.com/2014/04/ISIS-introduction.html.

We start by removing the static routing information on R4 and creating an ISIS routing process. We assign our NET - which is the area (49), system id (0001.010.010.010.010) and selector (00). Next, we enable our specific interfaces for ISIS:

```
R4#conf t
R4(config)#no ip route 0.0.0.0 0.0.0.0 10.2.4.1
R4(config)#router isis
R4(config-router)#is-type level-1
R4(config-router)#net 49.0001.010.010.010.010.00
R4(config-router)#int lo0
R4(config-if)#ip router isis
R4(config-if)#int gi1/0
R4(config-if)#ip router isis
```

```
R4(config-if)#
```

Similarly on PE2, we must start by removing our static information.

```
PE2#conf t
PE2(config)#no ip route vrf WHITE 10.2.4.0 255.255.255.0 10.2.4.2
PE2(config)#no ip route vrf WHITE 172.20.1.0 255.255.255.0 10.2.4.2
```

We also need to remove this from the BGP address family:

```
PE2(config)#router bgp 100
PE2(config-router)#address-family ipv4 vrf WHITE
PE2(config-router-af)#no redistribute connected
PE2(config-router-af)#no redistribute static
PE2(config-router-af)#exit
PE2(config-router)#exit
PE2(config)#
```

Next, on PE2, we create the ISIS process and assign it to our interface, in the same fashion as we did on R4. All we are doing is changing the system id.

```
PE2(config)#router isis
PE2(config-router)#is-type level-1
PE2(config-router)#net 49.0001.020.020.020.020.00
PE2(config-router)#int gi 3/0
PE2(config-if)#ip router isis
```

We should have the two routers talking to each other at this stage:

```
R4#sh isis neigh

System Id    Type Interface  IP Address   State Holdtime Circuit Id
PE2          L1   Gi1/0      10.2.4.1     UP    9        PE2.01
R4#
```

Next, we need to redistribute the IS-IS routes into BGP and the BGP routes into IS-IS. These will appear as level-1 routes.

```
PE2(config-if)#router bgp 100
PE2(config-router)#address-family ipv4 vrf WHITE
PE2(config-router-af)#redistribute isis level-1
PE2(config)#router isis
PE2(config-router)#redistribute bgp 100 ip level-1
```

If we now check the two routers, we should see a very healthy routing table, with R4 seeing R3's network, shown as ISIS level-1 which is denoted as "i L1":

```
R4#sh ip route | beg Gate
Gateway of last resort is not set

        10.0.0.0/8 is variably subnetted, 3 subnets, 2 masks
i L1    10.1.3.0/24 [115/10] via 10.2.4.1, 00:00:37, Gi1/0
C       10.2.4.0/24 is directly connected, GigabitEthernet1/0
L       10.2.4.2/32 is directly connected, GigabitEthernet1/0
        172.20.0.0/16 is variably subnetted, 2 subnets, 2 masks
C       172.20.1.0/24 is directly connected, Loopback0
L       172.20.1.1/32 is directly connected, Loopback0
i L1 192.168.1.0/24 [115/10] via 10.2.4.1, 00:00:37, Gi1/0
R4#
```

Likewise, R3 should also be able to see R3's network, appearing as EIGRP external (D EX):

```
R3#sh ip route | beg Gate
Gateway of last resort is not set

        10.0.0.0/8 is variably subnetted, 2 subnets, 2 masks
C       10.1.3.0/24 is directly connected, GigabitEthernet1/0
L       10.1.3.2/32 is directly connected, GigabitEthernet1/0
        172.20.0.0/24 is subnetted, 1 subnets
D EX    172.20.1.0 [170/2562816] via 10.1.3.1, 00:04:18, Gi1/0
        192.168.1.0/24 is variably subnetted, 2 subnets, 2 masks
C       192.168.1.0/24 is directly connected, Loopback0
L       192.168.1.1/32 is directly connected, Loopback0
R3#
```

As always, we should check reachability as well as visibility:

```
R3#ping 172.20.1.1 so lo0
Type escape sequence to abort.
Sending 5, 100-byte ICMP Echos to 172.20.1.1, timeout is 2 seconds:
Packet sent with a source address of 192.168.1.1
!!!!!
Success rate is 100 percent (5/5)
R3#
```

So now, we have gone through the different IGP and eBGP methods used to connect networks to an MPLS provider network. This is only part of the picture of how a network operates in real life. So far, we have dealt with very self-contained networks. In the next chapter, we will look at how the customers can share resources that belong to a different VRF and, also, at how we, as the service provider, can allow our customer's access to the Internet.

9. Services within an MPLS Cloud

Our examples so far have shown us how we can use different protocols to connect a customer to a service provider's MPLS network. Yet, as well all know, a company will also need to connect to the internet, not just to it's other offices. We will look at this shortly, but, first, we will look at how we can share resources within an MPLS cloud.

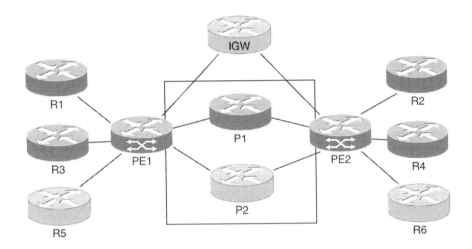

9.1 Customer Route Leaking

It has been a tough time for the WHITE company. Profits have been down for some time, and the RED company has bought them. Thankfully, everyone gets to keep their jobs, and the company name stays the same. Other things must change. The RED company has realized that they need access to the WHITE company's assets at the RED companies HQ's on the East and West coasts, Sadly, they need the newly purchased networks to change their IP addresses first, and then we can share their networks with the RED company. To make it a relatively simple change, R3 and R4 will only be incrementing the third octet on each internal network.

We start with R3, first removing the existing IP address (192.168.1.1/24) on the loopback interface and adding the new IP address (192.168.2.1/24):

```
R3#conf t
R3(config)#int lo0
R3(config-if)#no ip add 192.168.1.1 255.255.255.0
R3(config-if)#ip add 192.168.2.1 255.255.255.0
```

We must then advertise this new network in EIGRP:

```
R3(config-if)#router eigrp 3
R3(config-router)#network 192.168.2.0
R3(config-router)#no network 192.168.1.0
R3(config-router)#exit
R3(config)#exit
```

We will also quickly check that our IP addressing is correct:

```
R3(config-if)#do sh ip int bri | e un
Interface              IP-Address       OK? Method Status                Protocol
GigabitEthernet1/0     10.1.3.2         YES NVRAM  up                    up
Loopback0              192.168.2.1      YES manual up                    up

R3(config-if)#exit
R3#sh run | section eigrp
router eigrp 3
 network 10.1.3.0 0.0.0.255
 network 192.168.2.0
R3#
```

All looks good, so we can turn our attention to R4. The changes to R4 are much easier. We only need to change the loopback interface IP address from 172.20.1.1/24 to 172.20.2.1/24, as ISIS takes care of the advertisement of the prefix due to the command being configured at the interface level:

```
R4#conf t
R4(config)#int lo0
R4(config-if)#no ip add
R4(config-if)#ip add 172.20.2.1 255.255.255.0
R4(config-if)#
```

We can confirm that R3 can see the correct IP address for R4, as well as confirming reachability:

```
R3#sh ip route | beg Gate
Gateway of last resort is not set

      10.0.0.0/8 is variably subnetted, 3 subnets, 2 masks
C        10.1.3.0/24 is directly connected, GigabitEthernet1/0
L        10.1.3.2/32 is directly connected, GigabitEthernet1/0
D EX     10.2.4.0/24 [170/2562816] via 10.1.3.1, 00:03:32, Gi1/0
```

```
         172.20.0.0/24 is subnetted, 1 subnets
D EX      172.20.2.0 [170/2562816] via 10.1.3.1, 00:00:10, Gi1/0
         192.168.2.0/24 is variably subnetted, 2 subnets, 2 masks
C           192.168.2.0/24 is directly connected, Loopback0
L           192.168.2.1/32 is directly connected, Loopback0
R3#ping 172.20.2.1 so lo0
Type escape sequence to abort.
Sending 5, 100-byte ICMP Echos to 172.20.2.1, timeout is 2 seconds:
Packet sent with a source address of 192.168.2.1
!!!!!
Success rate is 100 percent (5/5)
R3#
```

The changes within the MPLS cloud are very simple. Recall from earlier that the route distinguisher (RD) is used to separate different companies within the MPLS network. It is this RD that maintains the uniqueness, the route target (RT) on the other hand is concerned with what network prefixes we are seeing from others and showing to others.

In order for the two different VRFs to be able to see each other, we can simply add another import statement to our VRF statements on our PE routers:

```
PE1#conf t
PE1(config)#ip vrf WHITE
PE1(config-vrf)#route-target import 100:1
PE1(config-vrf)#ip vrf RED
PE1(config-vrf)#route-target import 100:2
PE1(config-vrf)#

PE2#conf t
PE2(config)#ip vrf WHITE
PE2(config-vrf)#route-target import 100:1
PE2(config-vrf)#ip vrf RED
PE2(config-vrf)#route-target import 100:2
PE2(config-vrf)#
```

Once this additional command has been entered, we should start to see a few more entries on our customer routers (R1, R2, R3 and R4). R3 can see R1, R2 and R3:

```
R3#sh ip route | beg Gate
Gateway of last resort is not set

         10.0.0.0/8 is variably subnetted, 5 subnets, 2 masks
D EX      10.1.1.0/24 [170/2562816] via 10.1.3.1, 00:00:48, Gi1/0
C         10.1.3.0/24 is directly connected, GigabitEthernet1/0
L         10.1.3.2/32 is directly connected, GigabitEthernet1/0
D EX      10.2.2.0/24 [170/2562816] via 10.1.3.1, 00:00:48, Gi1/0
```

```
D EX      10.2.4.0/24 [170/2562816] via 10.1.3.1, 00:06:07, Gi1/0
          172.20.0.0/24 is subnetted, 2 subnets
D EX      172.20.1.0 [170/2562816] via 10.1.3.1, 00:00:48, Gi1/0
D EX      172.20.2.0 [170/2562816] via 10.1.3.1, 00:02:45, Gi1/0
D EX   192.168.1.0/24 [170/2562816] via 10.1.3.1, 00:00:48, Gi1/0
       192.168.2.0/24 is variably subnetted, 2 subnets, 2 masks
C         192.168.2.0/24 is directly connected, Loopback0
L         192.168.2.1/32 is directly connected, Loopback0
R3#
```

R4 can see R3, R1 and R2:

```
R4#sh ip route | beg Gate
Gateway of last resort is not set

      10.0.0.0/8 is variably subnetted, 5 subnets, 2 masks
i L1     10.1.1.0/24 [115/10] via 10.2.4.1, 00:00:43, Gi1/0
i L1     10.1.3.0/24 [115/10] via 10.2.4.1, 00:16:11, Gi1/0
i L1     10.2.2.0/24 [115/10] via 10.2.4.1, 00:00:43, Gi1/0
C        10.2.4.0/24 is directly connected, GigabitEthernet1/0
L        10.2.4.2/32 is directly connected, GigabitEthernet1/0
      172.20.0.0/16 is variably subnetted, 3 subnets, 2 masks
i L1     172.20.1.0/24 [115/10] via 10.2.4.1, 00:00:43, Gi1/0
C        172.20.2.0/24 is directly connected, Loopback0
L        172.20.2.1/32 is directly connected, Loopback0
i L1  192.168.1.0/24 [115/10] via 10.2.4.1, 00:00:43, Gi1/0
i L1  192.168.2.0/24 [115/10] via 10.2.4.1, 00:05:26, Gi1/0
R4#
```

R1 can see R2, R3 and R4:

```
R1#sh ip route | beg Gate
Gateway of last resort is not set

      10.0.0.0/8 is variably subnetted, 5 subnets, 2 masks
C        10.1.1.0/24 is directly connected, GigabitEthernet1/0
L        10.1.1.2/32 is directly connected, GigabitEthernet1/0
B        10.1.3.0/24 [20/0] via 10.1.1.1, 00:05:55
B        10.2.2.0/24 [20/0] via 10.1.1.1, 00:17:35
B        10.2.4.0/24 [20/0] via 10.1.1.1, 00:05:55
      172.20.0.0/24 is subnetted, 2 subnets
B        172.20.1.0 [20/0] via 10.1.1.1, 00:17:35
B        172.20.2.0 [20/0] via 10.1.1.1, 00:05:55
      192.168.1.0/24 is variably subnetted, 2 subnets, 2 masks
C        192.168.1.0/24 is directly connected, Loopback0
L        192.168.1.1/32 is directly connected, Loopback0
B     192.168.2.0/24 [20/0] via 10.1.1.1, 00:05:55
```

R1#

Finally, R2 can see R1, R3 and R4:

```
R2#sh ip route | beg Gate
Gateway of last resort is not set

      10.0.0.0/8 is variably subnetted, 5 subnets, 2 masks
B        10.1.1.0/24 [20/0] via 10.2.2.1, 00:18:52
B        10.1.3.0/24 [20/0] via 10.2.2.1, 00:07:11
C        10.2.2.0/24 is directly connected, GigabitEthernet1/0
L        10.2.2.2/32 is directly connected, GigabitEthernet1/0
B        10.2.4.0/24 [20/0] via 10.2.2.1, 00:07:11
      172.20.0.0/16 is variably subnetted, 3 subnets, 2 masks
C        172.20.1.0/24 is directly connected, Loopback0
L        172.20.1.1/32 is directly connected, Loopback0
B        172.20.2.0/24 [20/0] via 10.2.2.1, 00:07:11
B     192.168.1.0/24 [20/0] via 10.2.2.1, 00:18:52
B     192.168.2.0/24 [20/0] via 10.2.2.1, 00:07:11
R2#
```

Finally, we should make sure that we have reachability, which we can do mainly from R1:

```
R1#ping 172.20.1.1 so lo0
Type escape sequence to abort.
Sending 5, 100-byte ICMP Echos to 172.20.1.1, timeout is 2 seconds:
Packet sent with a source address of 192.168.1.1
!!!!!
Success rate is 100 percent (5/5)
R1#ping 172.20.2.1 so lo0
Type escape sequence to abort.
Sending 5, 100-byte ICMP Echos to 172.20.2.1, timeout is 2 seconds:
Packet sent with a source address of 192.168.1.1
!!!!!
Success rate is 100 percent (5/5)
R1#ping 192.168.2.1 so lo0
Type escape sequence to abort.
Sending 5, 100-byte ICMP Echos to 192.168.2.1, timeout is 2 seconds:
Packet sent with a source address of 192.168.1.1
!!!!!
Success rate is 100 percent (5/5)
R1#

R4#ping 172.20.1.1 so lo0
Type escape sequence to abort.
Sending 5, 100-byte ICMP Echos to 172.20.1.1, timeout is 2 seconds:
Packet sent with a source address of 172.20.2.1
```

```
!!!!!
Success rate is 100 percent (5/5)
R4#ping 192.168.2.1 so lo0
Type escape sequence to abort.
Sending 5, 100-byte ICMP Echos to 192.168.2.1, timeout is 2 seconds:
Packet sent with a source address of 172.20.2.1
!!!!!
Success rate is 100 percent (5/5)
R4#
```

Here, we have covered route leaking in MPLS where both sides can share the resources. Imagine a different scenario. Imagine two companies sharing a third company's network resources, but they should not have any visibility of each other. This is the idea of Central Services within an MPLS VPN environment, which we will cover next.

9.2 Central Services within MPLS

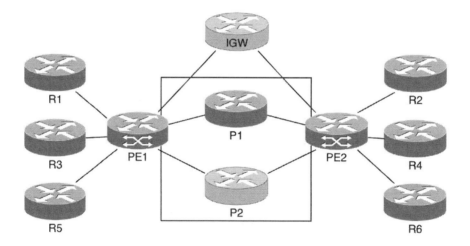

It's been a tough ride for the folks at the WHITE company's east coast office (R4). They have been taken over by the RED company, but the RED company has decided to sell off that part of the business. Don't feel sad for them, because they have been bought out by a fantastic start-up company called "SUPERNET", who offers a wide range of great products. These products are so great that the RED company (including what's left of the WHITE company) and the BLUE company have signed up to their services. Clearly, the RED company and the BLUE company are still very different businesses and should have no visibility of each other's networks. They both, however, need access to SUPERNET's services.

This is the whole idea behind what is known as Central Services in MPLS, sometimes referred to as "Common Services".

We will start by removing the WHITE VRF from PE2; one command will do the work for us:

```
PE2#conf t
PE2(config)#no ip vrf WHITE
Removing any distance ip and ip redistribution from router isis
% IPv4 addresses from all interfaces in VRF WHITE have been removed
PE2(config)#
```

Immediately, we can are told that redistribution from ISIS will be removed for us, but this also removes it from our BGP configuration:

```
PE2(config)#do sh run | section bgp
 redistribute bgp 100 subnets
router bgp 100
 bgp log-neighbor-changes
 neighbor 10.250.3.1 remote-as 100
 neighbor 10.250.3.1 update-source Loopback0
 !
 address-family vpnv4
  neighbor 10.250.3.1 activate
  neighbor 10.250.3.1 send-community extended
 exit-address-family
 !
 address-family ipv4 vrf BLUE
  network 2.2.2.6 mask 255.255.255.255
  redistribute ospf 3
 exit-address-family
 !
 address-family ipv4 vrf RED
  neighbor 10.2.2.2 remote-as 65001
  neighbor 10.2.2.2 activate
 exit-address-family
PE2(config)#
```

We will create a new VRF for R4, which we will call SUPERNET. This will export the route target 100:20 and will use the same numbers as the route distinguisher. We do not need to import our own RT in this case.

```
PE2(config)#ip vrf SUPERNET
PE2(config-vrf)#rd 100:20
PE2(config-vrf)#route-target export 100:20
PE2(config-vrf)#exit
```

Because we removed all the configuration from within BGP and for the interface connecting PE2 to R4 when we issued the command "no ip vrf WHITE", we must add these all back again:

```
PE2(config)#int gi 3/0
PE2(config-if)#ip vrf forwarding SUPERNET
PE2(config-if)#ip address 10.2.4.1 255.255.255.0
PE2(config-if)#ip router isis
PE2(config-if)#router isis
PE2(config-router)#redistribute bgp 100 level-1
PE2(config-router)#router bgp 100
PE2(config-router)#address-family ipv4 vrf SUPERNET
PE2(config-router-af)#redistribute isis level-1
```

Working on the same side of the topology, we need to get R2 and R6 to see the SUPERNET network first. We do this with a standard route-target import command:

```
PE2#conf t
PE2(config)#ip vrf BLUE
PE2(config-vrf)#route-target import 100:20
PE2(config-vrf)#ip vrf RED
PE2(config-vrf)#route-target import 100:20
```

The SUPERNET vrf obviously needs to have a return route back to the other networks:

```
PE2(config-vrf)#ip vrf SUPERNET
PE2(config-vrf)#route-target import 100:1
PE2(config-vrf)#route-target import 100:3
```

So far, we are almost there, but we have hit a roadblock.

The beauty of MPLS VPNs is that we can overlap IP addresses on as many customers as we want to. Each duplicate instance is wrapped within its own separate routing table courtesy of the VRF. The provider edge routers are happy with this overlap. The providers core routers (the "P" routers) are unaware and are happy just being the legs to the MP-BGP bridge that exists at each edge of the provider MPLS cloud. The road-block, however, is this: as soon as we start introducing any form of shared service we become unable to support this overlapping of IP space. Because our central services router (R4) exists outside the MPLS cloud, it is unaware of the VRFs and VPNs that enable us to use the same IP addressing schemes with abandon.

Let's look at R4's view of the world as our configuration currently stands.

```
R4#sh ip route | beg Gate
Gateway of last resort is not set

      1.0.0.0/24 is subnetted, 1 subnets
i L1    1.1.1.0 [115/10] via 10.2.4.1, 00:07:54, GigabitEthernet1/0
      2.0.0.0/32 is subnetted, 2 subnets
i L1    2.2.2.5 [115/10] via 10.2.4.1, 00:03:56, GigabitEthernet1/0
i L1    2.2.2.6 [115/10] via 10.2.4.1, 00:07:54, GigabitEthernet1/0
      10.0.0.0/8 is variably subnetted, 6 subnets, 2 masks
i L1    10.1.1.0/24 [115/10] via 10.2.4.1, 00:03:56, Gi1/0
i L1    10.1.5.0/24 [115/10] via 10.2.4.1, 00:03:56, Gi1/0
i L1    10.2.2.0/24 [115/10] via 10.2.4.1, 00:03:56, Gi1/0
C       10.2.4.0/24 is directly connected, GigabitEthernet1/0
L       10.2.4.2/32 is directly connected, GigabitEthernet1/0
i L1    10.2.6.0/24 [115/10] via 10.2.4.1, 00:07:54, Gi1/0
      172.20.0.0/16 is variably subnetted, 3 subnets, 2 masks
i L1    172.20.1.0/24 [115/10] via 10.2.4.1, 00:07:54, Gi1/0
C       172.20.2.0/24 is directly connected, Loopback0
L       172.20.2.1/32 is directly connected, Loopback0
i L1 192.168.1.0/24 [115/10] via 10.2.4.1, 00:03:56, Gi1/0
R4#
```

We do have routes to 172.20.1.0/24. But whom does it actually go to? We have two candidates; R2 and R6. We can check the routing table of both R2 and R6. We should see that both see R4's loopback network but only one will be able to ping it from their loopback interface:

```
R2#sh ip route | beg Gate
Gateway of last resort is not set

      10.0.0.0/8 is variably subnetted, 4 subnets, 2 masks
B       10.1.1.0/24 [20/0] via 10.2.2.1, 00:10:54
B       10.1.3.0/24 [20/0] via 10.2.2.1, 00:10:54
C       10.2.2.0/24 is directly connected, GigabitEthernet1/0
L       10.2.2.2/32 is directly connected, GigabitEthernet1/0
      172.20.0.0/16 is variably subnetted, 3 subnets, 2 masks
C       172.20.1.0/24 is directly connected, Loopback0
L       172.20.1.1/32 is directly connected, Loopback0
B       172.20.2.0/24 [20/0] via 10.2.2.1, 00:09:14
B    192.168.1.0/24 [20/0] via 10.2.2.1, 00:10:54
B    192.168.2.0/24 [20/0] via 10.2.2.1, 00:10:54
R2#ping 172.20.2.1 so lo0
Type escape sequence to abort.
Sending 5, 100-byte ICMP Echos to 172.20.2.1, timeout is 2 seconds:
Packet sent with a source address of 172.20.1.1
.....
Success rate is 0 percent (0/5)
```

```
R2#ping 172.20.2.1
Type escape sequence to abort.
Sending 5, 100-byte ICMP Echos to 172.20.2.1, timeout is 2 seconds:
!!!!!
Success rate is 100 percent (5/5)
R2#
```

R2 cannot ping R4's loopback from its loopback, but we know that we have reachability through our egress interface. Through a process of elimination, it should be R6 that has loopback to loopback reachability:

```
R6#sh ip route | beg Gate
Gateway of last resort is not set

      1.0.0.0/8 is variably subnetted, 2 subnets, 2 masks
C        1.1.1.0/24 is directly connected, GigabitEthernet2/0
L        1.1.1.2/32 is directly connected, GigabitEthernet2/0
      2.0.0.0/32 is subnetted, 2 subnets
O E2     2.2.2.5 [110/1] via 10.2.6.1, 01:08:05, GigabitEthernet1/0
O E2     2.2.2.6 [110/1] via 10.2.6.1, 01:08:25, GigabitEthernet1/0
      10.0.0.0/8 is variably subnetted, 3 subnets, 2 masks
O        10.1.5.0/24 [110/3] via 10.2.6.1, 01:08:00, Gi1/0
C        10.2.6.0/24 is directly connected, GigabitEthernet1/0
L        10.2.6.2/32 is directly connected, GigabitEthernet1/0
      172.20.0.0/16 is variably subnetted, 3 subnets, 2 masks
C        172.20.1.0/24 is directly connected, Loopback0
L        172.20.1.1/32 is directly connected, Loopback0
O E2     172.20.2.0/24 [110/1] via 10.2.6.1, 00:09:41, Gi1/0
O     192.168.1.0/24 [110/4] via 10.2.6.1, 01:08:00, Gi1/0
R6#ping 172.20.2.1 so lo0
Type escape sequence to abort.
Sending 5, 100-byte ICMP Echos to 172.20.2.1, timeout is 2 seconds:
Packet sent with a source address of 172.20.1.1
!!!!!
Success rate is 100 percent (5/5)
R6#
```

Clearly, we can only have one instance of the route 172.20.1.0/24 within our network, unless we use NAT, so customers sharing a resource must also use unique addresses. To avoid stepping into the realm of Network Address Translation (just yet), we are going to take the easy route and re-IP our customer networks on R6 (and later on R5). We will just change the third octet to match the router number:

```
R6#conf t
R6(config)#int lo0
R6(config-if)#no ip add
```

```
R6(config-if)#ip add 172.20.6.1 255.255.255.0
R6(config-if)#
```

Now, R2 can ping R4 from its loopback interface:

```
R2#ping 172.20.2.1 so lo0
Type escape sequence to abort.
Sending 5, 100-byte ICMP Echos to 172.20.2.1, timeout is 2 seconds:
Packet sent with a source address of 172.20.1.1
!!!!!
Success rate is 100 percent (5/5)
R2#
```

As can R6:

```
R6#ping 172.20.2.1 so lo0
Type escape sequence to abort.
Sending 5, 100-byte ICMP Echos to 172.20.2.1, timeout is 2 seconds:
Packet sent with a source address of 172.20.6.1
!!!!!
Success rate is 100 percent (5/5)
R6#
```

Now, let's extend this out to R1, R3 and R5. Starting with R1, we will import the RT of SUPERNET

```
PE1(config)#ip vrf RED
PE1(config-vrf)#route-target import 100:20
PE1(config-vrf)#
```

Now, R1 has visibility of R4. However, until we change R5's loopback interface IP address, we will not have loopback-to-loopback reachability:

```
R1#sh ip route | beg Gate
Gateway of last resort is not set

      10.0.0.0/8 is variably subnetted, 4 subnets, 2 masks
C        10.1.1.0/24 is directly connected, GigabitEthernet1/0
L        10.1.1.2/32 is directly connected, GigabitEthernet1/0
B        10.1.3.0/24 [20/0] via 10.1.1.1, 00:10:17
B        10.2.2.0/24 [20/0] via 10.1.1.1, 00:10:17
      172.20.0.0/24 is subnetted, 2 subnets
B        172.20.1.0 [20/0] via 10.1.1.1, 00:10:17
B        172.20.2.0 [20/0] via 10.1.1.1, 00:00:09
      192.168.1.0/24 is variably subnetted, 2 subnets, 2 masks
C        192.168.1.0/24 is directly connected, Loopback0
```

```
L        192.168.1.1/32 is directly connected, Loopback0
B        192.168.2.0/24 [20/0] via 10.1.1.1, 00:10:17
R1#ping 172.20.2.1 so lo0
Type escape sequence to abort.
Sending 5, 100-byte ICMP Echos to 172.20.2.1, timeout is 2 seconds:
Packet sent with a source address of 192.168.1.1
.....
Success rate is 0 percent (0/5)
R1#ping 172.20.2.1
Type escape sequence to abort.
Sending 5, 100-byte ICMP Echos to 172.20.2.1, timeout is 2 seconds:
!!!!!
Success rate is 100 percent (5/5)
R1#
```

If we change R5's loopback interface IP address:

```
R5#conf t
R5(config)#int lo0
R5(config-if)#no ip add
R5(config-if)#ip add 192.168.5.1 255.255.255.0
```

R1 has reachability:

```
R1#ping 172.20.2.1 so lo0
Type escape sequence to abort.
Sending 5, 100-byte ICMP Echos to 172.20.2.1, timeout is 2 seconds:
Packet sent with a source address of 192.168.1.1
!!!!!
Success rate is 100 percent (5/5)
R1#
```

With no overlap between R1 and R5's networks, we should have no problem with reachability between R5 and R4, once we import the route-target into our vrf:

```
PE1(config-vrf)#ip vrf BLUE
PE1(config-vrf)#route-target import 100:20
PE1(config-vrf)#

R5#sh ip route 172.20.2.0
Routing entry for 172.20.2.0/24
  Known via "ospf 3", distance 110, metric 1
  Tag Complete, Path Length == 1, AS 100, , type extern 2, forward
metric 1
  Last update from 10.1.5.1 on GigabitEthernet1/0, 00:00:53 ago
  Routing Descriptor Blocks:
```

```
        * 10.1.5.1, from 10.250.3.5, 00:00:53 ago, via GigabitEthernet1/0
            Route metric is 1, traffic share count is 1
            Route tag 3489661028
    R5#ping 172.20.2.1 so lo0
    Type escape sequence to abort.
    Sending 5, 100-byte ICMP Echos to 172.20.2.1, timeout is 2 seconds:
    Packet sent with a source address of 192.168.5.1
    !!!!!
    Success rate is 100 percent (5/5)
    R5#
```

Lastly, we need to add the SUPERNET RT to VRF WHITE and vice versa:

```
    PE1(config-vrf)#ip vrf WHITE
    PE1(config-vrf)#route-target import 100:20
    PE1(config-vrf)#

    PE2(config)#ip vrf SUPERNET
    PE2(config-vrf)#route-target import 100:2
```

Our last final loopback-to-loopback test shows that R3 has reachability to our central services network:

```
    R3#sh ip route 172.20.2.0
    Routing entry for 172.20.2.0/24
      Known via "eigrp 3", distance 170, metric 2562816, type external
      Redistributing via eigrp 3
      Last update from 10.1.3.1 on GigabitEthernet1/0, 00:00:13 ago
      Routing Descriptor Blocks:
        * 10.1.3.1, from 10.1.3.1, 00:00:13 ago, via GigabitEthernet1/0
            Route metric is 2562816, traffic share count is 1
            Total delay is 110 microseconds, minimum bandwidth is 1000 Kbit
            Reliability 100/255, minimum MTU 1500 bytes
            Loading 1/255, Hops 1
    R3#ping 172.20.2.1 so lo0
    Type escape sequence to abort.
    Sending 5, 100-byte ICMP Echos to 172.20.2.1, timeout is 2 seconds:
    Packet sent with a source address of 192.168.2.1
    !!!!!
    Success rate is 100 percent (5/5)
    R3#
```

Now, everyone has access to the SUPERNET network, and none of the companies have visibility to any other network, other than the ones they are supposed to. We know this, as we had to change the IP addresses to avoid any overlap.

This example has started to open up the bigger issues we face with MPLS VPNs, that being the segregation of the "standard" IPv4 routing table from the VPNs within the carrier network. We can overlap our VPNs as much as we (or to be more exact, the customer) desire, if these do in fact remain completely separated. Once we start to introduce and form of shared service, this starts to present an issue.

This becomes more of a factor when we try to extend our customers networks by offering them Internet access, which we will look at next.

9.3 Customer Internet Access

We come to the issue of how we, as the service provider, can provide our clients with Internet access. This can be achieved in a couple of different methods, and we will discuss and explore these options.

With static routing or through use of a routing protocol, it is usually very easy to supply a default route in order to reach another router, as the routes all exist within the same global routing space. When we use a VRF, we start to see that we need to take a number of extra steps.

Internet routing takes place within the BGP table, and this table lives in the global routing space. The global routing space is completely separate to the VRF context. As we have seen these VPN sites can communicate with someone in the same VPN, or to another VPN that we extend access to (as we saw earlier in this chapter). However, what these VPN sites cannot do by default is access anything within the global routing space of the provider's routers.

Therefore, we have a couple of options that we can implement.

The basic configuration for the IGW (Internet Gateway) router is as follows:

```
IGW(config)#ip route 0.0.0.0 0.0.0.0 null 0
IGW(config)#int lo0
IGW(config-if)#ip add 4.4.4.4 255.255.255.255
IGW(config-if)#int lo1
IGW(config-if)#ip add 5.5.5.5 255.255.255.255
IGW(config-if)#int Gi1/0
IGW(config-if)#ip add 10.20.1.1 255.255.255.0
IGW(config-if)#no shut
IGW(config-if)#int Gi2/0
IGW(config-if)#ip add 10.20.2.1 255.255.255.0
IGW(config-if)#no shut
```

We have a default route that we will be advertising out, as well as some IP addresses that we can use to test reachability with from our customer networks.

Providing Internet Access using a separate connection

We could have separate connections between the customer and our provider edge routers to carry the default routes we need in order to access the Internet. One link would carry the VRF traffic and another would be used for the default route out to the Internet. This could be costly for both the consumer and the supplier though, so this is less than ideal. This is not in our interest (certainly not from a financial standpoint).

So, we will move swiftly on to some more interesting options, which are to use a dedicated VRF, or to leak routes between the vrf and the global routing table.

Providing Internet Access through route leaking

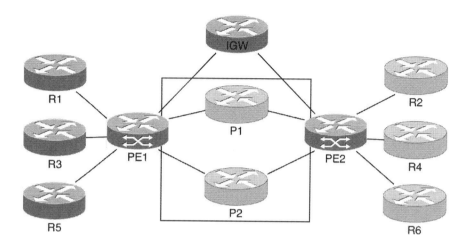

Despite the fact that routes that exist within a VRF and those that exist within the global routing table are separate, this is not to say that we cannot share from one to the other. We will see two examples of how we can accomplish it, using BGP and EIGRP. The same idea would be the same for OSPF and ISIS, or even RIP for that matter.

We start by setting PE1 to do some network address translation (NAT). NAT requires a couple of things to work. Firstly, we need an interface that we want to provide translation *for* (known as the "inside" interface). Secondly, we need an interface we want to translate *as* (known as the "outside" interface). The last thing we need is to specify some interesting traffic to actually translate.

Our "inside" interface will be Gi 2/0 on PE1, which is our connection to R1 and the "outside" connection will be Gi 6/0, our connection to the IGW router.

```
PE1(config)#int gi 2/0
PE1(config-if)#ip nat inside
*May 31 09:18:55.551: %LINEPROTO-5-UPDOWN: Line protocol on Interface
NVI0, changed state to up
PE1(config-if)#
PE1(config-if)#int gi 6/0
PE1(config-if)#ip nat outside
```

We must then define what we consider to be our interesting traffic, which will then in turn be translated. To do this, we create an access list with our subnets in it, and then use this as the source for translation within our nat statement:

```
PE1(config)#ip access-list standard VRF_RED_SUBNETS
PE1(config-std-nacl)#permit 10.1.1.0 0.0.0.255
PE1(config-std-nacl)#permit 192.168.1.0 0.0.0.255
PE1(config)#ip nat inside source list VRF_RED_SUBNETS interface Gi6/0 vrf RED overload
```

The NAT statement basically says that we would like to NAT any source within the list VRF_RED_SUBNETS to the global interface Gi 6/0 but only for the VRF RED. As more than one host will be connecting, we will allow them all to connect by specifying the "overload" keyword.

So far so good, but PE1 does not have a default route, and R1 will still be completely unaware of the IGW router.

The PE1 router requires a default route, which is just a standard ip route.

```
PE1(config)#ip route 0.0.0.0 0.0.0.0 10.20.1.1
```

The command for R1 is very similar, but instead of the default route being added to R1 (as we would normally do) the command is actually entered on the PE1 router. We use the same command as above, but with a couple of changes. We must specify the VRF that this route will live in and also specify the global keyword.

```
PE1(config)#ip route vrf RED 0.0.0.0 0.0.0.0 10.20.1.1 global
```

The "global" keyword means that the next hop resides in the global routing table (not in the VRF) - hence the route is "leaked" from the global routing table into the VRF routing table. The alternative would be to add a standard default route onto R1 and then leak a route to the IGW router through PE1. This which would mean that we have two static routes, rather than just the one.

Lastly, we need to make sure that this route is sent to our customer. To do this, we must redistribute the static route that we created above into the PE-CE routing protocol:

```
PE1(config)#router bgp 100
PE1(config-router)#address-family ipv4 vrf RED
PE1(config-router-af)#redistribute static
PE1(config-router-af)#default-information originate
PE1(config-router-af)#
```

If all is well, R1 should have a default route:

```
R1#sh ip route | beg Gateway
```

```
Gateway of last resort is 10.1.1.1 to network 0.0.0.0

B*      0.0.0.0/0 [20/0] via 10.1.1.1, 00:00:21
        10.0.0.0/8 is variably subnetted, 4 subnets, 2 masks
C          10.1.1.0/24 is directly connected, GigabitEthernet1/0
L          10.1.1.2/32 is directly connected, GigabitEthernet1/0
B          10.1.3.0/24 [20/0] via 10.1.1.1, 00:31:39
B          10.2.2.0/24 [20/0] via 10.1.1.1, 00:02:35
        172.20.0.0/24 is subnetted, 2 subnets
B          172.20.1.0 [20/0] via 10.1.1.1, 00:02:35
B          172.20.2.0 [20/0] via 10.1.1.1, 00:31:39
        192.168.1.0/24 is variably subnetted, 2 subnets, 2 masks
C          192.168.1.0/24 is directly connected, Loopback0
L          192.168.1.1/32 is directly connected, Loopback0
B       192.168.2.0/24 [20/0] via 10.1.1.1, 00:31:39
R1#sh ip route 0.0.0.0
Routing entry for 0.0.0.0/0, supernet
  Known via "bgp 65001", distance 20, metric 0, candidate default path
  Tag 100, type external
  Last update from 10.1.1.1 00:00:31 ago
  Routing Descriptor Blocks:
  * 10.1.1.1, from 10.1.1.1, 00:00:31 ago
      Route metric is 0, traffic share count is 1
      AS Hops 1
      Route tag 100
      MPLS label: none
R1#
```

We can then test reachability from our egress interface, as well as from our loopback network. We can also check the path that the packets take:

```
R1#ping 4.4.4.4
Type escape sequence to abort.
Sending 5, 100-byte ICMP Echos to 4.4.4.4, timeout is 2 seconds:
!!!!!
Success rate is 100 percent (5/5)
R1#ping 4.4.4.4 so lo0
Type escape sequence to abort.
Sending 5, 100-byte ICMP Echos to 4.4.4.4, timeout is 2 seconds:
Packet sent with a source address of 192.168.1.1
!!!!!
Success rate is 100 percent (5/5)
R1#trace 4.4.4.4
Type escape sequence to abort.
Tracing the route to 4.4.4.4
VRF info: (vrf in name/id, vrf out name/id)
  1 10.1.1.1 28 msec 84 msec 40 msec
```

```
   2 10.20.1.1 [AS 100] 128 msec 48 msec 52 msec
R1#
```

Extending this method to other routers, such as R2 follows the same logic. Because we have already assigned GI6/0 as our nat outside interface we do not need to do this step again.

We add the command "ip nat inside" to the interface connecting PE1 to R3:

```
PE1(config)#int gi 3/0
PE1(config-if)#ip nat inside
```

Next, we setup our access list to capture our interesting traffic, and again we tell the router that this is the traffic we wish to do NAT for.

```
PE1(config)#ip access-list standard VRF_WHITE_SUBNETS
PE1(config-std-nacl)#permit 10.1.3.0 0.0.0.255
PE1(config-std-nacl)#permit 192.168.2.0 0.0.0.255
PE1(config-std-nacl)#exit
PE1(config)#ip nat inside source list VRF_WHITE_SUBNETS interface gi6/0 vrf WHITE overload
```

Lastly, we need to create a static route for vrf WHITE, specifying that the next hop is outside of the VRF. Then, we need to redistribute this into our CE-PE routing protocol:

```
PE1(config)#ip route vrf WHITE 0.0.0.0 0.0.0.0 10.20.1.1 global
PE1(config)#router eigrp 3
PE1(config-router)#address-family ipv4 vrf WHITE
PE1(config-router-af)#redistribute static
```

R3 should now have a default route and be able to ping the loopback interfaces on the IGW router:

```
R3#sh ip route | beg Gate
Gateway of last resort is 10.1.3.1 to network 0.0.0.0

D*EX  0.0.0.0/0 [170/3072] via 10.1.3.1, 00:03:26, GigabitEthernet1/0
      10.0.0.0/8 is variably subnetted, 4 subnets, 2 masks
D EX     10.1.1.0/24 [170/2562816] via 10.1.3.1, 00:06:21, Gi1/0
C        10.1.3.0/24 is directly connected, GigabitEthernet1/0
L        10.1.3.2/32 is directly connected, GigabitEthernet1/0
D EX     10.2.2.0/24 [170/2562816] via 10.1.3.1, 00:06:21, Gi1/0
      172.20.0.0/24 is subnetted, 2 subnets
D EX     172.20.1.0 [170/2562816] via 10.1.3.1, 00:06:21, Gi1/0
D EX     172.20.2.0 [170/2562816] via 10.1.3.1, 00:06:21, Gi1/0
```

```
D EX    192.168.1.0/24 [170/2562816] via 10.1.3.1, 00:06:21, Gi1/0
        192.168.2.0/24 is variably subnetted, 2 subnets, 2 masks
C          192.168.2.0/24 is directly connected, Loopback0
L          192.168.2.1/32 is directly connected, Loopback0
R3#sh ip route 0.0.0.0
Routing entry for 0.0.0.0/0, supernet
  Known via "eigrp 3", distance 170, metric 3072, candidate default
path, type external
  Redistributing via eigrp 3
  Last update from 10.1.3.1 on GigabitEthernet1/0, 00:03:33 ago
  Routing Descriptor Blocks:
  * 10.1.3.1, from 10.1.3.1, 00:03:33 ago, via GigabitEthernet1/0
      Route metric is 3072, traffic share count is 1
      Total delay is 20 microseconds, minimum bandwidth is 1000000
Kbit
      Reliability 255/255, minimum MTU 1500 bytes
      Loading 1/255, Hops 1
R3#ping 4.4.4.4
Type escape sequence to abort.
Sending 5, 100-byte ICMP Echos to 4.4.4.4, timeout is 2 seconds:
!!!!!
Success rate is 100 percent (5/5)
R3#ping 4.4.4.4 so lo0
Type escape sequence to abort.
Sending 5, 100-byte ICMP Echos to 4.4.4.4, timeout is 2 seconds:
Packet sent with a source address of 192.168.2.1
!!!!!
Success rate is 100 percent (5/5)
R3#trace 4.4.4.4
Type escape sequence to abort.
Tracing the route to 4.4.4.4
VRF info: (vrf in name/id, vrf out name/id)
  1 10.1.3.1 28 msec 24 msec 28 msec
  2 10.20.1.1 92 msec 60 msec 60 msec
R3#
```

If we turn our attention to PE1, we can see that it is keeping a nice table of the translations that it is performing:

```
PE1#sh ip nat translations
Pro Inside global     Inside local      Outside local     Outside global
icmp 10.20.1.2:6      192.168.1.1:3     4.4.4.4:3         4.4.4.4:6
icmp 10.20.1.2:3      10.1.3.2:3        4.4.4.4:3         4.4.4.4:3
icmp 10.20.1.2:4      10.1.3.2:4        4.4.4.4:4         4.4.4.4:4
icmp 10.20.1.2:5      192.168.2.1:5     4.4.4.4:5         4.4.4.4:5
PE1#
```

These translations are fairly transient. Perform a couple of pings or increase the number of pings (*ping 4.4.4.4 rep 100*) so that you can see the translations on PE1. Now that we have sorted R1 and R3, we need to finish off the left hand side of our topology.

Part of our remit is that the BLUE Company should have no access to the RED Company (or the WHITE Company for that matter). So, if we extend Internet access to R5 (in the same manner as R1 and R3), can we still maintain this separation? Let's find out.

The commands follow exactly the same format as we used for the RED and WHITE routers:

```
PE1(config)#int gi 4/0
PE1(config-if)#ip nat inside
PE1(config-if)#ip access-list standard VRF_BLUE_SUBNETS
PE1(config-std-nacl)#permit 10.1.5.0 0.0.0.255
PE1(config-std-nacl)#permit 192.168.5.0 0.0.0.255
PE1(config-std-nacl)#exit
PE1(config)#ip route vrf BLUE 0.0.0.0 0.0.0.0 10.20.1.1 global
PE1(config)#ip nat inside source list VRF_BLUE_SUBNETS interface gi 6/0 vrf BLUE overload
PE1(config)#
```

The "default-information originate" just needs to be added in order for R5 to receive the route:

```
PE1(config)#router ospf 3 vrf BLUE
PE1(config-router)#default-information originate
PE1(config-router)#
```

Giving a few moments for the route to reach R5, we should now see the default route in its table:

```
R5#sh ip route | beg Gate
Gateway of last resort is 10.1.5.1 to network 0.0.0.0

O*E2  0.0.0.0/0 [110/1] via 10.1.5.1, 00:10:44, GigabitEthernet1/0
      1.0.0.0/8 is variably subnetted, 2 subnets, 2 masks
C        1.1.1.0/24 is directly connected, GigabitEthernet2/0
L        1.1.1.1/32 is directly connected, GigabitEthernet2/0
      2.0.0.0/32 is subnetted, 1 subnets
O E2     2.2.2.5 [110/1] via 10.1.5.1, 00:12:40, GigabitEthernet1/0
      10.0.0.0/8 is variably subnetted, 2 subnets, 2 masks
C        10.1.5.0/24 is directly connected, GigabitEthernet1/0
L        10.1.5.2/32 is directly connected, GigabitEthernet1/0
      192.168.5.0/24 is variably subnetted, 2 subnets, 2 masks
```

```
C       192.168.5.0/24 is directly connected, Loopback0
L       192.168.5.1/32 is directly connected, Loopback0
R5#
```

Just to make sure that all is well we can test out a couple of pings:

```
R5#ping 4.4.4.4
Type escape sequence to abort.
Sending 5, 100-byte ICMP Echos to 4.4.4.4, timeout is 2 seconds:
!!!!!
Success rate is 100 percent (5/5)
R5#ping 4.4.4.4 so lo0
Type escape sequence to abort.
Sending 5, 100-byte ICMP Echos to 4.4.4.4, timeout is 2 seconds:
Packet sent with a source address of 192.168.5.1
!!!!!
Success rate is 100 percent (5/5)
R5#
```

All looks good there, and PE1 has a nice set of translations:

```
PE1(config-router)#do sh ip nat translations
Pro Inside global      Inside local      Outside local      Outside global
icmp 10.20.1.2:6       192.168.5.1:6     4.4.4.4:6          4.4.4.4:6
icmp 10.20.1.2:5       192.168.1.1:5     4.4.4.4:5          4.4.4.4:5
icmp 10.20.1.2:3       192.168.2.1:3     4.4.4.4:3          4.4.4.4:3
PE1(config-router)#
```

If we try and hop from one company to another, we find that we are unable to:

```
R5#ping 192.168.1.1
Type escape sequence to abort.
Sending 5, 100-byte ICMP Echos to 192.168.1.1, timeout is 2 seconds:
UUUUU
Success rate is 0 percent (0/5)
R5#ping 192.168.2.1
Type escape sequence to abort.
Sending 5, 100-byte ICMP Echos to 192.168.3.1, timeout is 2 seconds:
UUUUU
Success rate is 0 percent (0/5)
R5#ping 10.1.1.2
Type escape sequence to abort.
Sending 5, 100-byte ICMP Echos to 10.1.1.2, timeout is 2 seconds:
UUUUU
Success rate is 0 percent (0/5)
R5#ping 10.1.3.2
```

```
Type escape sequence to abort.
Sending 5, 100-byte ICMP Echos to 10.1.3.2, timeout is 2 seconds:
UUUUU
Success rate is 0 percent (0/5)
R5#
```

Similarly, from R1 (as it never hurts to double-check, especially in the lab exam), the pings also fail:

```
R1#ping 192.168.5.1
Type escape sequence to abort.
Sending 5, 100-byte ICMP Echos to 192.168.5.1, timeout is 2 seconds:
UUUUU
Success rate is 0 percent (0/5)
R1#ping 10.1.5.2
Type escape sequence to abort.
Sending 5, 100-byte ICMP Echos to 10.1.5.2, timeout is 2 seconds:
UUU.U
Success rate is 0 percent (0/5)
R1#
```

This works exactly as we would like it to. So, what happens if we provide Internet Access as a separate VPN?

Providing Internet Access through a dedicated VRF

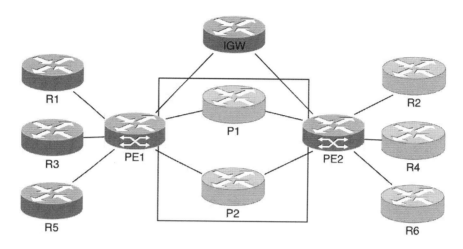

Keeping in with the theme of a previous topic where we looked at Central Services within an MPLS cloud, we could use the same logic to provide a separate VRF for internet access, which is what we will do now and extend this to all the customer routers in our network. We will start by removing most of the commands we used for the last exercise:

```
PE1(config)#int gi 2/0
PE1(config-if)#no ip nat inside
PE1(config-if)#int gi 3/0
PE1(config-if)#no ip nat inside
PE1(config-if)#int gi 4/0
PE1(config-if)#no ip nat inside
PE1(config-if)#int gi 6/0
PE1(config-if)#no ip nat outside
PE1(config-if)#exit
PE1(config)#no ip nat inside source list VRF_RED_SUBNETS interface Gi6/0 vrf RED overload
PE1(config)#no ip nat inside source list VRF_WHITE_SUBNETS interface Gi6/0 vrf WHITE overload
PE1(config)#no ip nat inside source list VRF_BLUE_SUBNETS interface Gi6/0 vrf BLUE overload
PE1(config)#no ip route vrf BLUE 0.0.0.0 0.0.0.0 10.20.1.1 global
PE1(config)#no ip route vrf RED 0.0.0.0 0.0.0.0 10.20.1.1 global
PE1(config)#no ip route vrf WHITE 0.0.0.0 0.0.0.0 10.20.1.1 global
```

I have left in the access lists created earlier, as we can reuse them.

We will create a BGP peering between the Internet router (IGW) and PE1 and PE2, advertising a default route and nothing else. From the viewpoint of PE1 and PE2, this will all take place within the vrf INTERNET, and we will use a route map to modify the prefixes we are exporting from our customers towards our Internet providing router.

```
IGW#conf t
IGW(config)#router bgp 200
IGW(config-router)#neighbor 10.20.1.2 remote-as 100
IGW(config-router)#neighbor 10.20.2.2 remote-as 100
IGW(config-router)#network 0.0.0.0
IGW(config-router)#
```

We start with what should be a familiar configuration. We define our vrf, set the route-distinguisher and route-targets, assign an interface to forward for this vrf, and then add this as an address family within BGP. Note, we are not importing any route targets.

```
PE1(config)#ip vrf INTERNET
PE1(config-vrf)#rd 100:200
PE1(config-vrf)#route-target export 100:200
PE1(config-vrf)#int gi 6/0
PE1(config-if)#ip vrf forwarding INTERNET
% Interface GigabitEthernet6/0 IPv4 disabled and address(es) removed
due to enabling VRF INTERNET
PE1(config-if)#ip add 10.20.1.2 255.255.255.0
PE1(config-if)#router bgp 100
PE1(config-router)#address-family ipv4 vrf INTERNET
PE1(config-router-af)#neigh 10.20.1.1 remote-as 200
PE1(config-router-af)#neigh 10.20.1.1 activate
PE1(config-router-af)#
*Jun  7 11:13:32.671: %BGP-5-ADJCHANGE: neighbor 10.20.1.1 vpn vrf
INTERNET Up
PE1(config-router-af)#
```

At this point, our BGP peering should come up.

The next task is to make our INTERNET VRF aware of the prefixes being sent from our customers. We will make it a bit more interesting than just importing the RT of the specific VRF. We might have a scenario where we do not want all of the networks within our customer's environment to have access to our Internet gateway. For example, we might want R1's egress interface to have access to the Internet, but not from the loopback network. Because we already have an access list in place for R1, we wont be selective on our routing at this point. This is, however, something we will look at a little later.

To make the INTERNET vrf aware of the prefixes exported by other vrfs, we will use an export map under the company vrf definition. The export-map will call a route-map, which will be used to mark routes that are to be imported into the INTERNET VRF. For R1, for example, we will then have routes with RT of 100:1 and routes with RT of 100:1 100:201. It is the second RT value (100:201) that will be used to import our routes into the INTERNET vrf.

We create a route-map, which will match our access list and then set an extended community value for the route-target on the prefixes that are matched. The keyword "additive" ensures that any existing extended community values are preserved.

Our previously used prefix-list is:

```
PE1(config)#ip access-list standard VRF_RED_SUBNETS
PE1(config-std-nacl)#permit 10.1.1.0 0.0.0.255
PE1(config-std-nacl)#permit 192.168.1.0 0.0.0.255
```

The route map that we will use is as follows:

```
PE1(config)#route-map VRF-RED-INTERNET permit 10
PE1(config-route-map)#match ip address VRF_RED_SUBNETS
PE1(config-route-map)#set extcommunity rt 100:201 additive
```

We now apply this route map to the vrf whose prefixes we want the Internet providing router to know about. Remember that the Internet router only has a default route pointing to null 0. Therefore, it needs to have these routes explicitly set within its routing table to be able to return any traffic sent to it. To accomplish this, we will export the routes from our VRF (using the route-map defined above) and also import the routes being exported from the INTERNET VRF, which should be just the default route using the standard route-target import command.

```
PE1(config-route-map)#ip vrf RED
PE1(config-vrf)#export map VRF-RED-INTERNET
PE1(config-vrf)#route-target import 100:200
PE1(config-vrf)#ip vrf INTERNET
PE1(config-vrf)#route-target import 100:201
```

Given a few moments, R1 receives the default route:

```
R1#sh ip route | beg Gate
Gateway of last resort is 10.1.1.1 to network 0.0.0.0

B*      0.0.0.0/0 [20/0] via 10.1.1.1, 00:00:43
        10.0.0.0/8 is variably subnetted, 3 subnets, 2 masks
```

```
C          10.1.1.0/24 is directly connected, GigabitEthernet1/0
L          10.1.1.2/32 is directly connected, GigabitEthernet1/0
B          10.1.3.0/24 [20/0] via 10.1.1.1, 01:03:13
           192.168.1.0/24 is variably subnetted, 2 subnets, 2 masks
C             192.168.1.0/24 is directly connected, Loopback0
L             192.168.1.1/32 is directly connected, Loopback0
B          192.168.2.0/24 [20/0] via 10.1.1.1, 01:03:13
R1#sh ip route 0.0.0.0
Routing entry for 0.0.0.0/0, supernet
  Known via "bgp 65001", distance 20, metric 0, candidate default path
  Tag 100, type external
  Last update from 10.1.1.1 00:00:08 ago
  Routing Descriptor Blocks:
  * 10.1.1.1, from 10.1.1.1, 00:00:08 ago
      Route metric is 0, traffic share count is 1
      AS Hops 2
      Route tag 100
      MPLS label: none
R1#sh ip bgp 0.0.0.0
BGP routing table entry for 0.0.0.0/0, version 2
Paths: (1 available, best #1, table default)
  Not advertised to any peer
  100 200
    10.1.1.1 from 10.1.1.1 (10.250.3.1)
      Origin IGP, localpref 100, valid, external, best
R1#
```

If we look at the route within the VRF context on PE1, we can see that it has the extended community value of 100:200, and it is sourced from AS 200:

```
PE1(config-vrf)#do sh bgp vpnv4 unicast vrf RED 0.0.0.0
BGP routing table entry for 100:1:0.0.0.0/0, version 168
Paths: (1 available, best #1, table RED)
  Advertised to update-groups:
     8
  200, imported path from 100:200:0.0.0.0/0
    10.20.1.1 (via INTERNET) from 10.20.1.1 (5.5.5.5)
      Origin IGP, metric 0, localpref 100, valid, external, best
      Extended Community: RT:100:200
PE1(config-vrf)#
```

With the default route happily sitting in the routing table of R1, we actually find that we cannot ping the Internet (the 4.4.4.4 IP address) from R1:

```
R1#ping 4.4.4.4
Type escape sequence to abort.
```

```
Sending 5, 100-byte ICMP Echos to 4.4.4.4, timeout is 2 seconds:
.....
Success rate is 0 percent (0/5)
R1#
```

Why is this? We are importing the correct route target(s), exporting the correct values, and we have the default route. So, what are we missing? If we look at the prefix that currently exists in the VPN, we can see that it is not being tagged with the extended community value we set:

```
PE1(config-vrf)#do sh bgp vpnv4 unicast vrf RED 192.168.1.0
BGP routing table entry for 100:1:192.168.1.0/24, version 50
Paths: (1 available, best #1, table RED)
  Not advertised to any peer
  65001
    10.1.1.2 from 10.1.1.2 (192.168.1.1)
      Origin IGP, metric 0, localpref 100, valid, external, best
      Extended Community: RT:100:1
      mpls labels in/out 23/nolabel
PE1(config-vrf)#
```

The extended community RT value still shows just the value of 100:1 and does not include the additional 100:201 that we set on our route-map. This is because the modification performed by the route map will not take effect until we clear the BGP process for the tagging to take place:

```
R1#clear ip bgp *
R1#
*Jun  7 11:24:46.287: %BGP-5-ADJCHANGE: neighbor 10.1.1.1 Down User reset
*Jun  7 11:24:46.291: %BGP_SESSION-5-ADJCHANGE: neighbor 10.1.1.1 IPv4 Unicast topology base removed from session  User reset
*Jun  7 11:24:46.791: %BGP-5-ADJCHANGE: neighbor 10.1.1.1 Up
R1#
```

Once the BGP peering comes back up again, we can see that the prefix now has two extended community values, the original 100:1 and the 100:201 we set in the route-map:

```
PE1(config-vrf)#do sh bgp vpnv4 unicast vrf RED 192.168.1.0
BGP routing table entry for 100:1:192.168.1.0/24, version 62
Paths: (1 available, best #1, table RED)
  Not advertised to any peer
  65001
    10.1.1.2 from 10.1.1.2 (192.168.1.1)
      Origin IGP, metric 0, localpref 100, valid, external, best
```

```
        Extended Community: RT:100:1 RT:100:201
        mpls labels in/out 16/nolabel
PE1(config-vrf)#
```

The routes are now visible on the Internet router (shown as "B"):

```
IGW(config-router)#do sh ip route | beg Gate
Gateway of last resort is 0.0.0.0 to network 0.0.0.0

S*     0.0.0.0/0 is directly connected, Null0
       4.0.0.0/32 is subnetted, 1 subnets
C         4.4.4.4 is directly connected, Loopback0
       5.0.0.0/32 is subnetted, 1 subnets
C         5.5.5.5 is directly connected, Loopback1
       10.0.0.0/8 is variably subnetted, 5 subnets, 2 masks
B         10.1.1.0/24 [20/0] via 10.20.1.2, 00:00:48
C         10.20.1.0/24 is directly connected, GigabitEthernet1/0
L         10.20.1.1/32 is directly connected, GigabitEthernet1/0
C         10.20.2.0/24 is directly connected, GigabitEthernet2/0
L         10.20.2.1/32 is directly connected, GigabitEthernet2/0
B      192.168.1.0/24 [20/0] via 10.20.1.2, 00:00:48
IGW(config-router)#do sh ip bgp | beg Network
   Network          Next Hop        Metric LocPrf Weight Path
*> 0.0.0.0          0.0.0.0              0         32768 i
*> 10.1.1.0/24      10.20.1.2                          0 100 65001 i
*> 192.168.1.0      10.20.1.2                          0 100 65001 i
IGW(config-router)#
```

And lastly, now that R1 has its VPN routes and a default route, it has reachability to the Internet (where we are using the IP address 4.4.4.4 to simulate the internet):

```
R1#sh ip route | beg Gate
Gateway of last resort is 10.1.1.1 to network 0.0.0.0

B*     0.0.0.0/0 [20/0] via 10.1.1.1, 00:02:15
       10.0.0.0/8 is variably subnetted, 3 subnets, 2 masks
C         10.1.1.0/24 is directly connected, GigabitEthernet1/0
L         10.1.1.2/32 is directly connected, GigabitEthernet1/0
B         10.1.3.0/24 [20/0] via 10.1.1.1, 00:02:15
       192.168.1.0/24 is variably subnetted, 2 subnets, 2 masks
C         192.168.1.0/24 is directly connected, Loopback0
L         192.168.1.1/32 is directly connected, Loopback0
B      192.168.2.0/24 [20/0] via 10.1.1.1, 00:02:15
R1#ping 4.4.4.4
Type escape sequence to abort.
Sending 5, 100-byte ICMP Echos to 4.4.4.4, timeout is 2 seconds:
```

```
!!!!!
Success rate is 100 percent (5/5)
R1#ping 4.4.4.4 so lo0
Type escape sequence to abort.
Sending 5, 100-byte ICMP Echos to 4.4.4.4, timeout is 2 seconds:
Packet sent with a source address of 192.168.1.1
!!!!!
Success rate is 100 percent (5/5)
R1#trace 4.4.4.4
Type escape sequence to abort.
Tracing the route to 4.4.4.4
VRF info: (vrf in name/id, vrf out name/id)
  1 10.1.1.1 20 msec 16 msec 20 msec
  2 10.20.1.1 [AS 200] 44 msec 28 msec 32 msec
R1#
```

Extending Internet access to R3 follows the same principles. We already have our access list defined from earlier. We will reuse the access list for our route map, which, in turn, will be used for our export map. vrf WHITE will import the route target of the INTERNET vrf, which will, in turn, import the route target specified by the export map (100:203).

```
PE1(config-vrf)#ip vrf WHITE
PE1(config-vrf)#export map VRF-WHITE-INTERNET
PE1(config-vrf)#route-target import 100:200
PE1(config-vrf)#route-map VRF-WHITE-INTERNET permit 10
PE1(config-route-map)#match ip address VRF_WHITE_SUBNETS
PE1(config-route-map)#set extcommunity rt 100:203 additive
PE1(config-route-map)#ip vrf INTERNET
PE1(config-vrf)#route-target import 100:203
PE1(config-vrf)#
```

After a few moments, router IGW will learn of the prefixes from R3:

```
IGW(config-router)#do sh ip route | beg Gate
Gateway of last resort is 0.0.0.0 to network 0.0.0.0

S*    0.0.0.0/0 is directly connected, Null0
      4.0.0.0/32 is subnetted, 1 subnets
C        4.4.4.4 is directly connected, Loopback0
      5.0.0.0/32 is subnetted, 1 subnets
C        5.5.5.5 is directly connected, Loopback1
      10.0.0.0/8 is variably subnetted, 6 subnets, 2 masks
B        10.1.1.0/24 [20/0] via 10.20.1.2, 00:06:59
B        10.1.3.0/24 [20/0] via 10.20.1.2, 00:00:03
C        10.20.1.0/24 is directly connected, GigabitEthernet1/0
L        10.20.1.1/32 is directly connected, GigabitEthernet1/0
```

```
C          10.20.2.0/24 is directly connected, GigabitEthernet2/0
L          10.20.2.1/32 is directly connected, GigabitEthernet2/0
B       192.168.1.0/24 [20/0] via 10.20.1.2, 00:06:59
B       192.168.2.0/24 [20/0] via 10.20.1.2, 00:00:03
IGW(config-router)#
```

R3 now has Internet access, courtesy of the default route:

```
R3#sh ip route | beg Gate
Gateway of last resort is 10.1.3.1 to network 0.0.0.0

D*EX   0.0.0.0/0 [170/2562816] via 10.1.3.1, 00:02:54, Gi1/0
       10.0.0.0/8 is variably subnetted, 3 subnets, 2 masks
D EX      10.1.1.0/24 [170/2562816] via 10.1.3.1, 00:06:49, Gi1/0
C         10.1.3.0/24 is directly connected, GigabitEthernet1/0
L         10.1.3.2/32 is directly connected, GigabitEthernet1/0
D EX   192.168.1.0/24 [170/2562816] via 10.1.3.1, 00:06:49, Gi1/0
       192.168.2.0/24 is variably subnetted, 2 subnets, 2 masks
C         192.168.2.0/24 is directly connected, Loopback0
L         192.168.2.1/32 is directly connected, Loopback0
R3#sh ip route 0.0.0.0
Routing entry for 0.0.0.0/0, supernet
  Known via "eigrp 3", distance 170, metric 2562816, candidate default
path
  Tag 200, type external
  Redistributing via eigrp 3
  Last update from 10.1.3.1 on GigabitEthernet1/0, 00:04:40 ago
  Routing Descriptor Blocks:
  * 10.1.3.1, from 10.1.3.1, 00:04:40 ago, via GigabitEthernet1/0
      Route metric is 2562816, traffic share count is 1
      Total delay is 110 microseconds, minimum bandwidth is 1000 Kbit
      Reliability 100/255, minimum MTU 1500 bytes
      Loading 1/255, Hops 1
      Route tag 200
R3#ping 4.4.4.4
Type escape sequence to abort.
Sending 5, 100-byte ICMP Echos to 4.4.4.4, timeout is 2 seconds:
!!!!!
Success rate is 100 percent (5/5)
R3#trace 192.168.1.1
Type escape sequence to abort.
Tracing the route to 192.168.1.1
VRF info: (vrf in name/id, vrf out name/id)
  1 10.1.3.1 8 msec 12 msec 12 msec
  2 10.1.1.2 32 msec 36 msec *
R3#
```

Now R3 has Internet access, whilst still retaining the most direct route to its partner network, so what will happen if we do the exact same thing on R5? The configuration follows the same steps as before:

```
PE1(config-vrf)#ip vrf BLUE
PE1(config-vrf)#export map VRF-BLUE-SUBNETS
PE1(config-vrf)#route-target import 100:200
PE1(config-vrf)#route-map VRF-BLUE-SUBNETS permit 10
PE1(config-route-map)#match ip address VRF_BLUE_SUBNETS
PE1(config-route-map)#set extcommunity rt 100:205 additive
PE1(config-route-map)#ip vrf INTERNET
PE1(config-vrf)#route-target import 100:205
PE1(config-vrf)#
```

R5 gets the default route and can ping the Internet:

```
R5#sh ip route | beg Gate
Gateway of last resort is 10.1.5.1 to network 0.0.0.0

O*E2  0.0.0.0/0 [110/1] via 10.1.5.1, 00:01:02, GigabitEthernet1/0
      1.0.0.0/8 is variably subnetted, 2 subnets, 2 masks
C        1.1.1.0/24 is directly connected, GigabitEthernet2/0
L        1.1.1.1/32 is directly connected, GigabitEthernet2/0
      2.0.0.0/32 is subnetted, 1 subnets
O E2     2.2.2.5 [110/1] via 10.1.5.1, 02:32:02, GigabitEthernet1/0
      10.0.0.0/8 is variably subnetted, 2 subnets, 2 masks
C        10.1.5.0/24 is directly connected, GigabitEthernet1/0
L        10.1.5.2/32 is directly connected, GigabitEthernet1/0
      192.168.5.0/24 is variably subnetted, 2 subnets, 2 masks
C        192.168.5.0/24 is directly connected, Loopback0
L        192.168.5.1/32 is directly connected, Loopback0
R5#ping 4.4.4.4
Type escape sequence to abort.
Sending 5, 100-byte ICMP Echos to 4.4.4.4, timeout is 2 seconds:
!!!!!
Success rate is 100 percent (5/5)
R5#
```

The IGW router has learnt about R5 through BGP:

```
IGW(config-router)#do sh ip route | i B
Codes: L - local, C - connected, S - static, R - RIP, M - mobile, B - BGP
B        10.1.1.0/24 [20/0] via 10.20.1.2, 00:14:57
B        10.1.3.0/24 [20/0] via 10.20.1.2, 00:08:01
B        10.1.5.0/24 [20/0] via 10.20.1.2, 00:01:01
```

```
B       192.168.1.0/24 [20/0] via 10.20.1.2, 00:14:57
B       192.168.2.0/24 [20/0] via 10.20.1.2, 00:08:01
B       192.168.5.0/24 [20/0] via 10.20.1.2, 00:01:01
IGW(config-router)#
```

So far, this is mission accomplished in terms of extending Internet access to the BLUE company. However, part of the remit is that BLUE's network should be separate from the other customers network.

However, BLUE has access to RED and WHITE, and vice versa:

```
R5#ping 192.168.1.1
Type escape sequence to abort.
Sending 5, 100-byte ICMP Echos to 192.168.1.1, timeout is 2 seconds:
!!!!!
Success rate is 100 percent (5/5)
R5#ping 192.168.2.1
Type escape sequence to abort.
Sending 5, 100-byte ICMP Echos to 192.168.2.1, timeout is 2 seconds:
!!!!!
Success rate is 100 percent (5/5)
R5#

R1#ping 192.168.5.1
Type escape sequence to abort.
Sending 5, 100-byte ICMP Echos to 192.168.5.1, timeout is 2 seconds:
!!!!!
Success rate is 100 percent (5/5)
R1#
```

Clearly, R1 does not have a defined route for R5 within its routing table, neither does R5 for R1.

```
R1#sh ip route 192.168.5.0
% Network not in table
R1#
```

All that each router has is the default route advertised to it by the various routing protocols. If we look at the BGP table on R1, we can see that the entry for 192.168.5.0/24 is encompassed in the default route:

```
R1#sh ip bgp 192.168.5.0
BGP routing table entry for 0.0.0.0/0, version 10
Paths: (1 available, best #1, table default)
  Not advertised to any peer
```

```
    100 200
      10.1.1.1 from 10.1.1.1 (10.250.3.1)
        Origin IGP, localpref 100, valid, external, best
R1#
```

By passing the traffic between R1 and R5, the network is doing exactly what it is configured to do. The IGW router is exporting the default route within RT 100:200 and importing the customer routes (100:201, 203 and 205) in order that their traffic may be returned to them. All the traffic that does not have a distinct route in the routing table of the individual company routers will be encompassed in the 100:200 default route:

```
PE1#sh ip bgp vpnv4 vrf RED 192.168.5.0
BGP routing table entry for 100:1:0.0.0.0/0, version 56
Paths: (1 available, best #1, table RED)
  Advertised to update-groups:
     8
  200, imported path from 100:200:0.0.0.0/0
    10.20.1.1 (via INTERNET) from 10.20.1.1 (5.5.5.5)
      Origin IGP, metric 0, localpref 100, valid, external, best
      Extended Community: RT:100:200
PE1#
```

The route that R1 receives does not match the one that R5 sends, hence the lack of the RT values of 100:5 or 100:205, it actually matches the default route sent by IGW. So, how can we overcome this inadvertent leakage? The options open to us are fairly limited, but before we look at the methods that work, let's discuss the ones that don't work, and more specifically, why they don't work. We will concentrate in R1 and R5.

Could we use, or modify, the route-target being exported from the IGW router?

We have seen how we can use a route map to set the extended community value, so could we match just the default route? Or, could we block the prefixes being sent from R5 being imported into the route target being exported from the IGW router? The answer to both of these questions is "no". R1 is just following the default route that it is being imported into its routing table through the BGP process on the PE router. We can still try by setting a specific route target value for the different company network prefixes and exporting that from the INTERNET vrf:

```
PE1(config)#route-map INTERNET-ONLY-ROUTES permit 10
PE1(config-route-map)#match ip address VRF_RED_SUBNETS
PE1(config-route-map)#set extcommunity rt 100:220
PE1(config-route-map)#route-map INTERNET-ONLY-ROUTES permit 20
PE1(config-route-map)#match ip address VRF_WHITE_SUBNETS
PE1(config-route-map)#set extcommunity rt 100:221
```

```
PE1(config-route-map)#route-map INTERNET-ONLY-ROUTES permit 30
PE1(config-route-map)#match ip address VRF_BLUE_SUBNETS
PE1(config-route-map)#set extcommunity rt 100:222
PE1(config-route-map)#route-map INTERNET-ONLY-ROUTES permit 40
PE1(config-route-map)#set extcommunity rt 100:200
PE1(config-route-map)#exit
PE1(config)#ip vrf INTERNET
PE1(config-vrf)#export map INTERNET-ONLY-ROUTES
```

Once we have cleared our BGP process and given it time to come back up again, we find that R1 still has access:

```
R1#sh ip bgp 192.168.5.0
BGP routing table entry for 0.0.0.0/0, version 16
Paths: (1 available, best #1, table default)
  Not advertised to any peer
  100 200
    10.1.1.1 from 10.1.1.1 (10.250.3.1)
      Origin IGP, localpref 100, valid, external, best
R1#ping 192.168.5.1
Type escape sequence to abort.
Sending 5, 100-byte ICMP Echos to 192.168.5.1, timeout is 2 seconds:
!!!!!
Success rate is 100 percent (5/5)
R1#
```

Again, this is because the route to 192.168.5.0/24 as seen by R1 is included in the 100:200 route target.

```
PE1(config-vrf)#do sh ip bgp vpnv4 vrf RED 192.168.5.0
BGP routing table entry for 100:1:0.0.0.0/0, version 22
Paths: (1 available, best #1, table RED)
  Advertised to update-groups:
     9
  200, imported path from 100:200:0.0.0.0/0
    10.20.1.1 (via INTERNET) from 10.20.1.1 (5.5.5.5)
      Origin IGP, metric 0, localpref 100, valid, external, best
      Extended Community: RT:100:200
PE1(config-vrf)#
```

So, let's try something else. We will remove the export statement on vrf INTERNET and the related route-map.

```
PE1(config-vrf)#no export map INTERNET-ONLY-ROUTES
PE1(config-vrf)#exit
PE1(config)#no route-map INTERNET-ONLY-ROUTES
```

```
PE1(config)#
```

Could we use a BGP route-map?

If the VRF is following what it has been told to, and exports just the default route, could we perform some change to this through BGP? We are using BGP as our entry point into and out of the MPLS cloud on both the IGW router and on R1. So, could we perform a change in say the community value, which under normal circumstances will remain with a prefix, as it passes through a network?

We could, again using a route map, set the community value on the routes as they exit out of R1, and using another route map match these values to deny the prefix being sent to R5. Under normal circumstances this would work; yet, we are still hitting the same challenge as we encountered above.

```
IGW(config)#access-list 101 permit ip 192.168.1.0 0.0.0.255 any
IGW(config)#access-list 101 permit ip 10.1.1.0 0.0.0.255 any
IGW(config)#route-map set-community permit 10
IGW(config-route-map)#match ip address 101
IGW(config-route-map)#set community 100:300
IGW(config-route-map)#route-map set-community permit 20
IGW(config-route-map)#exit
IGW(config)#router bgp 200
IGW(config-router)#neigh 10.20.1.2 send-community both
IGW(config-router)#neigh 10.20.1.2 route-map set-community in
IGW(config-router)#exit
IGW(config)#exit
IGW#clear ip bgp *
IGW#
```

Once the BGP neighbor relationship forms again, we can see that the route has the community value set. In the BGP world, 6553900 is the same as 100:300.

```
IGW#sh ip bgp 192.168.1.0
BGP routing table entry for 192.168.1.0/24, version 0
Paths: (1 available, no best path)
  Not advertised to any peer
  100 65001
    10.20.1.2 from 10.20.1.2 (10.250.3.1)
      Origin IGP, localpref 100, valid, external
      Community: 6553900
      Extended Community: RT:100:1 RT:100:201
IGW#
```

Recall that, in traditional BGP operation, the route would be propagated from one autonomous system (AS) to the next with the community unchanged (unless changed on purpose). In this case, the prefix 192.168.5.0/24 does not originate on IGW, nor is it technically being advertised by IGW. Therefore, a community value will not be carried with it, again because the specific prefix is not being advertised.

```
PE1(config-router-af)#do sh ip bgp vpnv4 vrf BLUE 192.168.1.0
BGP routing table entry for 100:3:0.0.0.0/0, version 79
Paths: (1 available, best #1, table BLUE)
  Not advertised to any peer
  200, imported path from 100:200:0.0.0.0/0
    10.20.1.1 (via INTERNET) from 10.20.1.1 (5.5.5.5)
      Origin IGP, metric 0, localpref 100, valid, external, best
      Extended Community: RT:100:200
PE1(config-router-af)#
```

The route is not actually being exported by BGP, only the default route is exported. Thus, our attempts to modify any route within the all-encompassing default route will fail.

The problem is that the IGW router is performing a U-Turn on the traffic.

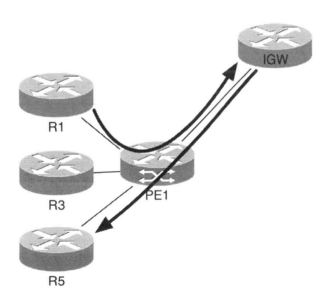

R1 does not have a matching route for 192.168.5.0/24 in its routing table; therefore, it sends the packet out to its default gateway (PE1). Similarily, PE1 forwards the packet onto its default gateway (IGW). The IGW router, not being vrf aware, does have a route to the subnet and forwards the packet back to PE1.

We are importing the 100:201, 203 and 205 route targets; and these are being exported as 100:200. Therefore, there are no modifications within BGP or MPLS that we can use to fix this issue. Thankfully for us, there are still methods we can use to prevent the different companies having access to each other.

Let's remove those last few commands and move on to some methods that will work:

```
IGW(config)#no access-list 101 permit ip 192.168.1.0 0.0.0.255 any
IGW(config)#no access-list 101 permit ip 10.1.1.0 0.0.0.255 any
IGW(config)#router bgp 200
IGW(config-router)#neigh 10.20.1.2 send-community both
IGW(config-router)#no neigh 10.20.1.2 route-map set-community in
IGW(config-router)#exit
IGW(config)#no route-map set-community
IGW(config)#exit
```

Preventing the U-Turn by black-holing the route

No matter how we try and tune our imports and exports, the fact is that the way it is set now is exactly how it needs to be. The default route is being imported by R1 (and the other routers). It is a default route, and, therefore, encompasses the prefixes for the networks that exist on R1, R3 and R5. The IGW router is not actually exporting these routes, just the route that happens to contain them all.

We can trick the routers and send them a dummy route, one that send the traffic in to a black hole. We have used this method before; we just need to set a route within the vrf and send it to null 0.

```
PE1(config)#ip route vrf RED 10.1.5.0 255.255.255.0 null 0
PE1(config)#ip route vrf RED 192.168.5.0 255.255.255.0 null 0
```

Now R1 will have no access to R5's networks:

```
R1(config-router)#do ping 10.1.5.2
Type escape sequence to abort.
Sending 5, 100-byte ICMP Echos to 10.1.5.2, timeout is 2 seconds:
UUUUU
Success rate is 0 percent (0/5)
R1(config-router)#do ping 192.168.5.1 so lo0
Type escape sequence to abort.
Sending 5, 100-byte ICMP Echos to 192.168.5.1, timeout is 2 seconds:
```

```
Packet sent with a source address of 192.168.1.1
UUUUU
Success rate is 0 percent (0/5)
R1(config-router)#
```

The problem with this approach is that, although it gives less access, it gives more visibility. R1 knows about these routes, as they appear in it's routing table, but it cannot reach them:

```
R1#sh ip route | beg Gate
Gateway of last resort is 10.1.1.1 to network 0.0.0.0

B*      0.0.0.0/0 [20/0] via 10.1.1.1, 00:00:45
        10.0.0.0/8 is variably subnetted, 4 subnets, 2 masks
C          10.1.1.0/24 is directly connected, GigabitEthernet1/0
L          10.1.1.2/32 is directly connected, GigabitEthernet1/0
B          10.1.3.0/24 [20/0] via 10.1.1.1, 00:00:45
B          10.1.5.0/24 [20/0] via 10.1.1.1, 00:00:45
        192.168.1.0/24 is variably subnetted, 2 subnets, 2 masks
C          192.168.1.0/24 is directly connected, Loopback0
L          192.168.1.1/32 is directly connected, Loopback0
B       192.168.2.0/24 [20/0] via 10.1.1.1, 00:00:45
B       192.168.5.0/24 [20/0] via 10.1.1.1, 00:00:45
R1#
```

So, really need to prevent access *and* stop R1 from even knowing about the routes.

Preventing the U-Turn using access-lists

Let's clear out our null routes, first:

```
PE1(config)#no ip route vrf RED 10.1.5.0 255.255.255.0 null 0
PE1(config)#no ip route vrf RED 192.168.5.0 255.255.255.0 null 0
```

Using an access list (ACL) makes a lot of sense as we can match on source or destination. The issue with using access lists is where to place the access list. Generally, best practice dictates that an access list should be placed as close to the source as possible. So, if the traffic to be denied is from R1 to R5, then the access list would be placed (ideally) on R1's egress interface. In this scenario, we cannot expect our customers to put ACLs on their equipment to prevent traffic that we should not be leaking to them in the first place. Therefore, the ACL should go on either PE1 or IGW. If we take the option of placing the ACL on PE1, then, as we extend our Internet access to the other side of our topology, we will also need another ACL, or set of ACLs, on PE2. Therefore, it makes sense that the ACL goes on the IGW router.

The next question is what do we include in our ACL? We could match on a source of 10.1.1.0/24 and a destination of 10.1.5.0/24, but then we would need another one to match a source of 10.1.3.0/24 and a destination of 10.1.5.0/24. We would have to continue this with all of our possible sources and destinations across our topology, making for quite a bloated ACL. Instead, we can actually keep things very simple. We can permit 0.0.0.0, and, due to the default implicit deny rule in each and every ACL, this will take care of the rest of it for us:

```
IGW(config)#access-list 1 permit 0.0.0.0
```

We, then, attach this (as an access-group) outbound from out IGW's interface connecting to PE1:

```
IGW(config)#int gi 1/0
IGW(config-if)#ip access-group 1 out
IGW(config-if)#
```

Now, if we test from R1, we can see that we still have access to the internet but not to R5.

```
R1#ping 4.4.4.4
Type escape sequence to abort.
Sending 5, 100-byte ICMP Echos to 4.4.4.4, timeout is 2 seconds:
!!!!!
Success rate is 100 percent (5/5)
R1#ping 192.168.5.1
Type escape sequence to abort.
Sending 5, 100-byte ICMP Echos to 192.168.5.1, timeout is 2 seconds:
.....
Success rate is 0 percent (0/5)
R1#
```

R5 also has access to the internet, but not to R1:

```
R5#ping 4.4.4.4
Type escape sequence to abort.
Sending 5, 100-byte ICMP Echos to 4.4.4.4, timeout is 2 seconds:
!!!!!
Success rate is 100 percent (5/5)
R5#ping 192.168.1.1
Type escape sequence to abort.
Sending 5, 100-byte ICMP Echos to 192.168.1.1, timeout is 2 seconds:
.....
Success rate is 0 percent (0/5)
R5#
```

Our last tests from R3 show that it has Internet access, access to it's other network (on R1), but no access to R5's networks from its own loopback network:

```
R3#ping 4.4.4.4
Type escape sequence to abort.
Sending 5, 100-byte ICMP Echos to 4.4.4.4, timeout is 2 seconds:
!!!!!
Success rate is 100 percent (5/5)
R3#ping 10.1.5.2 so lo0
Type escape sequence to abort.
Sending 5, 100-byte ICMP Echos to 10.1.5.2, timeout is 2 seconds:
Packet sent with a source address of 192.168.2.1
.....
Success rate is 0 percent (0/5)
R3#ping 192.168.5.1 so lo0
Type escape sequence to abort.
Sending 5, 100-byte ICMP Echos to 192.168.5.1, timeout is 2 seconds:
Packet sent with a source address of 192.168.2.1
.....
Success rate is 0 percent (0/5)
R3#ping 192.168.1.1
Type escape sequence to abort.
Sending 5, 100-byte ICMP Echos to 192.168.1.1, timeout is 2 seconds:
!!!!!
Success rate is 100 percent (5/5)
R3#
```

The next steps are to extend this to the rest of our network.

Completing Internet Access through a dedicated VRF

Now that we got over that hurdle and our customer are unaware of the trouble that could have been, we need to complete our Internet-as-a-VPN setup.

Barring a slight change in IP addresses, the configuration on PE2 is no different:

```
PE2(config)#ip vrf INTERNET
PE2(config-vrf)#rd 100:200
PE2(config-vrf)#route-target export 100:200
PE2(config-vrf)#int gi 6/0
PE2(config-if)#ip vrf forwarding INTERNET
PE2(config-if)#ip add 10.20.2.2 255.255.255.0
PE2(config-if)#no shut
```

```
PE2(config-if)#router bgp 100
PE2(config-router)#address-family ipv4 vrf INTERNET
PE2(config-router-af)#neighbor 10.20.2.1 remote-as 200
PE2(config-router-af)#neighbor 10.20.2.1 activate
PE2(config-router-af)#
*Jun  7 11:15:30.319: %BGP-5-ADJCHANGE: neighbor 10.20.2.1 vpn vrf
INTERNET Up
PE2(config-router-af)#
```

Next, we will set up vrf RED to export the route-target of 100:202, which is imported by vrf INTERNET. Conversely vrf RED will import the route target 100:200 that is being exported by the INTERNET vrf.

```
PE2(config-vrf)#ip vrf RED
PE2(config-vrf)#export map VRF-RED-SUBNETS
PE2(config-vrf)#route-target import 100:200
PE2(config-vrf)#route-map VRF-RED-SUBNETS permit 10
PE2(config-route-map)#match ip address VRF_RED_SUBNETS
PE2(config-route-map)#set extcommunity rt 100:202 additive
PE2(config-route-map)#ip vrf INTERNET
PE2(config-vrf)#route-target import 100:202
PE2(config-vrf)#
```

The set up for vrf BLUE is much the same:

```
PE2(config-vrf)#ip vrf BLUE
PE2(config-vrf)#export map VRF-BLUE-SUBNETS
PE2(config-vrf)#route-target import 100:200
PE2(config-vrf)#route-map VRF-BLUE-SUBNETS permit 10
PE2(config-route-map)#match ip address VRF_BLUE_SUBNETS
PE2(config-route-map)#set extcommunity rt 100:206 additive
PE2(config-route-map)#ip vrf INTERNET
PE2(config-vrf)#route-target import 100:206
PE2(config-vrf)#
```

Lastly, we just need the access lists for the route maps to work:

```
PE2(config)#ip access-list standard VRF_BLUE_SUBNETS
PE2(config-std-nacl)# permit 10.2.6.0 0.0.0.255
PE2(config-std-nacl)# permit 172.20.6.0 0.0.0.255
PE2(config-std-nacl)#ip access-list standard VRF_RED_SUBNETS
PE2(config-std-nacl)# permit 10.2.2.0 0.0.0.255
PE2(config-std-nacl)# permit 172.20.1.0 0.0.0.255
PE2(config-std-nacl)#exit
```

With this in place, R2 and R6 both get the default route.

```
R2#sh ip route | beg Gate
Gateway of last resort is 10.2.2.1 to network 0.0.0.0

B*      0.0.0.0/0 [20/0] via 10.2.2.1, 00:01:56
        10.0.0.0/8 is variably subnetted, 4 subnets, 2 masks
B          10.1.1.0/24 [20/0] via 10.2.2.1, 00:01:56
B          10.1.3.0/24 [20/0] via 10.2.2.1, 00:01:56
C          10.2.2.0/24 is directly connected, GigabitEthernet1/0
L          10.2.2.2/32 is directly connected, GigabitEthernet1/0
        172.20.0.0/16 is variably subnetted, 3 subnets, 2 masks
C          172.20.1.0/24 is directly connected, Loopback0
L          172.20.1.1/32 is directly connected, Loopback0
B          172.20.2.0/24 [20/0] via 10.2.2.1, 00:01:56
B       192.168.1.0/24 [20/0] via 10.2.2.1, 00:01:56
B       192.168.2.0/24 [20/0] via 10.2.2.1, 00:01:56
R2#

R6#sh ip route | beg Gate
Gateway of last resort is 10.2.6.1 to network 0.0.0.0

O*E2    0.0.0.0/0 [110/1] via 10.2.6.1, 00:10:41, GigabitEthernet1/0
        1.0.0.0/8 is variably subnetted, 2 subnets, 2 masks
C          1.1.1.0/24 is directly connected, GigabitEthernet2/0
L          1.1.1.2/32 is directly connected, GigabitEthernet2/0
        2.0.0.0/32 is subnetted, 2 subnets
O E2       2.2.2.5 [110/1] via 10.2.6.1, 00:12:28, GigabitEthernet1/0
O E2       2.2.2.6 [110/1] via 10.2.6.1, 00:21:09, GigabitEthernet1/0
        10.0.0.0/8 is variably subnetted, 3 subnets, 2 masks
O          10.1.5.0/24 [110/3] via 10.2.6.1, 00:12:22, Gi1/0
C          10.2.6.0/24 is directly connected, GigabitEthernet1/0
L          10.2.6.2/32 is directly connected, GigabitEthernet1/0
        172.20.0.0/16 is variably subnetted, 3 subnets, 2 masks
C          172.20.6.0/24 is directly connected, Loopback0
L          172.20.6.1/32 is directly connected, Loopback0
O E2       172.20.2.0/24 [110/1] via 10.2.6.1, 00:20:16, Gi1/0
O       192.168.5.0/24 [110/4] via 10.2.6.1, 00:12:22, Gi1/0
R6#
```

We need to run "*clear ip bgp **" on PE2 in order to pick up the changes. Once the BGP peering comes back up again, we can see that R2 cannot ping R5, either its loopback interface or the egress interface, but it can still reach R1 and R3, as well as the Internet:

```
R2#ping 192.168.5.1
Type escape sequence to abort.
Sending 5, 100-byte ICMP Echos to 192.168.5.1, timeout is 2 seconds:
UUUUU
```

```
Success rate is 0 percent (0/5)
R2#ping 192.168.1.1
Type escape sequence to abort.
Sending 5, 100-byte ICMP Echos to 192.168.1.1, timeout is 2 seconds:
!!!!!
Success rate is 100 percent (5/5)
R2#ping 192.168.2.1
Type escape sequence to abort.
Sending 5, 100-byte ICMP Echos to 192.168.2.1, timeout is 2 seconds:
!!!!!
Success rate is 100 percent (5/5)
R2#ping 10.1.5.2
Type escape sequence to abort.
Sending 5, 100-byte ICMP Echos to 10.1.5.2, timeout is 2 seconds:
UUUUU
Success rate is 0 percent (0/5)
R2#ping 4.4.4.4
Type escape sequence to abort.
Sending 5, 100-byte ICMP Echos to 4.4.4.4, timeout is 2 seconds:
!!!!!
Success rate is 100 percent (5/5)
R2#
```

However, R2 can reach R6:

```
R2#ping 10.2.6.2
Type escape sequence to abort.
Sending 5, 100-byte ICMP Echos to 10.2.6.2, timeout is 2 seconds:
!!!!!
Success rate is 100 percent (5/5)
R2#
```

R6 can reach the Internet and R5, but not R1 or R2 It can, however, reach R2:

```
R6#ping 4.4.4.4
Type escape sequence to abort.
Sending 5, 100-byte ICMP Echos to 4.4.4.4, timeout is 2 seconds:
!!!!!
Success rate is 100 percent (5/5)
R6#ping 192.168.5.1
Type escape sequence to abort.
Sending 5, 100-byte ICMP Echos to 192.168.5.1, timeout is 2 seconds:
!!!!!
Success rate is 100 percent (5/5)
R6#ping 192.168.1.1
Type escape sequence to abort.
Sending 5, 100-byte ICMP Echos to 192.168.1.1, timeout is 2 seconds:
```

```
UUUUU
Success rate is 0 percent (0/5)
R6#ping 192.168.2.1
Type escape sequence to abort.
Sending 5, 100-byte ICMP Echos to 192.168.2.1, timeout is 2 seconds:
UUUUU
Success rate is 0 percent (0/5)
R6#ping 10.2.2.2
Type escape sequence to abort.
Sending 5, 100-byte ICMP Echos to 10.2.2.2, timeout is 2 seconds:
!!!!!
Success rate is 100 percent (5/5)
```

Thankfully, the fix is easy; we have already created the access-list earlier. We just need to apply it to the second interface on IGW in order to get the results we need:

```
IGW(config)#int gi 2/0
IGW(config-if)#ip access-group 1 out
IGW(config-if)#
```

With this in place, R2 can no longer reach R6; though, it still can reach the Internet. Likewise, R6 can reach the internet but not R2.

```
R2#ping 10.2.6.2
Type escape sequence to abort.
Sending 5, 100-byte ICMP Echos to 10.2.6.2, timeout is 2 seconds:
.....
Success rate is 0 percent (0/5)
R2#ping 4.4.4.4
Type escape sequence to abort.
Sending 5, 100-byte ICMP Echos to 4.4.4.4, timeout is 2 seconds:
!!!!!
Success rate is 100 percent (5/5)
R2#

R6#ping 10.2.2.2
Type escape sequence to abort.
Sending 5, 100-byte ICMP Echos to 10.2.2.2, timeout is 2 seconds:
.....
Success rate is 0 percent (0/5)
R6#ping 4.4.4.4
Type escape sequence to abort.
Sending 5, 100-byte ICMP Echos to 4.4.4.4, timeout is 2 seconds:
!!!!!
Success rate is 100 percent (5/5)
R6#
```

We have now successfully provided Internet access through our network to all of our clients. Our clients are happy, and we are not breaching any contracts by leaking their networks into each other.

Let's move on now to some topics that will require a new topology but where we can explore loop prevention mechanisms in greater detail.

We will return to the current topology shortly. But, before we move on, we should probably recap this chapter, as well as the difference between the exam experience and real life experience.

This whole scenario may actually be a little more intensive than what may appear on the CCIE lab exam. It may use loopback IP addresses in order to simulate the internet and not require the same default route method that has been used here. Thus, the idea of the IGW router acting as a router-on-a-stick might never appear if we were exporting the 4.4.4.4/24 IP address from IGW, rather than a default route. The CCIE exam is design to tax you, to offer scenarios that may not reflect real-life, or even Cisco's view of what is considered "best practice". Certainly, this scenario would probably (well, hopefully) never appear in real-life, as the customers network would be protected behind a firewall, with proper network address translation and access rules to protect the network. We also would not be exporting or importing RFC 1918 addresses (the private addresses that we are using here). Exams are not designed to test real-life, just knowledge!

10. Filtering and loop prevention

In a Frame-Mode MPLS cloud, the LSRs use the TTL field within the MPLS header to avoid routing loops. This field is decremented at each LSR, and the packet will be discarded when the TTL reaches 0. This is the same method within a standard IP-routed network.

In Cell-Mode MPLS (which is MPLS in ATM networks), the ATM cell header does not have a TTL field. Instead, it uses a hop-count TLV, which gets increased at each router along the path. ATM based networks are not a component of the CCIE Routing and Switching exams, nor is it on the Service Provider exams (at the time of writing). Hence, we will not go through it here. Instead, we will turn our attention to loop-prevention mechanisms and filtering used by the different protocols within the MPLS VPN network.

10.1 Label Filtering using the Site-of-Origin

We have already seen that BGP has a very good loop prevention mechanism in the form of the AS_PATH, and we even had to override this back in chapter 8 in order to get routes from one site to another in the same autonomous system. We will, therefore, have a look at other methods of route filtering.

One of the features included in MP-BGP is the extended community attribute. We have seen this before and used it to set the route-target, using the command "set extcommunity rt" followed by the route target. There is another command we can use. This is "set extcommunity soo" followed by a number format the same as the route target such as "set extcommunity soo 100:100". SoO stands for Site-of-Origin, which is also known as the route origin. Itcan be used for routing loop prevention or as a way to filter routes.

We will have to step away from the main topology for this, but it is very important to understand why we are using a different topology. So, first we will try this out on our main topology to see why it does not work, for us, before we set up a new topology to see how it should work.

The Site of Origin is used for a site; yet, the actual definition of a site is not really that well defined and is actually very limited in scope. At best, we can say that the SoO is linked to a customer edge neighbor.

There are a couple of ways in which we can set the SoO; we can use a route-map within BGP (neighbor 1.1.1.1 route-map SetSOO in), directly on the neighbor (neighbor 1.1.1.1

soo 100:100), or through a sitemap under the connecting interface (ip vrf sitemap SetSOO). As you know, route maps allow us to set different attributes and manipulate routes as much as we want. Here is why SoO is a bit limited; SoO cannot be set per prefix, at least not in the way we need it to. We only, really, need the following routers for this test.

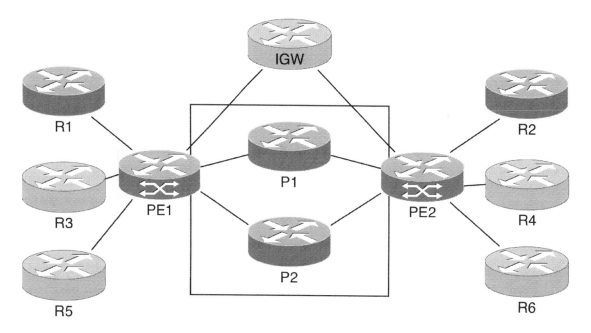

We can see this limitation in action by setting a new network on R1 (192.168.20.0/24), which, we will advertise through BGP. We will, however, try and prevent it from being imported into the routing table of R2.

```
R1(config)#int lo 1
R1(config-if)#ip add 192.168.20.1 255.255.255.0
R1(config-if)#router bgp 65001
R1(config-router)#network 192.168.20.0
R1(config-router)#
```

As expected, the route is quickly received by R2 and is reachable:

```
R2#sh ip route | i B
Codes: L - local, C - connected, S - static, R - RIP, M - mobile, B -
BGP
B*      0.0.0.0/0 [20/0] via 10.2.2.1, 00:16:55
B       10.1.1.0/24 [20/0] via 10.2.2.1, 00:16:57
B       10.1.3.0/24 [20/0] via 10.2.2.1, 00:17:10
B       172.20.2.0/24 [20/0] via 10.2.2.1, 00:17:10
```

```
B       192.168.1.0/24 [20/0] via 10.2.2.1, 00:16:57
B       192.168.2.0/24 [20/0] via 10.2.2.1, 00:05:22
B       192.168.20.0/24 [20/0] via 10.2.2.1, 00:00:44
R2#ping 192.168.20.1
Type escape sequence to abort.
Sending 5, 100-byte ICMP Echos to 192.168.20.1, timeout is 2 seconds:
!!!!!
Success rate is 100 percent (5/5)
R2#
```

We start with a route map that will match the network prefix and set the SOO value of 100:102. We have a second clause in the route map to permit all the other traffic, tagging it with an SOO of 100:101:

```
PE1(config)#route-map SetSOO permit 10
PE1(config-route-map)#match ip address 10
PE1(config-route-map)#set extcommunity soo 100:102
PE1(config-route-map)#exit
PE1(config)#route-map SetSOO permit 20
PE1(config-route-map)#set extcommunity soo 100:101
PE1(config-route-map)#exit
PE1(config)#access-list 10 permit 192.168.20.0 0.0.0.255
```

We, then, attach the route-map to our neighbor in BGP:

```
PE1(config)#router bgp 100
PE1(config-router)#address-family ipv4 vrf RED
PE1(config-router-af)#neigh 10.1.1.2 route-map SetSOO in
PE1(config-router-af)#
```

We need to clear the BGP peering for the changes to become active; but, once this is done, we can confirm that R2 is receiving the correct SoO setting within the Extended Community values:

```
PE2#sh ip bgp vpnv4 vrf RED 192.168.20.0
BGP routing table entry for 100:1:192.168.20.0/24, version 94
Paths: (1 available, best #1, table RED)
  Not advertised to any peer
  65001
    10.250.3.1 (metric 131072) from 10.250.3.1 (10.250.3.1)
      Origin IGP, metric 0, localpref 100, valid, internal, best
      Extended Community: SoO:100:102 RT:100:1 RT:100:201
      mpls labels in/out nolabel/22
PE2#
```

If we compare this prefix to another prefix that is also being advertised by R1, we can see that the route map has added the other SoO value:

```
PE2#sh ip bgp vpnv4 vrf RED 192.168.1.0
BGP routing table entry for 100:1:192.168.1.0/24, version 92
Paths: (1 available, best #1, table RED)
  Advertised to update-groups:
     4
  65001
    10.250.3.1 (metric 131072) from 10.250.3.1 (10.250.3.1)
      Origin IGP, metric 0, localpref 100, valid, internal, best
      Extended Community: SoO:100:101 RT:100:1 RT:100:201
      mpls labels in/out nolabel/21
PE2#
```

Therefore, we can have one prefix with one SoO value and another with a different one. So, why do I say that this doesn't work in the way that we need it to? We need to set up some similar rules on the other side of the network for this to become apparent.

We now need to set another route map on the other side of the cloud so that we can match (and then deny) routes based upon the SoO value. We will tag all of R2's routes with the same SoO as the one we have used on R1 for the 192.168.20.0/24 route:

```
PE2(config)#router bgp 100
PE2(config-router)#address-family ipv4 vrf RED
PE2(config-router-af)#neighbor 10.2.2.2 soo 100:102
PE2(config-router-af)#
```

Once we have cleared the BGP process on R2, our routes will become tagged with the same SoO value as the 192.168.20.0/24 route, and we can see that R2 does not import that route, but it has imported all the other routes (192.168.1.0/24 and 10.1.1.0/24):

```
R2#clear ip bgp *
R2#
*Jun  9 20:38:40.243: %BGP-5-ADJCHANGE: neighbor 10.2.2.1 Down User reset
*Jun  9 20:38:40.247: %BGP_SESSION-5-ADJCHANGE: neighbor 10.2.2.1 IPv4 Unicast topology base removed from session  User reset
*Jun  9 20:38:41.163: %BGP-5-ADJCHANGE: neighbor 10.2.2.1 Up
R2#sh ip route | i B
Codes: L - local, C - connected, S - static, R - RIP, M - mobile, B - BGP
B        10.1.1.0/24 [20/0] via 10.2.2.1, 00:01:26
B        10.1.3.0/24 [20/0] via 10.2.2.1, 00:01:26
B        172.20.2.0/24 [20/0] via 10.2.2.1, 00:01:26
```

```
B       192.168.1.0/24 [20/0] via 10.2.2.1, 00:01:26
B       192.168.2.0/24 [20/0] via 10.2.2.1, 00:01:26
R2#
```

This is good so far. We can actually perform filtering based on the SoO value. However, if we have a look at R1, we can see that R1 is now not importing any of the routes from R2:

```
R1#clear ip bgp *
R1#
R1#sh ip route | i B
Codes: L - local, C - connected, S - static, R - RIP, M - mobile, B - BGP
B*      0.0.0.0/0 [20/0] via 10.1.1.1, 00:09:21
B          10.1.3.0/24 [20/0] via 10.1.1.1, 00:09:21
B          172.20.2.0 [20/0] via 10.1.1.1, 00:09:21
B          192.168.2.0/24 [20/0] via 10.1.1.1, 00:09:21
R1#
```

Our one SoO tagging on R1 has caused all the routes from R2 with the same tag to be denied.

```
PE1#sh ip bgp vpnv4 vrf RED 172.20.1.0 | i SoO
        Extended Community: SoO:100:102 RT:100:1 RT:100:202
PE1#sh ip bgp vpnv4 vrf RED 192.168.1.0 | i SoO
        Extended Community: SoO:100:101 RT:100:1 RT:100:201
PE1#sh ip bgp vpnv4 vrf RED 192.168.20.0 | i SoO
        Extended Community: SoO:100:102 RT:100:1 RT:100:201
PE1#
```

As we have seen, although the SoO attribute can be used to filter routes, it really is not the best method in this particular case.

Let us instead see it work exactly as it should.

We have a new company, very unimaginatively called CompanyA. They have one site that is dual-homed to their ISP, using eBGP to peer from their routers in Los Angeles. Internally, they run EIGRP.

The network topology looks like this:

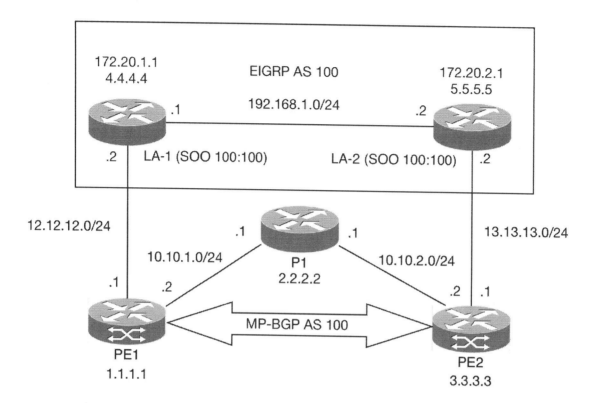

The configurations are as follows:

LA-1:

```
interface Loopback0
 ip address 4.4.4.4 255.255.255.255
!
interface Loopback1
 ip address 172.20.1.1 255.255.255.255
!
interface GigabitEthernet1/0
 description Link to PE1
 ip address 12.12.12.2 255.255.255.0
!
interface GigabitEthernet2/0
 ip address 192.168.1.1 255.255.255.0
!
router eigrp 200
 network 4.4.4.4 0.0.0.0
```

```
  network 172.20.1.1 0.0.0.0
  network 192.168.1.0
 !
 router bgp 65001
  bgp log-neighbor-changes
  network 4.4.4.4 mask 255.255.255.255
  network 172.20.1.1 mask 255.255.255.255
  neighbor 12.12.12.1 remote-as 100
  neighbor 12.12.12.1 allowas-in
```

LA-2:

```
 interface Loopback0
  ip address 5.5.5.5 255.255.255.255
 !
 interface Loopback1
  ip address 172.20.2.1 255.255.255.255
 !
 interface GigabitEthernet1/0
  description Link to PE2
  ip address 13.13.13.2 255.255.255.0
 !
 interface GigabitEthernet2/0
  ip address 192.168.1.2 255.255.255.0
 !
 router eigrp 200
  network 5.5.5.5 0.0.0.0
  network 172.20.2.1 0.0.0.0
  network 192.168.1.0
 !
 router bgp 65001
  bgp log-neighbor-changes
  network 5.5.5.5 mask 255.255.255.255
  network 172.20.2.1 mask 255.255.255.255
  neighbor 13.13.13.1 remote-as 100
  neighbor 13.13.13.1 allowas-in
```

PE1:

```
 ip vrf CompanyA
  rd 1:1
  route-target export 1:1
  route-target import 1:1
 !
 mpls label protocol ldp
 !
 interface Loopback0
```

```
 ip address 1.1.1.1 255.255.255.255
!
interface GigabitEthernet1/0
 description Link to LA-1
 ip vrf forwarding CompanyA
 ip address 12.12.12.1 255.255.255.0
!
interface GigabitEthernet2/0
 description Link to P1
 ip address 10.10.1.2 255.255.255.0
 mpls ip
!
router eigrp 100
 network 1.0.0.0
 network 10.10.1.0 0.0.0.255
!
router bgp 100
 bgp log-neighbor-changes
 neighbor 3.3.3.3 remote-as 100
 neighbor 3.3.3.3 update-source Loopback0
 !
 address-family vpnv4
  neighbor 3.3.3.3 activate
  neighbor 3.3.3.3 send-community extended
 exit-address-family
 !
 address-family ipv4 vrf CompanyA
  neighbor 12.12.12.2 remote-as 65001
  neighbor 12.12.12.2 activate
 exit-address-family
```

P1:

```
interface Loopback0
 ip address 2.2.2.2 255.255.255.255
!
interface GigabitEthernet1/0
 description Link to PE1
 ip address 10.10.1.1 255.255.255.0
 mpls ip
!
interface GigabitEthernet2/0
 description Link to PE2
 ip address 10.10.2.1 255.255.255.0
 mpls ip
!
router eigrp 100
```

```
    network 2.0.0.0
    network 10.10.1.0 0.0.0.255
    network 10.10.2.0 0.0.0.255
```

PE2:

```
ip vrf CompanyA
 rd 1:1
 route-target export 1:1
 route-target import 1:1
!
mpls label protocol ldp
!
interface Loopback0
 ip address 3.3.3.3 255.255.255.255
!
interface GigabitEthernet1/0
 description Link to P1
 ip address 10.10.2.2 255.255.255.0
 mpls ip
!
interface GigabitEthernet2/0
 description Link to LA-2
 ip vrf forwarding CompanyA
 ip address 13.13.13.1 255.255.255.0
!
router eigrp 100
 network 3.0.0.0
 network 10.10.2.0 0.0.0.255
!
router bgp 100
 bgp log-neighbor-changes
 neighbor 1.1.1.1 remote-as 100
 neighbor 1.1.1.1 update-source Loopback0
 !
 address-family vpnv4
  neighbor 1.1.1.1 activate
  neighbor 1.1.1.1 send-community extended
 exit-address-family
 !
 address-family ipv4 vrf CompanyA
  neighbor 13.13.13.2 remote-as 65001
  neighbor 13.13.13.2 activate
 exit-address-family
```

With this all in place, LA-1 and LA-2 see each other's advertised loopback networks through the eBGP link to the PE routers, rather than through their internal EIGRP network.

This is due to the eBGP routes being preferred due to the lower administrative distance (AD). eBGP's AD of 20 is much better than the AD of 90 for the EIGRP advertised routes; therefore, it is perceived as a more reliable route.

```
LA-1#sh ip route | i (5.5.5|172.20.2)
B        5.5.5.5 [20/0] via 12.12.12.1, 00:01:32
B        172.20.2.1 [20/0] via 12.12.12.1, 00:15:25
LA-1#

LA-2#sh ip route | i (4.4.4|172.20.1)
B        4.4.4.4 [20/0] via 13.13.13.1, 00:02:01
B        172.20.1.1 [20/0] via 13.13.13.1, 00:15:13
LA-2#
```

In this scenario, we do actually want to filter all of the routes from traversing the MPLS cloud; so, a Site of Origin will fit the requirements perfectly:

```
PE1(config)#router bgp 100
PE1(config-router)#address-family ipv4 vrf CompanyA
PE1(config-router-af)#neigh 12.12.12.2 soo 100:100
PE1(config-router-af)#do clear ip bgp *

PE2(config)#router bgp 100
PE2(config-router)#address-family ipv4 vrf CompanyA
PE2(config-router-af)#neigh 13.13.13.2 soo 100:100
PE2(config-router-af)#do clear ip bgp *
```

Now, LA-1 and LA-2 receive the routes through the EIGRP connection directly between them, rather than having the routes cross the MPLS network.

```
LA-1#sh ip route | i (5.5.5|172.20.2)
D        5.5.5.5 [90/130816] via 192.168.1.2, 00:22:06, Gi2/0
D        172.20.2.1 [90/130816] via 192.168.1.2, 00:22:06, Gi2/0
LA-1#

LA-2#sh ip route | i (4.4.4|172.20.1)
D        4.4.4.4 [90/130816] via 192.168.1.1, 00:23:22, Gi2/0
D        172.20.1.1 [90/130816] via 192.168.1.1, 00:23:22, Gi2/0
LA-2#
```

In this scenario, the site of origin value has worked in the manner intended. The routes will still be advertised through both routing protocols. If we follow the flow of the 4.4.4.4 prefix, it will pass from LA-1 to PE1, through the MP-BGP cloud to PE2. PE2 will match the SoO value of the 4.4.4.4 prefix against the SoO of the destination router (LA-2). Because they match, PE2 will not advertise the route to LA-2. This leaves the internal prefixes from LA-1 and LA-2 to pass along the EIGRP internal network, as shown in the diagram below. Returning to the example that didn't work with our main topology, is there another method we could use to filter that route from R2? Naturally, there is. We have look at this before to increase accessibility, either between customers, or to access shared services. It can also be used to reduce accessibility, which is what we will do next.

10.2 MP-BGP Prefix Filtering

If we want to filter routes out within the MPLS network, we can, Changing the extended community route target can do this. We have used this a number of times to increase the routes we can see from one network to the next. The same logic applies here; yet, instead of "RT additive", we can omit the additive keyword and use this functionality to provide a method of filtering the routes.

In this example, we will, return to our main topology, and export the 192.168.20.0/24 prefix from R1, but set it not to be imported by any other router.

We will start by removing the Site of Origin details we put in previously. From the previous example, all the routes from R2 were blocked from being imported into R1:

```
PE1(config)#router bgp 100
PE1(config-router)#address-family ipv4 vrf RED
PE1(config-router-af)#no neighbor 10.1.1.2 route-map SetSOO in
PE1(config-router-af)#do clear ip bgp *

PE2(config)#router bgp 100
PE2(config-router)#address-family ipv4 vrf RED

PE2(config-router-af)#no neighbor 10.2.2.2 soo 100:102
PE2(config-router-af)#do clear ip bgp *
```

We can see that R1 and R2 have their full compliment of routes back in their tables.

```
R1#sh ip route | i B
Codes: L - local, C - connected, S - static, R - RIP, M - mobile, B -
BGP
B        10.1.3.0/24 [20/0] via 10.1.1.1, 00:38:20
B        10.2.2.0/24 [20/0] via 10.1.1.1, 00:00:12
B        172.20.1.0 [20/0] via 10.1.1.1, 00:00:12
B        172.20.2.0 [20/0] via 10.1.1.1, 00:08:50
B     192.168.2.0/24 [20/0] via 10.1.1.1, 00:38:20
R1#
```

```
R2#sh ip route | i B
Codes: L - local, C - connected, S - static, R - RIP, M - mobile, B - 
BGP
B        10.1.1.0/24 [20/0] via 10.2.2.1, 00:08:45
B        10.1.3.0/24 [20/0] via 10.2.2.1, 00:08:45
B        172.20.2.0/24 [20/0] via 10.2.2.1, 00:08:45
B     192.168.1.0/24 [20/0] via 10.2.2.1, 00:08:45
B     192.168.2.0/24 [20/0] via 10.2.2.1, 00:08:45
B     192.168.20.0/24 [20/0] via 10.2.2.1, 00:00:19
R2#
```

We already have a route map on R1, so we can insert a clause into it. This clause will need to go at the beginning of the route map. Because of this, we will set this sequence number to 5, putting it before the existing rule at sequence 10. Here, we set the match command to match access list 10 which we created earlier and set the RT to 100:120. Note that we are omitting the "additive" keyword, so that this is the only RT for this particular prefix:

```
PE1(config)#route-map VRF-RED-INTERNET permit 5
PE1(config-route-map)#match ip address 10
PE1(config-route-map)#set extcommunity rt 100:120
```

This route map is already applied as an export map for the VRF, so we do not need to take any additional steps here:

```
PE1#sh run vrf RED
Building configuration...

Current configuration : 533 bytes
ip vrf RED
 rd 100:1
 export map VRF-RED-INTERNET
 route-target export 100:1
 route-target import 100:1
 route-target import 100:2
 route-target import 100:20
 route-target import 100:200
!
!
interface GigabitEthernet2/0
 ip vrf forwarding RED
 ip address 10.1.1.1 255.255.255.0
 negotiation auto
!
router bgp 100
```

```
!
address-family ipv4 vrf RED
 redistribute static
 neighbor 10.1.1.2 remote-as 65001
 neighbor 10.1.1.2 activate
 neighbor 10.1.1.2 send-community both
 default-information originate
exit-address-family
!
end

PE1#
```

Once we clear the BGP adjacencies on R1 (using the command "clear ip bgp *") we can see that the route only has the one RT value:

```
PE1#sh ip bgp vpnv4 vrf RED 192.168.20.0
BGP routing table entry for 100:1:192.168.20.0/24, version 244
Paths: (1 available, best #1, table RED)
  Advertised to update-groups:
     2
  65001
    10.1.1.2 from 10.1.1.2 (192.168.20.1)
      Origin IGP, metric 0, localpref 100, valid, external, best
      Extended Community: RT:100:120
      mpls labels in/out 32/nolabel
PE1#
```

Lastly, if we check R2, we can see that the route is not imported. Under the vrf definition we, have not set it to import 100:120.

```
R2#sh ip route | i B
Codes: L - local, C - connected, S - static, R - RIP, M - mobile, B - BGP
B        10.1.1.0/24 [20/0] via 10.2.2.1, 00:00:42
B        10.1.3.0/24 [20/0] via 10.2.2.1, 00:03:47
B        172.20.2.0/24 [20/0] via 10.2.2.1, 00:03:47
B     192.168.1.0/24 [20/0] via 10.2.2.1, 00:00:42
B     192.168.2.0/24 [20/0] via 10.2.2.1, 00:03:47
R2#
```

When working inside an MPLS cloud, we can filter based on the label attached to a particular route. This does not actually prevent the routes being advertised, which is what we will look at next.

10.3 Label filtering

It is important to point out that filtering labels in MPLS will not achieve the same thing as filtering a route out. The underlying IGP will still advertise the routes and they will still be reachable. Label filtering does serve one useful purpose, and that is to reduce the size of the LIB (Label Information Base).

We will see this in action with a simple three-router set up:

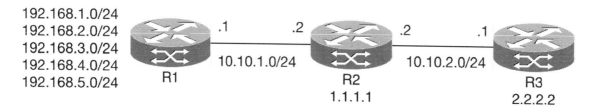

We will use R1 as our "major network." It will have five loopback interfaces, and our goal is to filter out the last two "networks" (192.168.4.0/24 and 192.168.5.0/24) from R3. The configuration for R1 is as follows:

```
R1(config)#int lo0
R1(config-if)#ip add 192.168.1.1 255.255.255.0
R1(config-if)#int lo1
R1(config-if)#ip add 192.168.2.1 255.255.255.0
R1(config-if)#int lo2
R1(config-if)#ip add 192.168.3.1 255.255.255.0
R1(config-if)#int lo3
R1(config-if)#ip add 192.168.4.1 255.255.255.0
R1(config-if)#int lo4
R1(config-if)#ip add 192.168.5.1 255.255.255.0
R1(config-if)#int gi 1/0
R1(config-if)#ip add 10.10.1.1 255.255.255.0
R1(config-if)#mpls ip
R1(config-if)#no shut
R1(config-if)#
```

R2's configuration:

```
R2(config)#int lo0
R2(config-if)#ip add 1.1.1.1 255.255.255.255
R2(config-if)#int gi 1/0
R2(config-if)#ip add 10.10.1.2 255.255.255.0
R2(config-if)#mpls ip
R2(config-if)#no shut
```

```
R2(config-if)#int gi 2/0
R2(config-if)#ip add 10.10.2.2 255.255.255.0
R2(config-if)#mpls ip
R2(config-if)#no shut
R2(config-if)#
```

Lastly we have R3:

```
R3(config)#int lo0
R3(config-if)#ip add 2.2.2.2 255.255.255.255
R3(config-if)#int gi 1/0
R3(config-if)#ip add 10.10.2.1 255.255.255.0
R3(config-if)#mpls ip
R3(config-if)#no shut
```

We will use OSPF as our IGP here. We can use two different methods to advertise all our networks; either explicitly, as we are doing with R1, or using one statement to advertise all possible networks, as we are doing on R2 and R3:

```
R1(config-if)#router ospf 1
R1(config-router)#network 10.10.1.0 0.0.0.255 area 0
R1(config-router)#network 192.168.1.0 0.0.0.255 area 0
R1(config-router)#network 192.168.2.0 0.0.0.255 area 0
R1(config-router)#network 192.168.3.0 0.0.0.255 area 0
R1(config-router)#network 192.168.4.0 0.0.0.255 area 0
R1(config-router)#network 192.168.5.0 0.0.0.255 area 0
R1(config-router)#

R2(config-if)#router ospf 1
R2(config-router)#network 0.0.0.0 255.255.255.255 area 0
R2(config-router)#

R3(config-if)#router ospf 1
R3(config-router)#network 0.0.0.0 255.255.255.255 area 0
R3(config-router)#
```

R3 can see the networks attached to R1, and has assigned labels to them:

```
R3(config-router)#do sh mpls forwarding-table
Local   Outgoing   Prefix            Bytes Label   Outgoing    Next Hop
Label   Label      or Tunnel Id      Switched      interface
16      16         192.168.5.1/32    0             Gi1/0       10.10.2.2
17      17         192.168.4.1/32    0             Gi1/0       10.10.2.2
18      18         192.168.3.1/32    0             Gi1/0       10.10.2.2
19      19         192.168.2.1/32    0             Gi1/0       10.10.2.2
20      20         192.168.1.1/32    0             Gi1/0       10.10.2.2
```

```
21       Pop Label  1.1.1.1/32    0             Gi1/0       10.10.2.2
22       Pop Label  10.10.1.0/24  0             Gi1/0       10.10.2.2
R3(config-router)#exit
```

Naturally, the LIB looks pretty healthy:

```
R3#sh mpls ldp bindings neighbor 1.1.1.1
  lib entry: 1.1.1.1/32, rev 16
      remote binding: lsr: 1.1.1.1:0, label: imp-null
  lib entry: 2.2.2.2/32, rev 2
      remote binding: lsr: 1.1.1.1:0, label: 21
  lib entry: 10.10.1.0/24, rev 18
      remote binding: lsr: 1.1.1.1:0, label: imp-null
  lib entry: 10.10.2.0/24, rev 4
      remote binding: lsr: 1.1.1.1:0, label: imp-null
  lib entry: 192.168.1.1/32, rev 14
      remote binding: lsr: 1.1.1.1:0, label: 20
  lib entry: 192.168.2.1/32, rev 12
      remote binding: lsr: 1.1.1.1:0, label: 19
  lib entry: 192.168.3.1/32, rev 10
      remote binding: lsr: 1.1.1.1:0, label: 18
  lib entry: 192.168.4.1/32, rev 8
      remote binding: lsr: 1.1.1.1:0, label: 17
  lib entry: 192.168.5.1/32, rev 6
      remote binding: lsr: 1.1.1.1:0, label: 16
R3#
```

Now we add an access list onto R3 to permit the first couple of labels from R1. By default, it will deny the rest:

```
R3(config)#access-list 1 permit 192.168.0.0 0.0.3.255
```

Then, we set this access list to specify which labels we want to accept from our neighboring LSR:

```
R3(config)#mpls ldp neighbor 1.1.1.1 labels accept 1
R3(config)#end
```

Now, if we look at the forwarding table, we can see that those unmatched routes have a "No Label" set:

```
R3#sh mpls forwarding-table
Local    Outgoing    Prefix             Bytes Label   Outgoing     Next Hop
Label    Label       or Tunnel Id       Switched      interface
16       No Label    192.168.5.1/32     0             Gi1/0        10.10.2.2
```

```
17          No Label    192.168.4.1/32    0           Gi1/0      10.10.2.2
18          18          192.168.3.1/32    0           Gi1/0      10.10.2.2
19          19          192.168.2.1/32    0           Gi1/0      10.10.2.2
20          20          192.168.1.1/32    0           Gi1/0      10.10.2.2
21          No Label    1.1.1.1/32        0           Gi1/0      10.10.2.2
22          No Label    10.10.1.0/24      0           Gi1/0      10.10.2.2
R3#
```

We should really include the other prefixes from R2 though, so that they receive a proper label action:

```
R3(config)#access-list 1 permit 1.1.1.1 0.0.0.0
R3(config)#access-list 1 permit 10.10.1.0 0.0.0.255
R3(config)#end
```

Now, if we check the forwarding table, we can see that we have fulfilled the requirements:

```
R3#sh mpls forwarding-table
Local    Outgoing    Prefix            Bytes Label    Outgoing    Next Hop
Label    Label       or Tunnel Id      Switched       interface
16       No Label    192.168.5.1/32    0              Gi1/0       10.10.2.2
17       No Label    192.168.4.1/32    0              Gi1/0       10.10.2.2
18       18          192.168.3.1/32    0              Gi1/0       10.10.2.2
19       19          192.168.2.1/32    0              Gi1/0       10.10.2.2
20       20          192.168.1.1/32    0              Gi1/0       10.10.2.2
21       Pop Label   1.1.1.1/32        0              Gi1/0       10.10.2.2
22       Pop Label   10.10.1.0/24      0              Gi1/0       10.10.2.2
R3#
```

Lastly, we can see that the LIB is reduced:

```
R3#sh mpls ldp bindings neighbor 1.1.1.1
  lib entry: 1.1.1.1/32, rev 16
      remote binding: lsr: 1.1.1.1:0, label: imp-null
  lib entry: 10.10.1.0/24, rev 18
      remote binding: lsr: 1.1.1.1:0, label: imp-null
  lib entry: 192.168.1.1/32, rev 14
      remote binding: lsr: 1.1.1.1:0, label: 20
  lib entry: 192.168.2.1/32, rev 12
      remote binding: lsr: 1.1.1.1:0, label: 19
  lib entry: 192.168.3.1/32, rev 10
      remote binding: lsr: 1.1.1.1:0, label: 18
R3#
```

Along with the loop preventions methods previously discussed, there is another one that we should discuss. This is the "down bit" when we use OSPF as our CE to PE IGP. This is particular to a concept of vrf-lite, which we will look at next.

11. VRF-Lite

As we have moved through the book so far, hopefully, you have got the feeling that MPLS is very flexible. We can add and remove things, such as network prefixes, or labels, very easily in just a few commands. So is there anything else that we can remove? Well, in the case of a layer 3 VPN, yes there is. We can remove MPLS completely which is known as VRF-lite.

With VRF-Lite, we are not dependent on MPLS. Instead, we just use VRFs (which because we are dealing with an IP-based network stands for *Virtual* Routing and Forwarding, rather than meaning *VPN* Routing and Forwarding in an MPLS based network).

11.1 Basic VRF-Lite configuration

We have a simple hub-and-spoke network topology here:

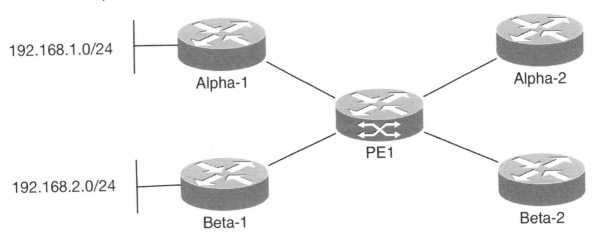

The Alpha routers will connect to each other, as will the Beta routers. We will use OSPF as our IGP, as well as advertising a couple of connected networks from Alpha-1 and Beta-1.

The initial configurations for the first two routers are very simple.

```
Alpha-1(config)#int gi 1/0
Alpha-1(config-if)#ip add 10.1.1.1 255.255.255.0
Alpha-1(config-if)#no shut
```

```
Alpha-1(config-if)#int lo0
Alpha-1(config-if)#ip add 192.168.1.1 255.255.255.0
Alpha-1(config-if)#ip ospf network point-to-point
Alpha-1(config-if)#

Beta-1(config)#int gi 1/0
Beta-1(config-if)#ip add 10.2.1.1 255.255.255.0
Beta-1(config-if)#no shut
Beta-1(config-if)#int lo0
Beta-1(config-if)#ip add 192.168.2.1 255.255.255.0
Beta-1(config-if)#ip ospf network point-to-point
Beta-1(config-if)#
```

The initial configuration for PE1 is also very simple, purely providing a connection to the routers either side of it:

```
PE1(config)#int gi 1/0
PE1(config-if)#ip add 10.1.1.2 255.255.255.0
PE1(config-if)#no shut
PE1(config-if)#int gi 2/0
PE1(config-if)#ip add 10.2.1.2 255.255.255.0
PE1(config-if)#no shut
PE1(config-if)#int gi 3/0
PE1(config-if)#ip add 10.10.1.2 255.255.255.0
PE1(config-if)#no shut
PE1(config-if)#int gi 4/0
PE1(config-if)#ip add 10.20.1.2 255.255.255.0
PE1(config-if)#no shut
PE1(config-if)#int lo0
PE1(config-if)#ip add 1.1.1.1 255.255.255.255
```

Lastly, the configurations for the final two routers again is just to set up the IP addresses on the connecting interfaces:

```
Alpha-2(config)#int gi 1/0
Alpha-2(config-if)#ip add 10.10.1.1 255.255.255.0
Alpha-2(config-if)#no shut

Beta-2(config)#int gi 1/0
Beta-2(config-if)#ip add 10.20.1.1 255.255.255.0
Beta-2(config-if)#no shut
```

The first steps we will take is to define the VRFs on the PE router, and to assign these to the interfaces. This is no different to how we have done this in any of the other examples we have covered so far:

```
PE1(config)#ip vrf ALPHA
PE1(config-vrf)#ip vrf BETA
PE1(config-vrf)#int gi 1/0
PE1(config-if)#ip vrf forwarding ALPHA
% Interface GigabitEthernet1/0 IPv4 disabled and address(es) removed
due to enabling VRF ALPHA
PE1(config-if)#ip add 10.1.1.2 255.255.255.0
PE1(config)#int gi 3/0
PE1(config-if)#ip vrf forwarding ALPHA
% Interface GigabitEthernet3/0 IPv4 disabled and address(es) removed
due to enabling VRF ALPHA
PE1(config-if)#ip add 10.10.1.2 255.255.255.0
PE1(config-if)#int gi 2/0
PE1(config-if)#ip vrf forwarding BETA
% Interface GigabitEthernet2/0 IPv4 disabled and address(es) removed
due to enabling VRF BETA
PE1(config-if)#ip add 10.2.1.2 255.255.255.0
PE1(config-if)#int gi 4/0
PE1(config-if)#ip vrf forwarding BETA
% Interface GigabitEthernet4/0 IPv4 disabled and address(es) removed
due to enabling VRF BETA
PE1(config-if)#ip add 10.20.1.2 255.255.255.0
```

In order to route anything from one side to another, we need to set up a routing protocol. We could use static routes, as these are also perfectly valid but not scalable. So, here, we will use OSPF for all of our links. We can use the same OSPF process on our connections from the customer routers to our provider routers, as these are only locally significant:

```
Alpha-1(config-if)#router ospf 1
Alpha-1(config-router)#router-id 10.1.1.1
Alpha-1(config-router)#network 10.1.1.0 0.0.0.255 area 0
Alpha-1(config-router)#network 192.168.1.0 0.0.0.255 area 0
Alpha-1(config-router)#

Beta-1(config-if)#router ospf 1
Beta-1(config-router)#router-id 10.2.1.1
Beta-1(config-router)#network 10.2.1.0 0.0.0.255 area 0
Beta-1(config-router)#network 192.168.2.0 0.0.0.255 area 0
Beta-1(config-router)#

Alpha-2(config-if)#router ospf 1
Alpha-2(config-router)#router-id 10.10.1.1
Alpha-2(config-router)#network 10.10.1.0 0.0.0.255 area 0
Alpha-2(config-router)#

Beta-2(config-if)#router ospf 2
Beta-2(config-router)#router-id 10.20.1.1
```

```
Beta-2(config-router)#network 10.20.1.0 0.0.0.255 area 0
Beta-2(config-router)#
```

On PE1, we will need to use different OSPF processes for each VRF that we create.

```
PE1(config-if)#router ospf 1 vrf ALPHA
PE1(config-router)#
PE1(config-router)#router-id 10.1.1.2
PE1(config-router)#network 10.1.1.0 0.0.0.255 area 0
PE1(config-router)#network 10.10.1.0 0.0.0.255 area 0
PE1(config-router)#
*Jul  7 08:05:25.323: %OSPF-5-ADJCHG: Process 1, Nbr 10.1.1.1 on
GigabitEthernet1/0 from LOADING to FULL, Loading Done
PE1(config-router)#
*Jul  7 08:06:59.623: %OSPF-5-ADJCHG: Process 1, Nbr 10.10.1.1 on
GigabitEthernet3/0 from LOADING to FULL, Loading Done
PE1(config-router)#router ospf 2 vrf BETA
PE1(config-router)#router-id 10.2.1.2
PE1(config-router)#network 10.2.1.0 0.0.0.255 area 0
PE1(config-router)#network 10.20.1.0 0.0.0.255 area 0
PE1(config-router)#
*Jul  7 08:09:06.907: %OSPF-5-ADJCHG: Process 2, Nbr 10.2.1.1 on
GigabitEthernet2/0 from LOADING to FULL, Loading Done
PE1(config-router)#
*Jul  7 08:10:59.487: %OSPF-5-ADJCHG: Process 2, Nbr 10.20.1.1 on
GigabitEthernet4/0 from LOADING to FULL, Loading Done
PE1(config-router)#
```

With our OSPF adjacencies formed, our customer routers have reachability from one side to the other:

```
Alpha-1#sh ip route | beg Gate
Gateway of last resort is not set

      10.0.0.0/8 is variably subnetted, 3 subnets, 2 masks
C        10.1.1.0/24 is directly connected, GigabitEthernet1/0
L        10.1.1.1/32 is directly connected, GigabitEthernet1/0
O        10.10.1.0/24 [110/2] via 10.1.1.2, 00:05:38, Gi1/0
      192.168.1.0/24 is variably subnetted, 2 subnets, 2 masks
C        192.168.1.0/24 is directly connected, Loopback0
L        192.168.1.1/32 is directly connected, Loopback0
Alpha-1#
Alpha-1#ping 10.10.1.1
Type escape sequence to abort.
Sending 5, 100-byte ICMP Echos to 10.10.1.1, timeout is 2 seconds:
!!!!!
Success rate is 100 percent (5/5)
```

```
Alpha-1#

Beta-1#sh ip route | beg Gate
Gateway of last resort is not set

     10.0.0.0/8 is variably subnetted, 3 subnets, 2 masks
C       10.2.1.0/24 is directly connected, GigabitEthernet1/0
L       10.2.1.1/32 is directly connected, GigabitEthernet1/0
O       10.20.1.0/24 [110/2] via 10.2.1.2, 00:02:57, Gi1/0
     192.168.2.0/24 is variably subnetted, 2 subnets, 2 masks
C       192.168.2.0/24 is directly connected, Loopback0
L       192.168.2.1/32 is directly connected, Loopback0
Beta-1#
Beta-1#ping 10.20.1.1
Type escape sequence to abort.
Sending 5, 100-byte ICMP Echos to 10.20.1.1, timeout is 2 seconds:
!!!!!
Success rate is 100 percent (5/5)
Beta-1#
```

On a purely one-to-one method, as above, this method is simplistic but still fulfills all the requirements. We have a VPN without any MPLS specific commands. So, how would we then extend this to include the sharing of routes between customers as we have done before? Well, in this instance, we would implement MP-BGP and use route distinguishers and route targets for the import and export of the routes. Even though we are only dealing with one provider router, we still require MP-BGP in order to export and import route targets.

Firstly, we set up the RD's and RT's:

```
PE1(config-router)#ip vrf ALPHA
PE1(config-vrf)#rd 100:100
PE1(config-vrf)#route-target export 100:100
PE1(config-vrf)#route-target import 100:100
PE1(config-vrf)#ip vrf BETA
PE1(config-vrf)#rd 100:200
PE1(config-vrf)#route-target import 100:200
PE1(config-vrf)#route-target export 100:200
```

Next, we set up MP-BGP. Note that we do not need to specify any neighbors, nor do we need to set up the vpnv4 address family as we did when we set up our layer 3 VPNs. We just set up the address families for the VRFs and redistribute from our OSPF processes:

```
PE1(config-vrf)#router bgp 100
PE1(config-router)#address-family ipv4 vrf ALPHA
```

```
PE1(config-router-af)#redistribute ospf 1 vrf ALPHA
PE1(config-router-af)#redistribute connected
PE1(config-router-af)#exit
PE1(config-router)#address-family ipv4 vrf BETA
PE1(config-router-af)#redistribute ospf 2 vrf BETA
PE1(config-router-af)#redistribute connected
PE1(config-router-af)#exit
```

The final step is to redistribute from BGP into OSPF:

```
PE1(config-router)#router ospf 1 vrf ALPHA
PE1(config-router)#redistribute bgp 100 subnets
PE1(config-router)#router ospf 2 vrf BETA
PE1(config-router)#redistribute bgp 100 subnets
```

With this setup alone, we will not see any difference in the routing table than we did previously, and we still have reachability:

```
Alpha-1#sh ip route | beg Gate
Gateway of last resort is not set

      10.0.0.0/8 is variably subnetted, 3 subnets, 2 masks
C        10.1.1.0/24 is directly connected, GigabitEthernet1/0
L        10.1.1.1/32 is directly connected, GigabitEthernet1/0
O        10.10.1.0/24 [110/2] via 10.1.1.2, 00:24:33, Gi1/0
      192.168.1.0/24 is variably subnetted, 2 subnets, 2 masks
C        192.168.1.0/24 is directly connected, Loopback0
L        192.168.1.1/32 is directly connected, Loopback0
Alpha-1#ping 10.10.1.1
Type escape sequence to abort.
Sending 5, 100-byte ICMP Echos to 10.10.1.1, timeout is 2 seconds:
!!!!!
Success rate is 100 percent (5/5)
Alpha-1#
```

Although everything looks the same, we have now opened up a world of possibilities to us. We can, as we have done before, use a route map to set the rt of a prefix so that it may be imported by another VRF. Here, we will add the RT of 100:200 to Alpha-1's loopback network so that the Beta routers will see it:

```
PE1(config)#ip prefix-list AddRT seq 5 permit 192.168.1.0/24
PE1(config)#
PE1(config)#route-map rm-AddRT permit 10
PE1(config-route-map)#match ip address prefix-list AddRT
PE1(config-route-map)#set extcommunity rt 100:200 additive
PE1(config-route-map)#exit
```

```
PE1(config)#ip vrf ALPHA
PE1(config-vrf)#export map rm-AddRT
PE1(config-vrf)#exit
```

Now, Beta-1 can see the loopback network:

```
Beta-1#sh ip route | beg Gate
Gateway of last resort is not set

        10.0.0.0/8 is variably subnetted, 3 subnets, 2 masks
C         10.2.1.0/24 is directly connected, GigabitEthernet1/0
L         10.2.1.1/32 is directly connected, GigabitEthernet1/0
O         10.20.1.0/24 [110/2] via 10.2.1.2, 00:25:57, Gi1/0
O E2    192.168.1.0/24 [110/2] via 10.2.1.2, 00:00:13, Gi1/0
        192.168.2.0/24 is variably subnetted, 2 subnets, 2 masks
C         192.168.2.0/24 is directly connected, Loopback0
L         192.168.2.1/32 is directly connected, Loopback0
Beta-1#ping 192.168.1.1
Type escape sequence to abort.
Sending 5, 100-byte ICMP Echos to 192.168.1.1, timeout is 2 seconds:
.....
Success rate is 0 percent (0/5)
Beta-1#
```

Beta-1 does not yet have reachability though, and this is because Alpha-1 has no knowledge of the networks that Beta-1 is sending traffic from. Using the same method as before, we can bring Beta-1's loopback network into Alpha-1's routing table:

```
PE1(config)#ip prefix-list AddRT2 seq 5 permit 192.168.2.0/24
PE1(config)#route-map rm-AddRT2 permit 10
PE1(config-route-map)#match ip address prefix-list AddRT2
PE1(config-route-map)#set extcommunity rt 100:100
PE1(config-route-map)#ip vrf BETA
PE1(config-vrf)#export map rm-AddRT2
PE1(config-vrf)#
```

Now that Alpha-1 has the route for Beta-1's loopback network, we also have reachability from one loopback interface to the other:

```
Beta-1#ping 192.168.1.1 so lo0
Type escape sequence to abort.
Sending 5, 100-byte ICMP Echos to 192.168.1.1, timeout is 2 seconds:
Packet sent with a source address of 192.168.2.1
!!!!!
Success rate is 100 percent (5/5)
Beta-1#
```

It would probably be a good idea to make this example a little more realistic. Although the topology we are working with is functional and does exactly what we need it to, it is hardly a scenario we are likely to encounter in the real world.

So, let's extend it out to include a more realistic provider network.

11.2 An expanded VRF-Lite scenario

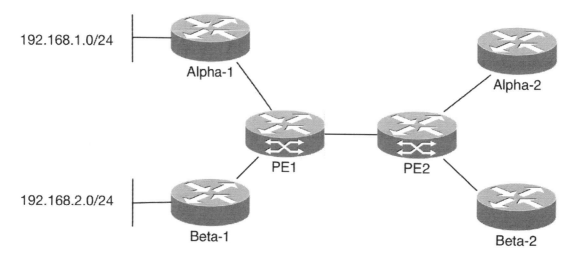

Starting back at the beginning with one provider router, it was easy to route between VRFs. So, now with our network as it stands, how would we route between VRFs?

Because we are expanding on the previous example, I will just include a few relevant outputs and not the whole configuration for the sake of brevity:

```
Alpha-1#sh ip int bri | i up
GigabitEthernet1/0      10.1.1.1        YES NVRAM  up      up
Loopback0               192.168.1.1     YES NVRAM  up      up
Alpha-1#

Beta-1#sh ip int bri | i up
GigabitEthernet1/0      10.2.1.1        YES NVRAM  up      up
Loopback0               192.168.2.1     YES NVRAM  up      up
Beta-1#

Alpha-2#sh ip int bri | i up
GigabitEthernet1/0      10.10.1.1       YES NVRAM  up      up
Loopback0               172.16.1.1      YES NVRAM  up      up
```

```
Alpha-2#

Beta-2#sh ip int bri | i up
GigabitEthernet1/0      10.20.1.1     YES NVRAM  up        up
Beta-2#

PE1#sh ip int bri | i up
GigabitEthernet1/0      10.1.1.2      YES NVRAM  up        up
GigabitEthernet2/0      10.2.1.2      YES NVRAM  up        up
GigabitEthernet3/0      unassigned    YES manual up        up
Loopback0               1.1.1.1       YES NVRAM  up        up
PE1#

PE2#sh ip int bri | i up
GigabitEthernet1/0      10.10.1.2     YES manual up        up
GigabitEthernet2/0      10.20.1.2     YES manual up        up
GigabitEthernet3/0      unassigned    YES manual up        up
PE2#
```

We start, as always, by creating our VRFs and assigning these to the appropriate interfaces:

```
PE1(config)#ip vrf ALPHA
PE1(config-vrf)#ip vrf BETA
```

If you want to save having to undo a lot of configuration (the reasons for why will be explained shortly) then do not assign IP addresses to the interfaces or set them up for vrf forwarding just yet.

```
PE1(config-vrf)#int gi 1/0
PE1(config-if)#ip vrf forwarding ALPHA
% Interface GigabitEthernet1/0 IPv4 disabled and address(es) removed
due to enabling VRF ALPHA
PE1(config-if)#ip add 10.1.1.2 255.255.255.0
PE1(config-if)#int gi 2/0
PE1(config-if)#ip vrf forwarding BETA
% Interface GigabitEthernet2/0 IPv4 disabled and address(es) removed
due to enabling VRF BETA
PE1(config-if)#ip add 10.2.1.2 255.255.255.0
PE1(config-if)#

PE2(config)#ip vrf ALPHA
PE2(config-vrf)#ip vrf BETA
PE2(config-vrf)#int gi 1/0
PE2(config-if)#ip vrf forwarding ALPHA
```

```
% Interface GigabitEthernet1/0 IPv4 disabled and address(es) removed
due to enabling VRF ALPHA
PE2(config-if)#ip add 10.10.1.2 255.255.255.0
PE2(config-if)#int gi 2/0
PE2(config-if)#ip vrf forwarding BETA
% Interface GigabitEthernet2/0 IPv4 disabled and address(es) removed
due to enabling VRF BETA
PE2(config-if)#ip add 10.20.1.2 255.255.255.0
PE2(config-if)#
```

Now, we will set up OSPF between our hosts again:

```
Alpha-1(config-if)#router ospf 1
Alpha-1(config-router)#router-id 10.1.1.1
Alpha-1(config-router)#network 10.1.1.0 0.0.0.255 area 0
Alpha-1(config-router)#network 192.168.1.0 0.0.0.255 area 0
Alpha-1(config-router)#

Beta-1(config-if)#router ospf 1
Beta-1(config-router)#router-id 10.2.1.1
Beta-1(config-router)#network 10.2.1.0 0.0.0.255 area 0
Beta-1(config-router)#network 192.168.2.0 0.0.0.255 area 0
Beta-1(config-router)#

Alpha-2(config-if)#router ospf 1
Alpha-2(config-router)#router-id 10.10.1.1
Alpha-2(config-router)#network 10.10.1.0 0.0.0.255 area 0
Alpha-2(config-router)#network 172.16.1.1 0.0.0.0 area 0

Beta-2(config-if)#router ospf 2
Beta-2(config-router)#router-id 10.20.1.1
Beta-2(config-router)#network 10.20.1.0 0.0.0.255 area 0
Beta-2(config-router)#

PE1(config-if)#router ospf 1 vrf ALPHA
PE1(config-router)#network 10.1.1.0 0.0.0.255 area 0
*Jul 12 10:13:48.523: %OSPF-5-ADJCHG: Process 1, Nbr 10.1.1.1 on
GigabitEthernet1/0 from LOADING to FULL, Loading Done
PE1(config-router)#router ospf 2 vrf BETA
PE1(config-router)#network 10.2.1.0 0.0.0.255 area 0
PE1(config-router)#
*Jul 12 10:14:06.091: %OSPF-5-ADJCHG: Process 2, Nbr 10.2.1.1 on
GigabitEthernet2/0 from LOADING to FULL, Loading Done
PE1(config-router)#

PE2(config-if)#router ospf 1 vrf ALPHA
PE2(config-router)#network 10.10.1.0 0.0.0.255 area 0
```

```
*Jul 12 10:14:15.411: %OSPF-5-ADJCHG: Process 1, Nbr 10.10.1.1 on
GigabitEthernet1/0 from LOADING to FULL, Loading Done
PE2(config-router)#router ospf 2 vrf BETA
PE2(config-router)#network 10.20.1.0 0.0.0.255 area 0
PE2(config-router)#
*Jul 12 10:14:28.019: %OSPF-5-ADJCHG: Process 2, Nbr 10.20.1.1 on
GigabitEthernet2/0 from LOADING to FULL, Loading Done
PE2(config-router)#
```

Our PE routes and our CE routers now have connectivity but only with their next-door neighbor. So how do we now join the two sides together?

We have two different VRFs, and we know that we can assign an IP address to a port and have it carry traffic for that particular VRF. So, we could do that and include the connecting interfaces of PE1 and PE2 in OSPF. However, that would only be good for one VRF, unless we start adding more interfaces and cables. At which stage it starts to get clumsy and uneconomical.

Instead, we will use a different method and assign dot1q VLAN id's to our interfaces. We can't assign a VLAN tag to the physical interface, so we will need to create sub interfaces. This means removing our existing IP addresses, creating the sub interfaces, and then configuring the interfaces with the IP addresses, VLAN id and in the case of the PE routers, assigning them to a VRF instance.

If you have saved your fingers from setting up the IP addresses as mentioned earlier, then join in now:

```
PE1(config-if)#int gi1/0
PE1(config-if)#no ip add
PE1(config-if)#
*Jul 12 10:20:33.971: %OSPF-5-ADJCHG: Process 1, Nbr 10.1.1.1 on
GigabitEthernet1/0 from FULL to DOWN, Neighbor Down: Interface down
or detached
PE1(config-if)#no ip vrf forwarding ALPHA
PE1(config-if)#int gi 1/0.100
PE1(config-subif)#encapsulation dot1Q 100
PE1(config-subif)#ip vrf forwarding ALPHA
PE1(config-subif)#ip add 10.1.1.2 255.255.255.0
PE1(config-subif)#no shut
```

We set Alpha-1 up to have the same VLAN id as PE1's connecting interface:

```
Alpha-1(config)#int gi 1/0
Alpha-1(config-if)#no ip add
```

```
Alpha-1(config-if)#int gi 1/0.100
Alpha-1(config-subif)#encapsulation dot1Q 100
Alpha-1(config-subif)#ip add 10.1.1.1 255.255.255.0
Alpha-1(config-subif)#no shut
Alpha-1(config-subif)#
```

Let's do the same for BETA-1:

```
PE1(config-subif)#int gi 2/0
PE1(config-if)#no ip add
*Jul 12 10:30:43.719: %OSPF-5-ADJCHG: Process 2, Nbr 10.2.1.1 on
GigabitEthernet2/0 from FULL to DOWN, Neighbor Down: Interface down
or detached
PE1(config-if)#no ip vrf forwarding BETA
PE1(config-if)#int gi 2/0.200
PE1(config-subif)#encapsulation dot1Q 200
PE1(config-subif)#ip vrf forwarding BETA
PE1(config-subif)#ip add 10.2.1.2 255.255.255.0
PE1(config-subif)#no shut
PE1(config-subif)#

Beta-1(config)#int gi 1/0
Beta-1(config-if)#no ip add
Beta-1(config-if)#int gi 1/0.200
Beta-1(config-subif)#encapsulation dot1q 200
Beta-1(config-subif)#ip add 10.2.1.1 255.255.255.0
Beta-1(config-subif)#no shut
Beta-1(config-subif)#
*Jul 12 10:33:45.399: %OSPF-5-ADJCHG: Process 1, Nbr 10.2.1.2 on
GigabitEthernet1/0.200 from LOADING to FULL, Loading Done
Beta-1(config-subif)#
```

Our OSPF adjacencies have re-established, so let's move on to creating out link between PE1 and PE2:

```
PE1(config-router)#int gi 3/0
PE1(config-if)#no shut
PE1(config-router)#int gi 3/0.100
PE1(config-subif)#encapsulation dot1Q 100
PE1(config-subif)#ip vrf forwarding ALPHA
PE1(config-subif)#ip add 10.1.3.1 255.255.255.0
PE1(config-subif)#no shut
PE1(config-subif)#int gi 3/0.200
PE1(config-subif)#encapsulation dot1Q 200
PE1(config-subif)#ip vrf forwarding BETA
PE1(config-subif)#ip add 10.2.3.1 255.255.255.0
```

```
PE1(config-subif)#no shut
PE1(config-subif)#

PE2(config-router)#int gi 3/0
PE2(config-if)#no shut
PE2(config-router)#int gi 3/0.100
PE2(config-subif)#encapsulation dot1Q 100
PE2(config-subif)#ip vrf forwarding ALPHA
PE2(config-subif)#ip add 10.1.3.2 255.255.255.0
PE2(config-subif)#no shut
PE2(config-subif)#int gi 3/0.200
PE2(config-subif)#encapsulation dot1Q 200
PE2(config-subif)#ip vrf forwarding BETA
PE2(config-subif)#ip add 10.2.3.2 255.255.255.0
PE2(config-subif)#no shut
```

We also need to extend our OSPF processes to include the new links:

```
PE1(config-subif)#router ospf 2 vrf BETA
PE1(config-router)#network 10.2.3.0 0.0.0.255 area 0
PE1(config-router)#router ospf 1 vrf ALPHA
PE1(config-router)#network 10.1.3.0 0.0.0.255 area 0

PE2(config-subif)#router ospf 2 vrf BETA
PE2(config-router)#network 10.2.3.0 0.0.0.255 area 0
PE2(config-router)#router ospf 1 vrf ALPHA
PE2(config-router)#network 10.1.3.0 0.0.0.255 area 0
PE2(config-router)#end
PE2#ping vrf ALPHA 10.1.3.1
Type escape sequence to abort.
Sending 5, 100-byte ICMP Echos to 10.1.3.1, timeout is 2 seconds:
!!!!!
Success rate is 100 percent (5/5)
PE2#

PE2#ping vrf BETA 10.2.3.1
Type escape sequence to abort.
Sending 5, 100-byte ICMP Echos to 10.2.3.1, timeout is 2 seconds:
!!!!!
Success rate is 100 percent (5/5)
PE2#
```

Moving on to the other side of the network, we'll set up PE2 and the other two customer routers in the same fashion as above:

```
PE2(config-subif)#int gi1/0
```

```
PE2(config-if)#no ip add
*Jul 12 10:36:32.879: %OSPF-5-ADJCHG: Process 1, Nbr 10.10.1.1 on
GigabitEthernet1/0 from FULL to DOWN, Neighbor Down: Interface down
or detached
PE2(config-if)#no ip vrf forwarding ALPHA
PE2(config-if)#int gi 1/0.100
PE2(config-subif)#encapsulation dot1Q 100
PE2(config-subif)#ip vrf forwarding ALPHA
PE2(config-subif)#ip add 10.10.1.2 255.255.255.0
PE2(config-subif)#no shut
PE2(config-subif)#int gi 2/0
PE2(config-if)#no ip add
*Jul 12 10:37:09.115: %OSPF-5-ADJCHG: Process 2, Nbr 10.20.1.1 on
GigabitEthernet2/0 from FULL to DOWN, Neighbor Down: Interface down
or detached
PE2(config-if)#no ip vrf forwarding BETA
PE2(config-if)#int gi 2/0.200
PE2(config-subif)#encapsulation dot1Q 200
PE2(config-subif)#ip vrf forwarding BETA
PE2(config-subif)#ip add 10.20.1.2 255.255.255.0
PE2(config-subif)#no shut
PE2(config-subif)#

Alpha-2(config)#int gi 1/0
Alpha-2(config-if)#no ip add
Alpha-2(config-if)#int gi 1/0.100
Alpha-2(config-subif)#encapsulation dot1Q 100
Alpha-2(config-subif)#ip add 10.10.1.1 255.255.255.0
Alpha-2(config-subif)#no shut
Alpha-2(config-subif)#
*Jul 12 10:39:13.867: %OSPF-5-ADJCHG: Process 1, Nbr 10.10.1.2 on
GigabitEthernet1/0.100 from LOADING to FULL, Loading Done
Alpha-2(config-subif)#

Beta-2(config)#int gi 1/0
Beta-2(config-if)#no ip add
Beta-2(config-if)#int gi 1/0.200
Beta-2(config-subif)#encapsulation dot1Q 200
Beta-2(config-subif)#ip add 10.20.1.1 255.255.255.0
Beta-2(config-subif)#no shut
Beta-2(config-subif)#
*Jul 12 10:39:48.463: %OSPF-5-ADJCHG: Process 1, Nbr 10.20.1.2 on
GigabitEthernet1/0.200 from LOADING to FULL, Loading Done
Beta-2(config-subif)#
```

Now, Alpha-1 has Alpha-2's networks in its routing table and also, more importantly, has reachability:

```
Alpha-1#sh ip route | beg Gate
Gateway of last resort is not set

      10.0.0.0/8 is variably subnetted, 4 subnets, 2 masks
C        10.1.1.0/24 is directly connected, GigabitEthernet1/0.100
L        10.1.1.1/32 is directly connected, GigabitEthernet1/0.100
O        10.1.3.0/24 [110/2] via 10.1.1.2, 00:28:49, Gi1/0.100
O        10.10.1.0/24 [110/3] via 10.1.1.2, 00:01:29, Gi1/0.100
      172.16.0.0/32 is subnetted, 1 subnets
O        172.16.1.1 [110/4] via 10.1.1.2, 00:01:29, Gi1/0.100
      192.168.1.0/24 is variably subnetted, 2 subnets, 2 masks
C        192.168.1.0/24 is directly connected, Loopback0
L        192.168.1.1/32 is directly connected, Loopback0
Alpha-1#ping 10.10.1.1 so lo0
Type escape sequence to abort.
Sending 5, 100-byte ICMP Echos to 10.10.1.1, timeout is 2 seconds:
Packet sent with a source address of 192.168.1.1
!!!!!
Success rate is 100 percent (5/5)
Alpha-1#
```

Similarly, Beta-1 can see and reach Beta-2:

```
Beta-1#sh ip route | beg Gate
Gateway of last resort is not set

      10.0.0.0/8 is variably subnetted, 4 subnets, 2 masks
C        10.2.1.0/24 is directly connected, GigabitEthernet1/0.200
L        10.2.1.1/32 is directly connected, GigabitEthernet1/0.200
O        10.2.3.0/24 [110/2] via 10.2.1.2, 00:00:39, Gi1/0.200
O        10.20.1.0/24 [110/3] via 10.2.1.2, 00:00:29, Gi1/0.200
      192.168.2.0/24 is variably subnetted, 2 subnets, 2 masks
C        192.168.2.0/24 is directly connected, Loopback0
L        192.168.2.1/32 is directly connected, Loopback0
Beta-1#ping 10.20.1.1 so lo0
Type escape sequence to abort.
Sending 5, 100-byte ICMP Echos to 10.20.1.1, timeout is 2 seconds:
Packet sent with a source address of 192.168.2.1
!!!!!
Success rate is 100 percent (5/5)
Beta-1#
```

If we wanted to share routes between our VRFs, we would have to set up MP-BGP between PE1 and PE2. So let's do that quickly. Apart from being good practice, it will return us nicely to the interaction between OSPF and BGP.

We start by adding to our VRFs the required route distinguishers and route targets:

```
PE1(config)#ip vrf ALPHA
PE1(config-vrf)#rd 100:100
PE1(config-vrf)#route-target both 100:100
PE1(config-vrf)#ip vrf BETA
PE1(config-vrf)#rd 100:200
PE1(config-vrf)#route-target both 100:200
PE1(config-vrf)#

PE2(config-router)#ip vrf ALPHA
PE2(config-vrf)#rd 100:100
PE2(config-vrf)#route-target both 100:100
PE2(config-vrf)#ip vrf BETA
PE2(config-vrf)#rd 100:200
PE2(config-vrf)#route-target both 100:200
PE2(config-vrf)#
```

We need to remove the sub interfaces between PE1 and PE2 we configured earlier:

```
PE1(config-vrf)#exit
PE1(config)#no int gi 3/0.100
%OSPF-5-ADJCHG: Process 1, Nbr 10.10.1.2 on GigabitEthernet3/0.100
from FULL to DOWN, Neighbor Down: Interface down or detached
PE1(config)#no int gi 3/0.200
PE1(config)#
%OSPF-5-ADJCHG: Process 2, Nbr 10.20.1.2 on GigabitEthernet3/0.200
from FULL to DOWN, Neighbor Down: Interface down or detached
PE1(config)#

PE2(config-vrf)#exit
PE2(config)#no int gi 3/0.100
%OSPF-5-ADJCHG: Process 1, Nbr 10.1.1.2 on GigabitEthernet3/0.100
from FULL to DOWN, Neighbor Down: Interface down or detached
PE2(config)#no int gi 3/0.200
PE2(config)#
%OSPF-5-ADJCHG: Process 2, Nbr 10.2.1.2 on GigabitEthernet3/0.200
from FULL to DOWN, Neighbor Down: Interface down or detached
PE2(config)#
```

Next, we to set up the physical connection between PE1 and PE2, as well as adding a loopback interface to PE2 that will be used to form our MP-BGP peering.

```
PE1(config)#int gi 3/0
PE1(config-if)#ip add 10.250.1.1 255.255.255.0
```

```
PE1(config-if)#mpls ip
PE1(config-if)#no shut
PE1(config-if)#

PE2(config)#int lo0
PE2(config-if)#ip add 2.2.2.2 255.255.255.255
PE2(config-if)#int gi 3/0
PE2(config-if)#ip add 10.250.1.2 255.255.255.0
PE2(config-if)#mpls ip
PE2(config-if)#no shut
```

We will create another OSPF process in order that we can join PE1 to PE2:

```
PE1(config)#router ospf 3
PE1(config-router)#network 1.1.1.1 0.0.0.0 area 0
PE1(config-router)#network 10.250.1.0 0.0.0.255 area 0

PE2(config)#router ospf 3
PE2(config-router)#network 2.2.2.2 0.0.0.0 area 0
PE2(config-router)#network 10.250.1.0 0.0.0.255 area 0
```

Now, we can set up our BGP neighbors:

```
PE1(config-router)#router bgp 100
PE1(config-router)#neigh 2.2.2.2 remote-as 100
PE1(config-router)#neigh 2.2.2.2 update-source lo0
PE1(config-router)#

PE2(config-router)#router bgp 100
PE2(config-router)#neigh 1.1.1.1 remote-as 100
PE2(config-router)#neigh 1.1.1.1 update-source lo0
PE2(config-router)#

PE1(config-router)#address-family vpnv4
PE1(config-router-af)#neigh 2.2.2.2 activate
PE1(config-router-af)#neigh 2.2.2.2 send-community extended
PE1(config-router-af)#exit
PE1(config-router)#address-family ipv4 vrf ALPHA
PE1(config-router-af)#redistribute ospf 1 vrf ALPHA metric 10
PE1(config-router-af)#router ospf 1 vrf ALPHA
PE1(config-router)#redistribute bgp 100 metric-type 1 metric 10 subnets
PE1(config-router)#router bgp 100
PE1(config-router)#address-family ipv4 vrf BETA
PE1(config-router-af)#redistribute ospf 2 vrf BETA metric 10
PE1(config-router-af)#router ospf 2 vrf BETA
PE1(config-router)#redistribute bgp 100 subnets
```

```
PE2(config-router)#address-family vpnv4
PE2(config-router-af)#neigh 1.1.1.1 activate
PE2(config-router-af)#neigh 1.1.1.1 send-community extended
PE2(config-router-af)#exit
PE2(config-router)#address-family ipv4 vrf ALPHA
PE2(config-router-af)#redistribute ospf 1 vrf ALPHA metric 10
PE2(config-router-af)#router ospf 1 vrf ALPHA
PE2(config-router)#redistribute bgp 100 metric-type 1 metric 10
subnets
PE2(config-router)#router bgp 100
PE2(config-router)#address-family ipv4 vrf BETA
PE2(config-router-af)#redistribute ospf 2 vrf BETA metric 10
PE2(config-router-af)#router ospf 2 vrf BETA
PE2(config-router)#redistribute bgp 100 subnets
```

At this stage, Alpha-1 and Beta-1 should be able to reach their counterpart (note that in the sake of formatting, I have changed "GigabitEthernet" to "Gi" in the output):

```
Alpha-1#sh ip route ospf | beg Gate
Gateway of last resort is not set

      10.0.0.0/8 is variably subnetted, 3 subnets, 2 masks
O IA     10.10.1.0/24 [110/11] via 10.1.1.2, 00:01:37, Gi1/0.100
      172.16.0.0/32 is subnetted, 1 subnets
O IA     172.16.1.1 [110/11] via 10.1.1.2, 00:01:37, Gi1/0.100
Alpha-1#ping 10.10.1.1
Type escape sequence to abort.
Sending 5, 100-byte ICMP Echos to 10.10.1.1, timeout is 2 seconds:
!!!!!
Success rate is 100 percent (5/5)
Alpha-1#


Beta-1#sh ip route ospf | beg Gate
Gateway of last resort is not set

      10.0.0.0/8 is variably subnetted, 3 subnets, 2 masks
O IA     10.20.1.0/24 [110/2] via 10.2.1.2, 00:01:54, Gi1/0.200
Beta-1#ping 10.20.1.1
Type escape sequence to abort.
Sending 5, 100-byte ICMP Echos to 10.20.1.1, timeout is 2 seconds:
!!!!!
Success rate is 100 percent (5/5)
Beta-1#
```

As we have seen in previous chapters, we use prefix lists and route maps to change the value for the route target, which is sent across in the extended community:

```
PE1(config)#ip prefix-list AddRT-Alpha-Beta seq 5 permit 192.168.1.0/24
PE1(config)#route-map AddRoute-Alpha-Beta permit 10
PE1(config-route-map)#match ip address prefix-list AddRT-Alpha-Beta
PE1(config-route-map)#set extcommunity rt 100:200 additive
PE1(config-route-map)#ip vrf ALPHA
PE1(config-vrf)#export map AddRoute-Alpha-Beta
PE1(config-vrf)#exit

PE1(config)#ip prefix-list AddRT-Beta-Alpha seq 5 permit 192.168.2.0/24
PE1(config)#route-map AddRoute-Beta-Alpha permit 10
PE1(config-route-map)#match ip address prefix-list AddRT-Beta-Alpha
PE1(config-route-map)#set extcommunity rt 100:100 additive
PE1(config-route-map)#ip vrf BETA
PE1(config-vrf)#export map AddRoute-Beta-Alpha
PE1(config-vrf)#
```

Now Alpha-1 and Beta-1 will be able to see the new routes:

```
Alpha-1#sh ip route ospf | beg Gate
Gateway of last resort is not set

      10.0.0.0/8 is variably subnetted, 3 subnets, 2 masks
O IA     10.10.1.0/24 [110/11] via 10.1.1.2, 00:05:57, Gi1/0.100
      172.16.0.0/32 is subnetted, 1 subnets
O IA     172.16.1.1 [110/11] via 10.1.1.2, 00:05:57, Gi1/0.100
O E1  192.168.2.0/24 [110/11] via 10.1.1.2, 00:00:03, Gi1/0.100
Alpha-1#

Beta-1#sh ip route ospf | beg Gate
Gateway of last resort is not set

      10.0.0.0/8 is variably subnetted, 3 subnets, 2 masks
O IA     10.20.1.0/24 [110/2] via 10.2.1.2, 00:05:43, Gi1/0.200
O E2  192.168.1.0/24 [110/10] via 10.2.1.2, 00:01:35, Gi1/0.200
Beta-1#
```

They should also have reachability from just their loopback interfaces:

```
Alpha-1#ping 192.168.2.1
Type escape sequence to abort.
Sending 5, 100-byte ICMP Echos to 192.168.2.1, timeout is 2 seconds:
```

```
.....
Success rate is 0 percent (0/5)
Alpha-1#ping 192.168.2.1 so lo0
Type escape sequence to abort.
Sending 5, 100-byte ICMP Echos to 192.168.2.1, timeout is 2 seconds:
Packet sent with a source address of 192.168.1.1
!!!!!
Success rate is 100 percent (5/5)
Alpha-1#

Beta-1#ping 192.168.1.1
Type escape sequence to abort.
Sending 5, 100-byte ICMP Echos to 192.168.1.1, timeout is 2 seconds:
.....
Success rate is 0 percent (0/5)
Beta-1#ping 192.168.1.1 so lo0
Type escape sequence to abort.
Sending 5, 100-byte ICMP Echos to 192.168.1.1, timeout is 2 seconds:
Packet sent with a source address of 192.168.2.1
!!!!!
Success rate is 100 percent (5/5)
Beta-1#
```

Beta-2 and Alpha-2 will not have reachability at the moment. Although they can see the new routes, Beta-1 and Alpha-1 do not have any knowledge of them. We can sort this out using the same commands above to set up prefix lists and route maps to add the RT values (as additive) to PE2:

```
PE2(config)#ip prefix-list AddRT-Alpha-Beta seq 5 permit
172.16.1.1/32
PE2(config)#route-map AddRoute-Alpha-Beta permit 10
PE2(config-route-map)#match ip address prefix-list AddRT-Alpha-Beta
PE2(config-route-map)#set extcommunity rt 100:200 additive
PE2(config-route-map)#ip vrf ALPHA
PE2(config-vrf)#export map AddRoute-Alpha-Beta
PE2(config-vrf)#exit
PE2(config)#
```

Given a few moments for the routes to refresh, Beta-1 can now see the loopback interface of Alpha-2 its routing table:

```
Beta-1#sh ip route ospf | beg Gate
Gateway of last resort is not set

      10.0.0.0/8 is variably subnetted, 3 subnets, 2 masks
O IA     10.20.1.0/24 [110/2] via 10.2.1.2, 00:00:02, Gi1/0.200
```

```
                 172.16.0.0/32 is subnetted, 1 subnets
O E2        172.16.1.1 [110/10] via 10.2.1.2, 00:00:03, Gi1/0.200
O E2     192.168.1.0/24 [110/10] via 10.2.1.2, 00:04:52, Gi1/0.200
Beta-1#
```

And, we have reachability:

```
Alpha-2#ping 192.168.2.1 so lo0
Type escape sequence to abort.
Sending 5, 100-byte ICMP Echos to 192.168.2.1, timeout is 2 seconds:
Packet sent with a source address of 172.16.1.1
!!!!!
Success rate is 100 percent (5/5)
Alpha-2#
```

We do not have any loopback interfaces on Beta-2 to test with, so we will have to use the physical interface instead:

```
PE2(config)#ip prefix-list AddRT-Beta-Alpha seq 5 permit 10.20.1.0/24
PE2(config)#route-map AddRoute-Beta-Alpha permit 10
PE2(config-route-map)#match ip address prefix-list AddRT-Beta-Alpha
PE2(config-route-map)#set extcommunity rt 100:100 additive
PE2(config-route-map)#ip vrf BETA
PE2(config-vrf)#export map AddRoute-Beta-Alpha
PE2(config-vrf)#exit
PE2(config)#
```

Again, given a few moments, Alpha-1 will get Beta-2s information into the routing table:

```
Alpha-1#sh ip route ospf | beg Gate
Gateway of last resort is not set

         10.0.0.0/8 is variably subnetted, 4 subnets, 2 masks
O IA      10.10.1.0/24 [110/11] via 10.1.1.2, 00:01:57, Gi1/0.100
O E1      10.20.1.0/24 [110/11] via 10.1.1.2, 00:00:07, Gi1/0.100
         172.16.0.0/32 is subnetted, 1 subnets
O IA       172.16.1.1 [110/11] via 10.1.1.2, 00:01:57, Gi1/0.100
O E1     192.168.2.0/24 [110/11] via 10.1.1.2, 00:05:47, Gi1/0.100
Alpha-1#
```

And Beta-2 will have reachability:

```
Beta-2#ping 192.168.1.1
Type escape sequence to abort.
Sending 5, 100-byte ICMP Echos to 192.168.1.1, timeout is 2 seconds:
!!!!!
```

```
Success rate is 100 percent (5/5)
Beta-2#
```

We have a bit of a mix of OSPF route types here. We have the Alpha routers with IA (Inter-area) and E1 (external type 1), and the Beta routes with IA and E2 (external type 2) routes. When we performed the redistribution from BGP into OSPF for the ALPHA VRF, we used the following:

```
PE2(config-router-af)#router ospf 1 vrf ALPHA
PE2(config-router)#redistribute bgp 100 metric-type 1 metric 10 subnets
```

The metric-type of 1 explains why the routes appear as external type 1 routes. For the BETA VRF, we did not specify a metric-type; therefore, they will be redistributed as type 2 by default.

```
PE2(config-router-af)#router ospf 2 vrf BETA
PE2(config-router)#redistribute bgp 100 subnets
```

We can change the route type using the same commands as we used for the ALPHA VRF:

```
PE1(config)#router ospf 2 vrf BETA
PE1(config-router)#redistribute bgp 100 metric 10 metric-type 1 subnets
PE1(config-router)#

PE2(config)#router ospf 2 vrf BETA
PE2(config-router)#redistribute bgp 100 metric 10 metric-type 1 subnets
PE2(config-router)#
```

Now, Beta-1 and Beta-2 see the routes that were E2 as E1 instead:

```
Beta-1#sh ip route ospf | beg Gate
Gateway of last resort is not set

      10.0.0.0/8 is variably subnetted, 3 subnets, 2 masks
O IA     10.20.1.0/24 [110/11] via 10.2.1.2, 00:02:44, Gi1/0.200
      172.16.0.0/32 is subnetted, 1 subnets
O E1     172.16.1.1 [110/11] via 10.2.1.2, 00:02:44, Gi1/0.200
O E1  192.168.1.0/24 [110/11] via 10.2.1.2, 00:02:44, Gi1/0.200
Beta-1#

Beta-2#sh ip route ospf | beg Gate
```

```
Gateway of last resort is not set

      10.0.0.0/8 is variably subnetted, 3 subnets, 2 masks
O IA     10.2.1.0/24 [110/11] via 10.20.1.2, 00:03:03, Gi1/0.200
      172.16.0.0/32 is subnetted, 1 subnets
O E1     172.16.1.1 [110/11] via 10.20.1.2, 00:03:03, Gi1/0.200
O E1  192.168.1.0/24 [110/11] via 10.20.1.2, 00:03:03, Gi1/0.200
O IA  192.168.2.0/24 [110/11] via 10.20.1.2, 00:05:47, Gi1/0.200
Beta-2#
```

As you can see VRF-lite is as highly configurable as MPLS is, yet without the need for the labels used in MPLS.

11.3 The DN bit and capability vrf-lite

So far, we have used OSPF as our CE-to-PE routing protocol with no issues. With RFC 4577, which defines "OSPF as the Provider/Customer Edge Protocol for BGP/MPLS IP Virtual Private Networks (VPNs)," we encounter some interesting constraints. Consider the following extract from the RFC:

"If a route sent from a PE router to a CE router could then be received by another PE router from one of its own CE routers, it would be possible for routing loops to occur. To prevent this, a PE sets the DN bit [OSPF-DN] in any LSA that it sends to a CE, and a PE ignores any LSA received from a CE that already has the DN bit sent."

So what does this mean for us, and, more particularly, why should we care? To understand this and to actually see this work as we need it to, we need a very basic topology:

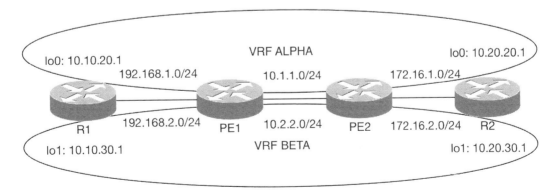

How though does this setting of the DN bit (which is the Downbit) affect our topology? None of our routers are multi-homed, therefore we will not encounter a traditional routing loop. Yet, when we use VRF-lite, the CE acts as a PE, and the methods defined in the RFC still apply here. So we will break it down a bit and see this in action.

When we redistribute between BGP and OSPF, the down bit must be set for type 3 and type 5 LSAs, with type 3 being a Summary LSA and type 5 being an External LSA. Cisco, however, only sets this in type 3 LSAs and uses route tagging for type 5 and type 7 LSAs. We have already seen that the MPLS network acts as a "superbackbone" for OSPF, and the PE routers act as an ABR (Area Border Router) between the super backbone and the OSPF area. Therefore, when a PE router receives a route, a type 3 LSA will be generated.

A PE router will set the down bit on a type 3 LSA, if the routes have come over an MPLS cloud through MP-BGP, and are redistributed into OSPF. Because the DN bit is set, the information within the LSA will not be used in the OSPF route calculation, and the LSA does not get translated into a route.

Let's lab this up. We will be using the same two VRFs as before. ALPHA will use an RD of 100:100, with the same RT, and will have a VLAN tag of 100. BETA will use 200:200 for both the VRF particulars and 200 as the VLAN tag.

The initial router configurations are below:

R1

```
R1(config)#ip vrf ALPHA
R1(config-vrf)#rd 100:100
R1(config-vrf)#exit
R1(config)#ip vrf BETA
R1(config-vrf)#rd 200:200
R1(config-vrf)#exit
R1(config)#int gi 1/0
R1(config-if)#no shut
R1(config-subif)#int lo0
R1(config-if)#ip vrf for ALPHA
R1(config-if)#ip add 10.10.20.1 255.255.255.255
R1(config-if)#int lo1
R1(config-if)#ip vrf for BETA
R1(config-if)#ip add 10.10.30.1 255.255.255.255
R1(config-if)#int gi 1/0.1
R1(config-subif)#ip vrf for ALPHA
R1(config-subif)#encap dot 100
R1(config-subif)#ip add 192.168.1.1 255.255.255.0
R1(config-subif)#int gi 1/0.2
R1(config-subif)#ip vrf for BETA
R1(config-subif)#encap dot 200
```

```
R1(config-subif)#ip add 192.168.2.1 255.255.255.0
R1(config-subif)#router ospf 100 vrf ALPHA
R1(config-router)#network 10.10.20.1 0.0.0.0 area 0
R1(config-router)#network 192.168.1.0 0.0.0.255 area 0
R1(config-router)#router ospf 200 vrf BETA
R1(config-router)#network 10.10.30.1 0.0.0.0 area 0
R1(config-router)#network 192.168.2.0 0.0.0.255 area 0
R1(config-router)#
```

R2

```
R2(config)#ip vrf ALPHA
R2(config-vrf)#rd 100:100
R2(config-vrf)#exit
R2(config)#ip vrf BETA
R2(config-vrf)#rd 200:200
R2(config-vrf)#exit
R2(config)#int gi 1/0
R2(config-if)#no shut
R2(config-subif)#int lo0
R2(config-if)#ip vrf for ALPHA
R2(config-if)#ip add 10.20.20.1 255.255.255.255
R2(config-if)#int lo1
R2(config-if)#ip vrf for BETA
R2(config-if)#ip add 10.20.30.1 255.255.255.255
R2(config-if)#int gi 1/0.1
R2(config-subif)# ip vrf for ALPHA
R2(config-subif)#encap dot 100
R2(config-subif)#ip add 172.16.1.1 255.255.255.0
R2(config-subif)#int gi 1/0.2
R2(config-subif)#encap dot 200
R2(config-subif)#ip vrf for BETA
R2(config-subif)#ip add 172.16.2.1 255.255.255.0
R2(config-subif)#router ospf 100 vrf ALPHA
R2(config-router)#network 10.20.20.1 0.0.0.0 area 0
R2(config-router)#network 172.16.1.0 0.0.0.255 area 0
R2(config-router)#router ospf 200 vrf BETA
R2(config-router)#network 10.20.30.1 0.0.0.0 area 0
R2(config-router)#network 172.16.2.0 0.0.0.255 area 0
R2(config-router)#
```

PE1

```
PE1(config)#ip vrf ALPHA
PE1(config-vrf)#rd 100:100
PE1(config-vrf)#exit
PE1(config)#ip vrf BETA
```

```
PE1(config-vrf)#rd 200:200
PE1(config-vrf)#exit
PE1(config)#int gi 1/0
PE1(config-if)#no shut
PE1(config-if)#int gi 1/0.1
PE1(config-subif)#encap dot1q 100
PE1(config-subif)#ip vrf for ALPHA
PE1(config-subif)#int gi 1/0.2
PE1(config-subif)#encap dot 200
PE1(config-subif)#ip vrf for BETA
PE1(config-subif)#int Gi 1/0.1
PE1(config-subif)#encap dot 100
PE1(config-subif)#ip vrf for ALPHA
PE1(config-subif)#ip add 192.168.1.2 255.255.255.0
PE1(config-subif)#int gi 1/0.2
PE1(config-subif)#ip vrf for BETA
PE1(config-subif)#encap dot 200
PE1(config-subif)#ip add 192.168.2.2 255.255.255.0
PE1(config-subif)#int gi 2/0
PE1(config-if)#no shut
PE1(config-if)#int gi 2/0.1
PE1(config-subif)#encap dot 100
PE1(config-subif)#ip vrf for ALPHA
PE1(config-subif)#ip add 10.1.1.1 255.255.255.0
PE1(config-subif)#int gi 2/0.2
PE1(config-subif)#encap dot 200
PE1(config-subif)#ip vrf for BETA
PE1(config-subif)#ip add 10.2.2.1 255.255.255.0
PE1(config-subif)#router ospf 100 vrf ALPHA
PE1(config-router)#network 192.168.1.0 0.0.0.255 area 0
PE1(config-router)#redistribute bgp 100 subnets metric 10
PE1(config-router)#router ospf 200 vrf BETA
PE1(config-router)#network 192.168.2.0 0.0.0.255 area 0
PE1(config-router)#redistribute bgp 100 subnets metric 10
PE1(config-router)#router bgp 100
PE1(config-router)#bgp router-id 1.1.1.1
PE1(config-router)#address-family ipv4 vrf ALPHA
PE1(config-router-af)#neigh 10.1.1.2 remote-as 100
PE1(config-router-af)#neigh 10.1.1.2 activate
PE1(config-router-af)#redistribute ospf 100 metric 10 match int ext
PE1(config-router-af)#address-family ipv4 vrf BETA
PE1(config-router-af)#neigh 10.2.2.2 remote-as 100
PE1(config-router-af)#neigh 10.2.2.2 activate
PE1(config-router-af)#redistribute ospf 200 metric 10 match int ext
PE1(config-router-af)#
*Aug 22 22:30:19.647: %OSPF-5-ADJCHG: Process 200, Nbr 10.10.30.1 on
GigabitEthernet1/0.2 from LOADING to FULL, Loading Done
```

```
*Aug 22 22:30:26.075: %OSPF-5-ADJCHG: Process 100, Nbr 10.10.20.1 on
GigabitEthernet1/0.1 from LOADING to FULL, Loading Done
PE1(config-router-af)#
*Aug 22 22:30:56.739: %BGP-5-ADJCHANGE: neighbor 10.1.1.2 vpn vrf
ALPHA Up
*Aug 22 22:30:57.075: %BGP-5-ADJCHANGE: neighbor 10.2.2.2 vpn vrf
BETA Up
PE1(config-router-af)#
```

PE2

```
PE2(config)#ip vrf ALPHA
PE2(config-vrf)#rd 100:100
PE2(config-vrf)#exit
PE2(config)#ip vrf BETA
PE2(config-vrf)#rd 200:200
PE2(config-vrf)#exit
PE2(config)#int gi 1/0
PE2(config-if)#no shut
PE2(config-if)#int gi 1/0.1
PE2(config-subif)#encap dot 100
PE2(config-subif)#ip vrf for ALPHA
PE2(config-subif)#ip add 172.16.1.2 255.255.255.0
PE2(config-subif)#int gi 1/0.2
PE2(config-subif)#encap dot 200
PE2(config-subif)#ip vrf for BETA
PE2(config-subif)#ip add 172.16.2.2 255.255.255.0
PE2(config-subif)#int gi 2/0
PE2(config-if)#no shut
PE2(config-if)#int gi 2/0.1
PE2(config-subif)#encap dot 100
PE2(config-subif)#ip vrf for ALPHA
PE2(config-subif)#ip add 10.1.1.2 255.255.255.0
PE2(config-subif)#int gi 2/0.2
PE2(config-subif)#encap dot 200
PE2(config-subif)#ip vrf for BETA
PE2(config-subif)#ip add 10.2.2.2 255.255.255.0
PE2(config-subif)#router ospf 100 vrf ALPHA
PE2(config-router)#network 172.16.1.0 0.0.0.255 area 0
PE2(config-router)#redistribute bgp 100 subnets metric 10
PE2(config-router)#router ospf 200 vrf BETA
PE2(config-router)#network 172.16.2.0 0.0.0.255 area 0
PE2(config-router)#redistribute bgp 100 subnets metric 10
PE2(config-router)#router bgp 100
PE2(config-router)#bgp router-id 2.2.2.2
PE2(config-router)#address-family ipv4 vrf ALPHA
PE2(config-router-af)#neigh 10.1.1.1 remote-as 100
```

```
PE2(config-router-af)#neigh 10.1.1.1 activate
PE2(config-router-af)#redistribute ospf 100 metric 10 match int ext
PE2(config-router-af)#address-family ipv4 vrf BETA
PE2(config-router-af)#neigh 10.2.2.1 remote-as 100
PE2(config-router-af)#neigh 10.2.2.1 activate
PE2(config-router-af)#redistribute ospf 200 metric 10 match int ext
PE2(config-router-af)#
*Aug 22 22:30:57.287: %BGP-5-ADJCHANGE: neighbor 10.1.1.1 vpn vrf
ALPHA Up
*Aug 22 22:30:57.463: %BGP-5-ADJCHANGE: neighbor 10.2.2.1 vpn vrf
BETA Up
PE2(config-router-af)#
```

At this stage, we should have full OSPF adjacencies between R1 and PE1 and between R2 and PE2. We should also have BGP adjacencies between PE1 and PE2 for both VRFs. BGP and OSPF should be redistributing between each other. What we shouldn't have are any OSPF routes on R1 or R2 though:

```
R1#sh ip route vrf ALPHA | beg Gate
Gateway of last resort is not set

      10.0.0.0/32 is subnetted, 1 subnets
C        10.10.20.1 is directly connected, Loopback0
      192.168.1.0/24 is variably subnetted, 2 subnets, 2 masks
C        192.168.1.0/24 is directly connected, GigabitEthernet1/0.1
L        192.168.1.1/32 is directly connected, GigabitEthernet1/0.1
R1#
R1#sh ip route vrf BETA | beg Gate
Gateway of last resort is not set

      10.0.0.0/32 is subnetted, 1 subnets
C        10.10.30.1 is directly connected, Loopback1
      192.168.2.0/24 is variably subnetted, 2 subnets, 2 masks
C        192.168.2.0/24 is directly connected, GigabitEthernet1/0.2
L        192.168.2.1/32 is directly connected, GigabitEthernet1/0.2
R1#
```

Because we are redistributing between BGP and OSPF in a VRF-lite network, the downbit (DN bit) is checked:

```
PE1#sh ip ospf 100 data external 10.20.20.1

            OSPF Router with ID (192.168.1.2) (Process ID 100)

        Type-5 AS External Link States
```

```
    LS age: 1618
    Options: (No TOS-capability, DC, Downward)
    LS Type: AS External Link
    Link State ID: 10.20.20.1 (External Network Number )
    Advertising Router: 192.168.1.2
    LS Seq Number: 80000003
    Checksum: 0xC989
    Length: 36
    Network Mask: /32
          Metric Type: 2 (Larger than any link state path)
          MTID: 0
          Metric: 10
          Forward Address: 0.0.0.0
          External Route Tag: 3489661028

PE1#
```

The DN bit can be seen above, shown as "Downward," set in the options field. Although the route is received by R1, due to the checks performed, the route is ignored by R1. We can change this behavior using the ospf process command "capability vrf-lite", which disables the DN-bit check and allows the route to be installed in the routing table.

```
R1(config)#router ospf 100 vrf ALPHA
R1(config-router)#capability vrf-lite
R1(config-router)#router ospf 200 vrf BETA
R1(config-router)#capability vrf-lite
R1(config-router)#end

R2(config)#router ospf 100 vrf ALPHA
R2(config-router)#cap v
R2(config-router)#router ospf 200 vrf BETA
R2(config-router)#cap v
R2(config-router)#end
```

If we now look again at R1s routing table, we can see that the routes have been installed into the routing tables for the different VRFs, and we have reachability:

```
R1#sh ip route vrf ALPHA | beg Gate
Gateway of last resort is not set

      10.0.0.0/32 is subnetted, 2 subnets
C        10.10.20.1 is directly connected, Loopback0
O E2     10.20.20.1 [110/10] via 192.168.1.2, 00:00:02, Gi1/0.1
      172.16.0.0/24 is subnetted, 1 subnets
O E2     172.16.1.0 [110/10] via 192.168.1.2, 00:00:26, Gi1/0.1
      192.168.1.0/24 is variably subnetted, 2 subnets, 2 masks
```

```
C        192.168.1.0/24 is directly connected, GigabitEthernet1/0.1
L        192.168.1.1/32 is directly connected, GigabitEthernet1/0.1
R1#ping vrf ALPHA 10.20.20.1
Type escape sequence to abort.
Sending 5, 100-byte ICMP Echos to 10.20.20.1, timeout is 2 seconds:
!!!!!
Success rate is 100 percent (5/5)
R1#

R1#sh ip route vrf BETA | beg Gate
Gateway of last resort is not set

         10.0.0.0/32 is subnetted, 2 subnets
C           10.10.30.1 is directly connected, Loopback1
O E2        10.20.30.1 [110/10] via 192.168.2.2, 00:05:07, Gi1/0.2
         172.16.0.0/24 is subnetted, 1 subnets
O E2        172.16.2.0 [110/10] via 192.168.2.2, 00:05:16, Gi1/0.2
         192.168.2.0/24 is variably subnetted, 2 subnets, 2 masks
C           192.168.2.0/24 is directly connected, GigabitEthernet1/0.2
L           192.168.2.1/32 is directly connected, GigabitEthernet1/0.2
R1#ping vrf BETA 10.20.30.1
Type escape sequence to abort.
Sending 5, 100-byte ICMP Echos to 10.20.30.1, timeout is 2 seconds:
!!!!!
Success rate is 100 percent (5/5)
R1#ping vrf ALPHA 10.20.20.1 so lo0
Type escape sequence to abort.
Sending 5, 100-byte ICMP Echos to 10.20.20.1, timeout is 2 seconds:
Packet sent with a source address of 10.10.20.1
!!!!!
Success rate is 100 percent (5/5)
R1#ping vrf BETA 10.20.30.1 so lo1
Type escape sequence to abort.
Sending 5, 100-byte ICMP Echos to 10.20.30.1, timeout is 2 seconds:
Packet sent with a source address of 10.10.30.1
!!!!!
Success rate is 100 percent (5/5)
R1#
```

We will look again at VRF-lite when we discuss IPv6, but for the moment lets move on to layer 2 technologies.

12. MPLS and Layer 2

Up until now, we have concentrated on Layer 3 technologies such as VPNs and VRF-lite. MPLS can be used to extend the layer 2 network. There are a number of ways MPLS can operate at this level; through layer 2 tunnels (L2TPv3) which use pseudowires, Any Transport over MPLS (AToM), and by extension; Ethernet over MPLS (EoMPLS), Virtual Private LAN Services (VPLS), and Overlay Transport Virtualization (OTV).

From the CCIE syllabus the above fall into two categories, and actually we are only required to be able to describe them for the written exam, as they do not feature on the lab exam:

```
4.1.g Describe basic layer 2 VPN — wireline
4.1.g (i) L2TPv3 general principals
4.1.g (ii) ATOM general principals
4.1.h Describe basic L2VPN — LAN services
4.1.h (i) MPLS-VPLS general principals
4.1.h (ii) OTV general principals
```

Even though we only need to describe the general principles, we will actually go through some examples of the technologies. L2TPv3 and AToM can be tested out using native GNS3 routers, such as the 7200 series. VPLS and OTV are only fully available on higher end devices; so, regrettably, they are out of scope for this book.

There is a distinction between the technologies as they fall into one of two categories: wireline or LAN services. Wireline services provide point-to-point connections between two CE devices and are termed Virtual Private Wire Services (VPWS). LAN services emulate a LAN using a mesh of point-to-point pseudowires, creating a Virtual Private LAN Service (VPLS), or more recently using an IP overlay mechanism.

We will start with L2TPv3 and then have a look at AToM and EoMPLS, before discussing VPLS and OTV.

12.1 L2TPv3

Layer 2 Tunnel Protocol version 3 (L2TPv3) is an industry standard protocol and can transport any payload within the encapsulated packet. Although L2TPv3 does not require MPLS to function, we are going to look at it in respect to MPLS.

In the diagram below, we have a simple MPLS network. We have two provider routers sitting either side of R5. We also have two provider edge routers connecting to our customer routers. The customer routers will have IP addresses in the 192.168.1.0/24 range, with the goal is to make it appear as it they are directly connected.

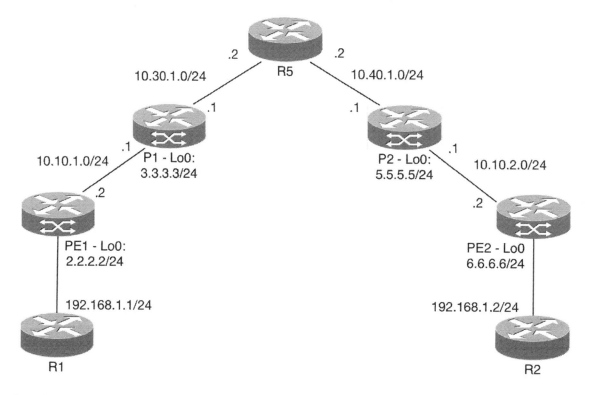

R5 will not be partaking in the MPLS network. This is so that we can explore the concept of LDP targeted discovery; the idea being that we can be selective as to which routers will run MPLS. For example, we can make P1 form an LDP adjacency directly with P2 while R5 just provides layer 3 connectivity for the MPLS enabled routers.

Starting with the configuration of R5, we start to build our EIGRP topology that will include all of our provider routers. As you can see, none of the interfaces on R5 are enabled for MPLS:

R5:

```
interface FastEthernet0/0
 description Link to P1
 ip address 10.30.1.2 255.255.255.0
 duplex auto
 speed auto
!
interface FastEthernet0/1
 description Link to P2
 ip address 10.40.1.2 255.255.255.0
 duplex auto
 speed auto
!
!
router eigrp 100
 network 10.30.1.0 0.0.0.255
 network 10.40.1.0 0.0.0.255
 no auto-summary
!
```

We then move on to P1, creating the required loopback interface for LDP to form adjacencies. Then we set up the interfaces and continue to expand our EIGRP AS:

P1:

```
interface Loopback0
 ip address 3.3.3.3 255.255.255.0
!
interface FastEthernet0/0
 description Link to PE1
 ip address 10.10.1.1 255.255.255.0
 duplex auto
 speed auto
 mpls ip
!
interface FastEthernet0/1
 description link to R5
 ip address 10.30.1.1 255.255.255.0
 duplex auto
 speed auto
 mpls ip
!
!
router eigrp 100
 network 3.3.3.0 0.0.0.255
```

```
  network 10.10.1.0 0.0.0.255
  network 10.30.1.0 0.0.0.255
  no auto-summary
```

Now, we need to add a couple of lines to specify whom our LDP neighbor will be. So far, we have just used directly connected neighbors, but here, as our neighbor (P2) is not directly connected, we need to specify that we are using targeted LDP along with the neighbor's ldp router-id.

```
P1(config)#mpls ldp router-id Loopback0 force
P1(config)#mpls ldp neigh 5.5.5.5 targeted ldp
P1(config)#mpls ldp discovery targeted-hello accept
P1(config)#
```

We use a targeted hello message in this instance. If the neighbor was directly connected, the router would send out LDP Hello messages, using UDP, to all the routers within the subnet. This is called an LDP Link Hello. Because our neighbor is more than one hop away, we need to send the same kind of message but this time as a unicast message destined for the specified router. This is the targeted hello.

P2:

P2's initial configuration is very similar to P1:

```
interface Loopback0
 ip address 5.5.5.5 255.255.255.0
!
interface FastEthernet0/0
 description link to R5
 ip address 10.40.1.1 255.255.255.0
 duplex auto
 speed auto
 mpls ip
!
interface FastEthernet0/1
 description link to PE2
 ip address 10.10.2.1 255.255.255.0
 duplex auto
 speed auto
 mpls ip
!
!
router eigrp 100
 network 5.5.5.0 0.0.0.255
 network 10.10.2.0 0.0.0.255
```

```
network 10.40.1.0 0.0.0.255
no auto-summary
```

Again, we need to perform the same steps as P1 and specify who our LDP neighbor will be:

```
P2(config)#mpls ldp router-id Loopback0 force
P2(config)#mpls ldp neigh 3.3.3.3 targeted ldp
*Mar  1 00:08:56.895: %LDP-5-NBRCHG: LDP Neighbor 3.3.3.3:0 (1) is UP
P2(config)#mpls ldp discovery targeted-hello accept
P2(config)#
```

We can then confirm that our LDP adjacency has formed. Indeed, as expected, it is showing as targeted:

```
P1#sh mpls ldp neigh
    Peer LDP Ident: 5.5.5.5:0; Local LDP Ident 3.3.3.3:0
        TCP connection: 5.5.5.5.11584 - 3.3.3.3.646
        State: Oper; Msgs sent/rcvd: 8/8; Downstream
        Up time: 00:01:34
        LDP discovery sources:
          Targeted Hello 3.3.3.3 -> 5.5.5.5, active, passive
        Addresses bound to peer LDP Ident:
          10.40.1.1       5.5.5.5
P1#
```

Jumping over to our customer routers, we are just going to specify an IP address. Both the routers will be in the same subnet:

```
R1(config)#int fa 0/0
R1(config-if)#ip add 192.168.1.1 255.255.255.0
R1(config-if)#no shut
R1(config-if)#desc Connection to PE1
R1(config-if)#

R2(config)#int fa 0/0
R2(config-if)#ip add 192.168.1.2 255.255.255.0
R2(config-if)#no shut
R2(config-if)#desc Connection to PE2
R2(config-if)#
```

Both PE1 and PE2 will have a basic initial configuration, setting the IP addresses, enabling the interface connecting to the provider routers for MPLS and expanding the EIGRP AS so that we send and receive the routes that we need:

PE1:

```
interface Loopback0
 ip address 2.2.2.2 255.255.255.0
!
interface FastEthernet0/0
 description Link to R1
 no ip address
 duplex auto
 speed auto
!
interface FastEthernet0/1
 description link to P1
 ip address 10.10.1.2 255.255.255.0
 duplex auto
 speed auto
 mpls ip
!
!
router eigrp 100
 network 2.2.2.0 0.0.0.255
 network 10.10.1.0 0.0.0.255
 no auto-summary
```

PE2:

```
interface Loopback0
 ip address 6.6.6.6 255.255.255.0
!
interface FastEthernet0/0
 description link to P2
 ip address 10.10.2.2 255.255.255.0
 duplex auto
 speed auto
 mpls ip
!
interface FastEthernet0/1
 description Link to R2
 no ip address
 duplex auto
 speed auto
!
router eigrp 100
 network 6.6.6.0 0.0.0.255
 network 10.10.2.0 0.0.0.255
 no auto-summary
```

Now we need to create our tunnel. To do this, we create a pseudowire class (which identifies the type of pseudowire), under global configuration, setting the encapsulation to Layer 2 tunneling protocol version 3 (l2tpv3) and setting the interface to be our loopback interface.

```
PE1(config)#pseudowire-class PW-CLASS
PE1(config-pw-class)#encapsulation l2tpv3
PE1(config-pw-class)#ip local interface lo0

PE2(config)#pseudowire-class PW-CLASS
PE2(config-pw-class)#encapsulation l2tpv3
PE2(config-pw-class)#ip local interface lo0
```

The local interface command set the IP address that the pseudowire will be listening on, or to term it another way, it would be our local endpoint.

We then go into the interface connecting our PE routers to the customer and create the tunnel, specifying the IP address of the other PE router, the virtual circuit ID (100) and the pseudowire class we created above:

```
PE1(config-pw-class)#int fa 0/0
PE1(config-if)#xconnect 6.6.6.6 100 pw-class PW-CLASS
PE1(config-if-xconn)#

PE2(config-pw-class)#int fa0/1
PE2(config-if)#xconnect 2.2.2.2 100 pw-class PW-CLASS
PE2#
```

We can then check that our tunnel is up:

```
PE1#sh l2tun tunnel all

L2TP Tunnel Information Total tunnels 1 sessions 1

Tunnel id 47358 is up, remote id is 15107, 1 active sessions
  Locally initiated tunnel
  Tunnel state is established, time since change 00:00:10
  Tunnel transport is IP (L2TP) (115)
  Remote tunnel name is PE2
    Internet Address 6.6.6.6, port 0
  Local tunnel name is PE1
    Internet Address 2.2.2.2, port 0
  L2TP class for tunnel is l2tp_default_class
  Counters, taking last clear into account:
    0 packets sent, 0 received
```

```
        0 bytes sent, 0 received
        Last clearing of counters never
      Counters, ignoring last clear:
        0 packets sent, 0 received
        0 bytes sent, 0 received
      Control Ns 5, Nr 4
      Local RWS 128 (default), Remote RWS 128 (max)
      Control channel Congestion Control is disabled
      Tunnel PMTU checking disabled
      Retransmission time 1, max 1 seconds
      Unsent queuesize 0, max 0
      Resend queuesize 0, max 2
      Total resends 0, ZLB ACKs sent 2
      Total peer authentication failures 0
      Current no session pak queue check 0 of 5
      Retransmit time distribution: 0 0 0 0 0 0 0 0 0
      Control message authentication is disabled
    PE1#
```

We can confirm that R1 has reachability to R2 and that ARP is working correctly, as well as R2 appearing to only be one hop away:

```
    R1#ping 192.168.1.2

    Type escape sequence to abort.
    Sending 5, 100-byte ICMP Echos to 192.168.1.2, timeout is 2 seconds:
    .!!!!
    Success rate is 80 percent (4/5)
    R1#sh cdp neigh | beg Device
    Device ID    Local Intrfce   Holdtme    Capability   Platform   Port ID
    PE1          Fas 0/0         157        R S I        3745       Fas 0/0
    R2           Fas 0/0         175        R S I        3745       Fas 0/0
    R1#sh arp
    Protocol   Address          Age (min)  Hardware Addr   Type   Interface
    Internet   192.168.1.1        -        c401.5c6c.0000  ARPA   Fa0/0
    Internet   192.168.1.2        1        c406.3540.0000  ARPA   Fa0/0
    R1#trace 192.168.1.2
    Type escape sequence to abort.
    Tracing the route to 192.168.1.2

      1 192.168.1.2 212 msec 208 msec *
    R1#
```

We can also look at the xconnect(s) that we have configured on our routers using the command "sh xconnect all"

```
PE1#sh xconnect all
  Legend: XC ST=Xconnect State, S1=Segment1 State, S2=Segment2 State
  UP=Up, DN=Down, AD=Admin Down, IA=Inactive, NH=No Hardware
  XC ST  Segment 1              S1 Segment 2                        S2
  ------+----------------------+--+-----------------------------+--
  UP     ac   Fa0/0(Ethernet)   UP l2tp 6.6.6.6:100                 UP
  PE1#

PE2#sh xconnect all
  Legend: XC ST=Xconnect State, S1=Segment1 State, S2=Segment2 State
  UP=Up, DN=Down, AD=Admin Down, IA=Inactive, NH=No Hardware
  XC ST  Segment 1              S1 Segment 2                        S2
  ------+----------------------+--+-----------------------------+--
  UP     ac   Fa0/1(Ethernet)   UP l2tp 2.2.2.2:100                 UP
  PE2#
```

L2TPv3 is very similar to AToM (and EoMPLS) in many respects; both use xconnects, and both carry layer 2 frames. The major difference is that AToM (specifically EoMPLS in the example we will look at) carries the layer 2 frames inside an MPLS packet, rather than an IPv4 packet.

12.2 AToM

AToM, which stands for Any Transport over MPLS, provides a way of setting up layer 2 circuits across the MPLS backbone. AToM can transport ATM, Ethernet, Frame Relay, PPP and HDLC traffic, hence being called "*Any Transport*". Ethernet over MPLS is very similar, yet as the name suggests transports Ethernet.

With a simplified topology to the one we previously used, we can set up an xconnect between PE1 and PE2 without the need for a pseudowire class. Instead, we define a virtual circuit ID and set the encapsulation to MPLS, using the interface command "xconnect <peer-id> <vc number> encapsulation mpls".

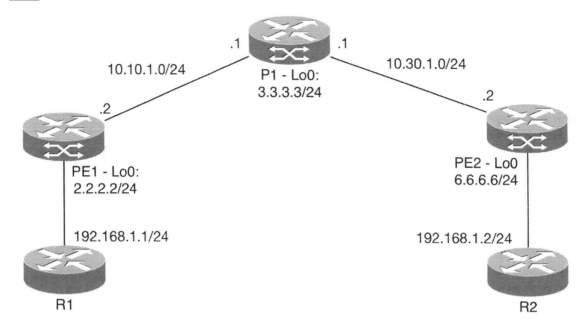

The difference between here, and when we used L2TPv3, is that we need to pay closer attention to how we are advertising our loopback interfaces. If we keep much the same configuration as before, with our loopbacks being advertised through EIGRP as a /24, we may not see our tunnels come up:

PE1:

```
interface Loopback0
 ip address 2.2.2.2 255.255.255.0
!
interface FastEthernet0/0
 description Link to R1
 no ip address
 duplex auto
 speed auto
 xconnect 6.6.6.6 100 encapsulation mpls
!
interface FastEthernet0/1
 description link to P1
 ip address 10.10.1.2 255.255.255.0
 duplex auto
 speed auto
 mpls ip
!
!
router eigrp 100
```

```
 network 2.2.2.0 0.0.0.255
 network 10.10.1.0 0.0.0.255
 no auto-summary
!
mpls ldp router-id Loopback0 force
```

P1:

```
interface Loopback0
 ip address 3.3.3.3 255.255.255.0
!
interface FastEthernet0/0
 description Link to PE1
 ip address 10.10.1.1 255.255.255.0
 duplex auto
 speed auto
 mpls ip
!
interface FastEthernet0/1
 description link to PE2
 ip address 10.30.1.1 255.255.255.0
 duplex auto
 speed auto
 mpls ip
!
!
router eigrp 100
 network 3.3.3.0 0.0.0.255
 network 10.10.1.0 0.0.0.255
 network 10.30.1.0 0.0.0.255
 no auto-summary
!
mpls ldp router-id Loopback0 force
```

PE2:

```
interface Loopback0
 ip address 6.6.6.6 255.255.255.0
!
interface FastEthernet0/0
 ip address 10.30.1.2 255.255.255.0
 duplex auto
 speed auto
 mpls ip
!
interface FastEthernet0/1
 description Link to R2
```

```
 no ip address
 duplex auto
 speed auto
 xconnect 2.2.2.2 100 encapsulation mpls
!
!
router eigrp 100
 network 6.6.6.0 0.0.0.255
 network 10.30.1.0 0.0.0.255
 no auto-summary
!
mpls ldp router-id Loopback0 force
```

If we look at the virtual circuit details, we can have different results. It may come up immediately, or it may not. Why do we have a potential for different results? If we look at the Cisco guide for Any Transport over MPLS for IOS 15.2S[3], then, we can see that under the restrictions we should use a /32 for our loopback interfaces:

"*Address format: Configure the Label Distribution Protocol (LDP) router ID on all PE routers to be a loopback address with a /32 mask. Otherwise, some configurations might not function properly.*"

The key here, is "might not". Your VC may be up, and working perfectly. Mileage can vary here. When I first tried this it failed. When Beau tried it, it worked, until he reloaded his routers and found that one side was up and the other was down. When I tried it again it worked straight away. However, we will continue with this example as it we have encountered an issue.

The details for VC 100 show that the output interface being "unknown", and the status is "down":

```
PE2#sh mpls l2transport vc 100 detail
Local interface: Fa0/1 up, line protocol up, Ethernet up
  Destination address: 2.2.2.2, VC ID: 100, VC status: down
    Output interface: unknown, imposed label stack {}
  Create time: 00:04:53, last status change time: 00:01:21
  Signaling protocol: LDP, peer 2.2.2.2:0 up
    MPLS VC labels: local 19, remote 19
    Group ID: local 0, remote 0
    MTU: local 1500, remote 1500
```

---

[3] http://www.cisco.com/en/US/docs/ios-xml/ios/mp_l2_vpns/configuration/15-2s/mp-any-transport.html#GUID-13EE58D4-75E3-4808-9AB6-D9996042723D

```
      Remote interface description: Link to R1
    Sequencing: receive disabled, send disabled
    VC statistics:
      packet totals: receive 0, send 0
      byte totals:   receive 0, send 0
      packet drops:  receive 0, seq error 0, send 24
```

The virtual circuit still shows as down on both sides:

```
PE2#sh mpls l2transport vc 100

Local intf   Local circuit         Dest address     VC ID      Status
------------ --------------------- ---------------- ---------- -------
Fa0/1        Ethernet              2.2.2.2          100        DOWN
PE2#sh mpls l2trans bind
  Destination Address: 2.2.2.2,  VC ID: 100
    Local Label: 19
        Cbit: 1,    VC Type: Ethernet,    GroupID: 0
        MTU: 1500,  Interface Desc: n/a
        VCCV: CC Type: CW [1], RA [2]
              CV Type: LSPV [2]
    Remote Label: 19
        Cbit: 1,    VC Type: Ethernet,    GroupID: 0
        MTU: 1500,  Interface Desc: Link to R1
        VCCV: CC Type: CW [1], RA [2]
              CV Type: LSPV [2]
PE2#
```

If we look closer at the LDP details, we can see that we have "no host route" to our peers:

```
PE2#sh mpls ldp disc
Local LDP Identifier:
    6.6.6.6:0
    Discovery Sources:
    Interfaces:
        FastEthernet0/0 (ldp): xmit/recv
            LDP Id: 3.3.3.3:0; no host route
    Targeted Hellos:
        6.6.6.6 -> 2.2.2.2 (ldp): active/passive, xmit/recv
            LDP Id: 2.2.2.2:0; no host route
PE2#
```

We have reachability, but this just proves that our underlying IGP is working.

```
PE2#ping 2.2.2.2 so lo0
```

```
Type escape sequence to abort.
Sending 5, 100-byte ICMP Echos to 2.2.2.2, timeout is 2 seconds:
Packet sent with a source address of 6.6.6.6
!!!!!
Success rate is 100 percent (5/5)
PE2#
```

Let us now follow Cisco at their word, and advertise our loopback interfaces as a /32, rather than a /24, which is actually a requirement of AToM. So, let's go ahead and change our set up by removing the IP addresses assigned to our loopbacks and the network currently advertised in EIGRP. We will change both to be a /32:

```
P1(config)#int lo0
P1(config-if)#no ip add
P1(config-if)#ip add 3.3.3.3 255.255.255.255
P1(config-if)#router eigrp 100
P1(config-router)#no net 3.3.3.0 0.0.0.255
P1(config-router)#net 3.3.3.3 0.0.0.0

PE1(config)#int lo0
PE1(config-if)#no ip add
PE1(config-if)#ip add 2.2.2.2 255.255.255.255
PE1(config-if)#router eigrp 100
PE1(config-router)#no net 2.2.2.0 0.0.0.255
PE1(config-router)#netw 2.2.2.2 0.0.0.0

PE2(config)#int lo0
PE2(config-if)#no ip add
PE2(config-if)#ip add 6.6.6.6 255.255.255.255
PE2(config-if)#router eigrp 100
PE2(config-router)#no network 6.6.6.0 0.0.0.255
PE2(config-router)#network 6.6.6.6 0.0.0.0
```

If we look again at the LDP discovery, we should see that we no longer have "no host route" messages, and our virtual circuit comes up:

```
PE2#sh mpls ldp disc
Local LDP Identifier:
    6.6.6.6:0
    Discovery Sources:
    Interfaces:
        FastEthernet0/0 (ldp): xmit/recv
            LDP Id: 3.3.3.3:0
    Targeted Hellos:
        6.6.6.6 -> 2.2.2.2 (ldp): active/passive, xmit/recv
            LDP Id: 2.2.2.2:0
```

```
PE2#
PE2#sh mpls l2transport vc 100

Local intf    Local circuit          Dest address     VC ID      Status
----------    -----------------      -------------    --------   -------
Fa0/1         Ethernet               2.2.2.2          100        UP
PE2# sh mpls l2transport vc 100 detail
Local interface: Fa0/1 up, line protocol up, Ethernet up
  Destination address: 2.2.2.2, VC ID: 100, VC status: up
    Next hop: 10.30.1.1
    Output interface: Fa0/0, imposed label stack {19 19}
  Create time: 00:38:24, last status change time: 00:13:23
  Signaling protocol: LDP, peer 2.2.2.2:0 up
    MPLS VC labels: local 19, remote 19
    Group ID: local 0, remote 0
    MTU: local 1500, remote 1500
    Remote interface description: Link to R1
  Sequencing: receive disabled, send disabled
  VC statistics:
    packet totals: receive 135, send 180
    byte totals:   receive 14741, send 18249
    packet drops:  receive 0, seq error 0, send 229

PE2#
```

R1 now sees R2 as a directly connected neighbor:

```
R1#trace 192.168.1.2

Type escape sequence to abort.
Tracing the route to 192.168.1.2

  1 192.168.1.2 164 msec 248 msec *
R1#sh cdp neigh | beg Device
Device ID    Local Intrfce    Holdtme    Capability    Platform    Port ID
PE1          Fas 0/0          151        R S I         3745        Fas 0/0
R2           Fas 0/0          120        R S I         3745        Fas 0/0
R1#
```

Before we move on to VPLS and OTV, we should briefly look at AToM tunnels and EoMPLS. We saw previously that we could create a tunnel between two end-points. What happens if we have two tunnels? Well, although this does bring us nicely into the subject of MPLS Traffic Engineering (MPLS-TE). MPLS-TE is a topic of concentration on the Service Provider track. Why, then, am I talking about overlapping between the two exams? Well, although MPLS-TE isn't on the exam, we do need to know about it in order to fully understand the tunnels component of the R&S exam.

The next example will be the least complex one we have come across yet, in terms of the number of devices to configure. Using just two routers, we will create an adjacency using the first link between them. Using a different physical link between the two, we will create a couple of tunnels using traffic engineering to set some preferences for how our xconnect between the two will connect.

Our topology for this is very simple; two routers with two gigabit ethernet interfaces connected to each other (R1 Gi 1/0 to R2 Gi 1/0 and Gi2/0 to Gi 2/0). The IOS does need to be quite recent:

```
R1#sh ver | i IOS
Cisco IOS Software, 7200 Software (C7200-ADVIPSERVICESK9-M), Version 15.2(4)S5, RELEASE SOFTWARE (fc1)
R1#
```

I found that the preferred-path command was not available in the 15.1 IOS release I tried.

The configurations are below. We start with R1 by defining our label protocol of LDP, and enabling traffic engineering for tunnels:

```
R1(config)#mpls label protocol ldp
R1(config)#mpls traffic-eng tunnels
```

Next, we start to create our pseudowire classes, called PW-class1 and PW-class2. We can use the command preferred-path to start engineering how our traffic will flow around the network. Preferred-path takes one of two options; interface or peer. We will use both options:

```
R1(config)#pseudowire-class PW-class1
R1(config-pw-class)#encapsulation mpls
R1(config-pw-class)#preferred-path interface Tunnel1
% Invalid tunnel interface
R1(config-pw-class)#
*Jul 29 20:52:40.387: %LINEPROTO-5-UPDOWN: Line protocol on Interface Tunnel1, changed state to down
R1(config-pw-class)#pseudowire-class PW-class2
R1(config-pw-class)#encapsulation mpls
R1(config-pw-class)#preferred-path peer 10.18.18.18
```

Note that, although we receive an error that the tunnel interface is invalid, the IOS will actually create the interface for us. Next we create our loopback interface that will be used to control our tunnels:

```
R1(config-pw-class)#int lo0
R1(config-if)#ip add 10.2.2.2 255.255.255.255
R1(config-if)#no ip directed-broadcast
```

Now we can create our tunnels, and here we start to encounter some traffic engineering commands. Firstly, we will start by borrowing the IP address from our loopback interface and setting the option "no ip directed broadcast", which disables directed broadcasts. For our tunnel we need to specify a destination, which is 10.16.16.16.

```
R1(config-if)#interface Tunnel1
R1(config-if)#ip unnumbered loopback 0
R1(config-if)#no ip directed-broadcast
R1(config-if)#tunnel destination 10.16.16.16
```

We need to enable the tunnel for MPLS-TE by setting the tunnel mode. We can also set priorities for setup and for hold. The setup priority (the first number) is used when signaling a label switch path for the tunnel. If there is an existing tunnel, it can be preempted. For the setup priority, which ranges from 0 to 7, a lower value is preferred. The second priority number is for the hold-priority. Again, a lower value is preferred, and 7 is the least preferred value. The hold priority is used once a tunnel is established. The next command sets the tunnel bandwidth. This can either be a fixed value for the interface in kbps (as we have here), or this can be set as a percentage using the command "tunnel mpls traffic-eng percent 80", which would set the maximum percentage of the link bandwidth that could be used by the tunnel.

```
R1(config-if)#tunnel mode mpls traffic-eng
R1(config-if)#tunnel mpls traffic-eng priority 7 7
R1(config-if)#tunnel mpls traffic-eng bandwidth 1500
```

The final command is to set the path options for our tunnel. Each path option is numbered, starting at 1, As shown in the configuration snippet below, each path can be setup dynamically, or explicitly, where we can fine-tune our paths around the network. This is why we have idea of "traffic engineering". For our example, we will set our first tunnel to be explicit and point it to an explicit path, which we will configure in a moment:

```
R1(config-if)#tunnel mpls traffic-eng path-option 1 ?
   dynamic   setup based on dynamically calculcated path
   explicit  setup based on preconfigured path
R1(config-if)#tunnel mpls traffic-eng path-option 1 explicit name
path-tunnel-1
```

Tunnel 2 is set up almost identically; although, we will use dynamic paths for the path-option:

```
R1(config-if)#interface tunnel 2
*Jul 29 21:01:55.923: %LINEPROTO-5-UPDOWN: Line protocol on Interface
Tunnel2, changed state to downlo0
R1(config-if)#ip unnumbered lo0
R1(config-if)#no ip directed-broadcast
R1(config-if)#tunnel destination 10.16.16.16
R1(config-if)#tunnel mode mpls traffic-eng
R1(config-if)#tunnel mpls traffic-eng pri 7 7
R1(config-if)#tunnel mpls traffic-eng bandwidth 1500
R1(config-if)#tunnel mpls traffic-eng path-option 1 dynamic
```

Because we are using Ethernet over MPLS here, which is a subcomponent of AToM, we need to use sub interfaces to pass our vlans over the tunnel. We can then create a virtual circuit using an xconnect and link that to our pseudowire-class, which we created a few moments ago:

```
R1(config-if)#int gi 1/0
R1(config-if)#no shut
R1(config-if)#int gi 1/0.1
R1(config-subif)#encapsulation dot1Q 500
R1(config-subif)#no ip directed-broadcast
R1(config-subif)#xconnect 10.16.16.16 100 pw-class PW-class1
R1(config-subif-xconn)#
*Jul 29 21:06:05.895: %LINEPROTO-5-UPDOWN: Line protocol on Interface
pseudowire0, changed state to up
```

Our second interface, gi 2/0, will be used for the core of our traffic. It will be used for LDP signaling; we will also enable it for MPLS TE tunnels and enable RSVP so that we may have some control over how much bandwidth we allocate to our tunnel. By default RSVP, is disabled and can be enabled by using the command "ip rsvp bandwidth". The numbers in the command are for the bandwidth reservation for the tunnel in kbps (up to 75% of the total bandwidth of the interface) and the second number is for a single flow limit in kbps. We will run OSPF between R1 and R2:

```
R1(config-subif-xconn)#int gi 2/0
R1(config-if)#no shut
*Jul 29 21:06:59.991: %LINK-3-UPDOWN: Interface GigabitEthernet2/0,
changed state to up
*Jul 29 21:07:00.991: %LINEPROTO-5-UPDOWN: Line protocol on Interface
GigabitEthernet2/0, changed state to up
R1(config-if)#ip add 10.0.0.1 255.255.255.0
R1(config-if)#mpls ip
R1(config-if)#mpls traffic-eng tunnels
R1(config-if)#ip rsvp bandwidth 15000 15000
R1(config-if)#exit
R1(config)#router ospf 1
```

```
R1(config-router)#network 10.0.0.0 0.0.0.255 area 0
R1(config-router)#network 10.2.2.2 0.0.0.0 area 0
```

MPLS tunnels need an IP address, so we will again use that of loopback 0. Finally, we state that we want to use traffic-engineering for OSPF area 0:

```
R1(config-router)#mpls traffic-eng router-id lo0
R1(config-router)#mpls traffic-eng area 0
```

We are very nearly finished with R1. The last couple of commands we need to do is to set a route up to explicitly use tunnel 2 for and to create the explicit path we are using for tunnel 1. Our explicit path will just have the outgoing interface on it, which is Gi 2/0. However, in a longer path, we would reference the LDP router-id of each hop:

```
R1(config-router)#ip route 10.18.18.18 255.255.255.255 tunnel 2
R1(config)#ip explicit-path name path-tunnel-1 enable
R1(cfg-ip-expl-path)#next-address 10.0.0.1
Explicit Path name path-tunnel-1:
    1: next-address 10.0.0.1
R1(config-if)#
*Jul 29 21:23:22.463: %LINEPROTO-5-UPDOWN: Line protocol on Interface Tunnel1, changed state to up
*Jul 29 21:23:22.543: %LINEPROTO-5-UPDOWN: Line protocol on Interface Tunnel2, changed state to up
```

With R1's tunnels up, we can move on to R2. I have removed all the line protocol messages to make it easier to read, but the steps are very much the same just simplified:

```
R2(config)#mpls label proto ldp
R2(config)#mpls traffic-eng tunnels
R2(config)#mpls ldp router-id lo0
R2(config)#int lo0
R2(config-if)#ip add 10.16.16.16 255.255.255.255
R2(config-if)#no ip directed-broadcast
R2(config-if)#int lo1
R2(config-if)#ip add 10.18.18.18 255.255.255.255
R2(config-if)#no ip directed-broadcast
R2(config-if)#int gi 1/0
R2(config-if)#no shut
R2(config-if)#int gi 1/0.1
R2(config-subif)#encapsulation dot1Q 500
R2(config-subif)#no ip directed-broadcast
R2(config-subif)#no cdp enable
R2(config-subif)#xconnect 10.2.2.2 100 pw-class PW-class1
Please make sure pw-class PW-class1 is configured
```

```
Please make sure pw-class PW-class1 is configured and valid [Unknown
pseudo-wire class name]
R2(config-subif)#
R2(config-subif)#pseudowire-class PW-class1
R2(config-pw-class)#encapsulation mpls
R2(config-pw-class)#int gi 2/0
R2(config-if)#ip add 10.0.0.2 255.255.255.0
R2(config-if)#no shut
R2(config-if)#mpls traffic-eng tunnels
R2(config-if)#mpls ip
R2(config-if)#ip rsvp bandwidth 15000 15000
R2(config-if)#router ospf 1
R2(config-router)#network 10.0.0.0 0.0.0.255 area 0
R2(config-router)#network 10.16.16.16 0.0.0.0 area 0
R2(config-router)#mpls traffic-eng router-id lo0
R2(config-router)#mpls traffic-eng area 0
R2(config-router)#end
```

All our tunnels and virtual circuits should be up now, and we can make sure that R1 has access to 10.18.18.18 through its secondary tunnel:

```
R1#sh ip route | beg Gate
Gateway of last resort is not set

      10.0.0.0/8 is variably subnetted, 5 subnets, 2 masks
C        10.0.0.0/24 is directly connected, GigabitEthernet2/0
L        10.0.0.1/32 is directly connected, GigabitEthernet2/0
C        10.2.2.2/32 is directly connected, Loopback0
O        10.16.16.16/32 [110/2] via 10.0.0.2, 00:37:09, Gi2/0
S        10.18.18.18/32 is directly connected, Tunnel2
R1#ping 10.18.18.18
Type escape sequence to abort.
Sending 5, 100-byte ICMP Echos to 10.18.18.18, timeout is 2 seconds:
!!!!!
Success rate is 100 percent (5/5)
R1#
```

We can also check that our virtual circuit is up and using the preferred path across tunnel 1:

```
R1#sh mpls l2transport vc 100

Local intf     Local circuit        Dest address      VC ID    Status
----------     -----------------    --------------    -------  ---------
Gi1/0.1        Eth VLAN 500         10.16.16.16       100      UP
```

```
R1#sh mpls l2transport vc 100 detail
Local interface: Gi1/0.1 up, line protocol up, Eth VLAN 500 up
  Destination address: 10.16.16.16, VC ID: 100, VC status: up
    Output interface: Tu1, imposed label stack {16}
    Preferred path: Tunnel1,  active
    Default path: disabled
    Next hop: point2point
  Create time: 00:51:58, last status change time: 00:19:22
    Last label FSM state change time: 00:35:31
  Signaling protocol: LDP, peer 10.16.16.16:0 up
    Targeted Hello: 10.2.2.2(LDP Id) -> 10.16.16.16, LDP is UP
    Status TLV support (local/remote)   : enabled/supported
      LDP route watch                   : enabled
      Label/status state machine        : established, LruRru
      Last local dataplane   status rcvd: No fault
      Last BFD dataplane     status rcvd: Not sent
      Last BFD peer monitor  status rcvd: No fault
      Last local AC  circuit status rcvd: No fault
      Last local AC  circuit status sent: No fault
      Last local PW i/f circ status rcvd: No fault
      Last local LDP TLV     status sent: No fault
      Last remote LDP TLV    status rcvd: No fault
      Last remote LDP ADJ    status rcvd: No fault
    MPLS VC labels: local 16, remote 16
    Group ID: local 0, remote 0
    MTU: local 1500, remote 1500
    Remote interface description:
  Sequencing: receive disabled, send disabled
  Control Word: On (configured: autosense)
  Dataplane:
    SSM segment/switch IDs: 4100/4096 (used), PWID: 1
  VC statistics:
    transit packet totals: receive 0, send 0
    transit byte totals:   receive 0, send 0
    transit packet drops:  receive 0, seq error 0, send 0

R1#
```

So what happens when tunnel 1 goes down? Remember this is an explicit path, so in the event that one of our LDP hops goes down the tunnel will collapse. We can simulate this by shutting down the tunnel 1 interface:

```
R1(config)#int tunnel 1
R1(config-if)#shut
R1(config-if)#end
R1#
```

```
*Jul 27 09:21:14.127: %SYS-5-CONFIG_I: Configured from console by
console
R1#
*Jul 27 09:21:14.939: %LINEPROTO-5-UPDOWN: Line protocol on Interface
Tunnel1, changed state to down
*Jul 27 09:21:14.943: %LINK-5-CHANGED: Interface Tunnel1, changed
state to administratively down
R1#sh mpls l2transport vc detail
Local interface: Gi1/0.1 up, line protocol up, Eth VLAN 500 up
  Destination address: 10.16.16.16, VC ID: 100, VC status: up
    Output interface: Gi2/0, imposed label stack {16}
    Preferred path: Tunnel1,  no route
    Default path: active
    Next hop: 10.0.0.2
  Create time: 00:00:45, last status change time: 00:00:45
    Last label FSM state change time: 00:00:45
  Signaling protocol: LDP, peer 10.16.16.16:0 up
    Targeted Hello: 10.2.2.2(LDP Id) -> 10.16.16.16, LDP is UP
    Status TLV support (local/remote)   : enabled/supported
     LDP route watch                    : enabled
     Label/status state machine         : established, LruRru
     Last local dataplane   status rcvd: No fault
     Last BFD dataplane     status rcvd: Not sent
     Last BFD peer monitor  status rcvd: No fault
     Last local AC  circuit status rcvd: No fault
     Last local AC  circuit status sent: No fault
     Last local PW i/f circ status rcvd: No fault
     Last local LDP TLV     status sent: No fault
     Last remote LDP TLV    status rcvd: No fault
     Last remote LDP ADJ    status rcvd: No fault
    MPLS VC labels: local 19, remote 16

R1#
```

We can see that the VC will now take any available path and stays up in the event that the tunnel 1 interface is down. If we turn the tunnel interface back up, our VC switches back over to the preferred tunnel.

```
R1(config)#int tunnel 1
R1(config-if)#no shut
R1(config-if)#
*Jul 27 09:25:29.283: %LINEPROTO-5-UPDOWN: Line protocol on Interface
Tunnel1, changed state to up
R1(config-if)#
R1(config-if)#end
R1#sh mpls l2transport vc detail
Local interface: Gi1/0.1 up, line protocol up, Eth VLAN 500 up
```

```
      Destination address: 10.16.16.16, VC ID: 100, VC status: up
        Output interface: Tu1, imposed label stack {16}
        Preferred path: Tunnel1,  active
        Default path: ready
        Next hop: point2point
      Create time: 00:04:56, last status change time: 00:04:55
        Last label FSM state change time: 00:04:55
      Signaling protocol: LDP, peer 10.16.16.16:0 up
        Targeted Hello: 10.2.2.2(LDP Id) -> 10.16.16.16, LDP is UP
        Status TLV support (local/remote)   : enabled/supported
          LDP route watch                   : enabled
          Label/status state machine        : established, LruRru
          Last local dataplane   status rcvd: No fault
          Last BFD dataplane     status rcvd: Not sent
          Last BFD peer monitor  status rcvd: No fault
          Last local AC  circuit status rcvd: No fault
          Last local AC  circuit status sent: No fault
          Last local PW i/f circ status rcvd: No fault
          Last local LDP TLV     status sent: No fault
          Last remote LDP TLV    status rcvd: No fault
          Last remote LDP ADJ    status rcvd: No fault
        MPLS VC labels: local 19, remote 16
        Group ID: local 0, remote 0
        MTU: local 1500, remote 1500
        Remote interface description:
      Sequencing: receive disabled, send disabled
      Control Word: On (configured: autosense)
      Dataplane:
        SSM segment/switch IDs: 4100/4099 (used), PWID: 1
      VC statistics:
        transit packet totals: receive 0, send 0
        transit byte totals:   receive 0, send 0
        transit packet drops:  receive 0, seq error 0, send 0
```

Assume for a moment though that in the event that tunnel 1 goes down, we want the VC to remain down. Well, we can achieve this by using the option "disable-fallback" on the preferred path command:

```
R1(config)#pseudowire-class PW-class1
R1(config-pw-class)#preferred-path interface tunnel 1 disable-fallback
R1(config-pw-class)#end
R1#conf t
R1(config)#int tunnel 1
R1(config-if)#shut
R1(config-if)#
*Jul 27 09:27:20.695: %LINEPROTO-5-UPDOWN: Line protocol on Interface Tunnel1, changed state to down
```

```
*Jul 27 09:27:20.699: %LINK-5-CHANGED: Interface Tunnel1, changed
state to administratively down
R1(config-if)#
R1(config-if)#end
R1#
*Jul 27 09:27:23.847: %SYS-5-CONFIG_I: Configured from console by
console
R1#
R1#sh mpls l2transport vc detail
Local interface: Gi1/0.1 up, line protocol up, Eth VLAN 500 up
  Destination address: 10.16.16.16, VC ID: 100, VC status: down
    Last error: MPLS dataplane reported a fault to the nexthop
    Output interface: none, imposed label stack {}
    Preferred path: Tunnel1,  no route
    Default path: disabled
    No adjacency
  Create time: 00:03:15, last status change time: 00:03:15
    Last label FSM state change time: 00:02:49
  Signaling protocol: LDP, peer 10.16.16.16:0 up
    Targeted Hello: 10.2.2.2(LDP Id) -> 10.16.16.16, LDP is UP
    Status TLV support (local/remote)   : enabled/supported
      LDP route watch                   : enabled
      Label/status state machine        : activating, LruRruD
      Last local dataplane   status rcvd: DOWN(pw-tx-fault)
      Last BFD dataplane     status rcvd: Not sent
      Last BFD peer monitor  status rcvd: No fault
      Last local AC  circuit status rcvd: No fault
      Last local AC  circuit status sent: DOWN(pw-rx-fault)
      Last local PW i/f circ status rcvd: No fault
      Last local LDP TLV     status sent: DOWN(pw-tx-fault)
      Last remote LDP TLV    status rcvd: No fault
      Last remote LDP ADJ    status rcvd: No fault
  MPLS VC labels: local 16, remote 16
  Group ID: local 0, remote 0
  MTU: local 1500, remote 1500
  Remote interface description:
  Sequencing: receive disabled, send disabled
  Control Word: On (configured: autosense)
  Dataplane:
    SSM segment/switch IDs: 4103/4102 (used), PWID: 1
  VC statistics:
    transit packet totals: receive 0, send 0
    transit byte totals:   receive 0, send 0
    transit packet drops:  receive 0, seq error 0, send 0

R1#
```

Before we leave AToM and move on to VPLS and OTV, we should briefly look at the control word. The control word, as we can see above sitting between "Sequencing:" and "Dataplane:", is a feature of pseudowires. It is optional in most layer 2 protocols but required for Frame Relay (and ATM AAL5). In AToM, the control word sits between the VC label and the layer 2 frame. The purpose of the control word is to carry protocol control information and sequence numbers. Enabling the control word is very simple. (It is required to have the pseudowire class encapsulation set to MPLS, this has already been done in the previous configurations):

```
R1(config)#pseudowire-class PW-class1
R1(config-pw-class)#control-word
R1(config-pw-class)#exit
```

Then, we can see it in the packet as a C-bit. Within the Pseudowire FEC TLV (where TLV stands for type-length-value) is the virtual Circuit ID and the VC type (Ethernet VLAN).

```
▽ Notification Message
      0... .... = U bit: Unknown bit not set
      Message Type: Notification Message (0x1)
      Message Length: 42
      Message ID: 0x00000023
   ▷ Status TLV
   ▷ PW Status TLV
   ▽ Forwarding Equivalence Classes TLV
      00.. .... = TLV Unknown bits: Known TLV, do not Forward (0x00)
      TLV Type: Forwarding Equivalence Classes TLV (0x100)
      TLV Length: 12
      ▽ FEC Elements
         ▽ FEC Element 1 VCID: 100
            FEC Element Type: Virtual Circuit FEC (128)
            1... .... = C-bit: Control Word Present
            .000 0000 0000 0100 = VC Type: Ethernet VLAN (0x0004)
            VC Info Length: 4
            Group ID: 0
            VC ID: 100
```

12.3 VPLS and OTV

Despite being two very different technologies, in many ways it is easier to discuss VPLS and OTV together. Again, it is important to stress that the CCIE (v5) exam only requires basic knowledge of VPLS and OTV, but it does not require actual lab configuration.

We have seen that we can use xconnect technology in L2TPv3 and AToM to provide layer 2 VPNs. We have configured these during the last couple of examples. VPLS is the carrier grade version of these and is available on higher end devices only. These include the XR 12000 series, 7600 series, and ME3600 series for IOS; ASR 1000 series for IOS XE; ASR 9000 for IOS XR; and the Nexus 7000 range for NX-OS. OTV is supported on the Nexus 7000 range and the ASR 1000, which regrettably limits the ability to practice these technologies. Therefore, we will just look at the technologies and the differences between them.

VPLS provides point-to-multipoint and multipoint-to-multipoint sites with a way to join their Ethernet-based LANs together to form an extended LAN through the service provider's network. Again, we use the concept of virtual circuits for which VPLS simulates a virtual bridge providing the connectivity.

OTV, or Overlay Transport Virtualization, is similar to VPLS, in that it is designed to carry layer 2 networks. However, it does have a number of differences. Whereas VPLS had a more organic growth, with extensions being created over the years to add the features needed that were not in the original specification, OTV was designed from the ground up to address the issues found in VPLS.

VPLS requires a full mesh in order to work but loses a degree of autonomy on each site in the mesh. VPLS will flood MAC address reachability information, and fully supports MAC address aging, whereas OTV will carry MAC address reachability in a control protocol. Therefore, unknown unicast traffic does not need to travel over the overlay, meaning that flooding can be limited to a single site.

Along with suppressing flooding, ARP storms will also not travel across an overlay, whereas VPLS does not have an ability to control this traffic. VPLS does cope well with suppressing STP and VTP but cannot suppress HSRP, VRRP or GBLP messages, and it will, very happily, replicate both broadcast and multicast traffic. If you have followed my blog about the battles I had with a QinQ link[4], then you'll know that keeping HSRP traffic localized to a site is very important. Thankfully OTV will prevent such traffic propagating between sites.

VPLS is dependent on some form of label-switching protocol to function, such as MPLS or GRE. OTV, on the other hand, will work over any transport that can forward an IP packet. In order to have multihoming, VPLS requires additional protocols, such as BGP or VSS (Virtual Switching System); whereas OTV includes the ability to multi-home within the control protocol. OTV uses native IP multicast and can load balance. VPLS uses a mesh

---

[4] http://www.802101.com/2013/10/fun-with-qinq-tunnels-part-3-why-hsrp.html

of point-to-multipoint tunnels and cannot perform per-flow load balancing (unless using VSS).

Designed to include between 40 and 60 devices, VPLS is far less scalable than OTV. Though running Hierarchical VPLS (H-VPLS) can lend itself to support more devices, it does require EoMPLS or a QinQ link. BGP signaling in VPLS (RFC 4761) does alleviate some of those issues. OTV, however, was designed to scale to the hundreds of devices, without adding the extra complexity of additional routing protocols. (As stated OTV will run across any network if there is end-to-end IP reachability).

When it comes to VLANs, VPLS carries a single VLAN per VPLS instance, unless using QinQ which means a lot more CLI configuration than with OTV. OTV, on the other hand, can carry multiple VLANs across a single overlay. Whilst we are on the subject of CLI complexity, OTV is actually a very automated process. The configuration of OTV is often referred to as "single-touch." The edge device is configured at the new data centre and will automatically establish OTV connections to the other data centres in the same overlay domain.

It is a shame that we cannot look at VPLS and OTV, especially as OTV is such an exciting technology, which is bound to be popular in the coming years, if the hardware range supporting it grows. Instead, let us turn to look at something else that will be more popular in the coming years that we can actually configure; IPv6.

13. IPv6 over MPLS

IPv6 is supported by MPLS but still requires an IPv4 core; as LDP is still only IPv4 compatible, although there is a draft out there for an IPv6 supporting version. We can use IPv6 in two ways: either with the customer focus that we are used to, called 6VPE, or as a method of transporting IPv6 global addresses over an MPLS cloud, called 6PE.

13.1 6VPE

Let's return to our main topology.

The Blue company has decided to embrace IPv6 in a big way, taking the very brave and audacious decision that they want only IPv6 connections into your provider network. Thankfully, moving to IPv6 is not a major task. In fact, nothing in the core of the network actually needs to change. MP-BGP will happily carry IPv6 traffic without needing any major work. If you have read the first volume of this series, you'll already be aware of how easy it is to set up IPv6 and BGP. In this scenario, this is referred to as "6VPE" or IPv6 VPN over MPLS.

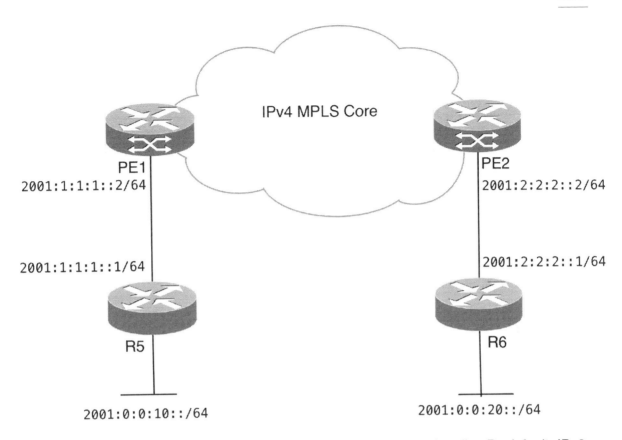

The first steps are to enable a couple of items for basic IPv6 functionality. By default, IPv6 is disabled, so we need to enable it using the following:

    R5(config)#ipv6 unicast-routing

    PE1(config)#ipv6 unicast-routing

    PE2(config)#ipv6 unicast-routing

    R6(config)#ipv6 unicast-routing

Next, we need to set up a couple of things on our PE devices. These are the basic things we need for our MPLS labels to work and a method for them to cross between the PE devices.

Recall from earlier that CEF is a requirement for MPLS. Well, IPv6 has a CEF equivalent; the command for which is "ipv6 cef":

    PE1(config)#ipv6 cef

```
PE2(config)#ipv6 cef
```

The second requirement is the transport between PE1 and PE2. For IPv4, this is through a vpn address family (address-family vpnv4), and for IPv6 it is no different. First, however, we must change the default behavior of BGP, which is to be IPv4 only. After which, we can create our VPNv6 address family, which will carry the customer VPN traffic between PE1 and PE2:

```
PE1(config)#router bgp 100
PE1(config-router)#no bgp default ipv4-unicast
PE1(config-router)#address-family vpnv6

PE2(config)#router bgp 100
PE2(config-router)#no bgp default ipv4-unicast
PE2(config-router)#address-family vpnv6
```

Once we have created our address family, we need to specify our neighbors. This is in the same way we have done previously. Note that we do not need to make these neighbors IPv6 neighbors, as IPv4 will be the medium that carries our IPv6 VPN traffic:

```
PE1(config-router-af)#neigh 10.250.4.1 activate
PE1(config-router-af)#neighbor 10.250.4.1 send-community extended

PE2(config-router-af)#neigh 10.250.3.1 activate
PE2(config-router-af)#neighbor 10.250.3.1 send-community extended
```

With this in place, lets get started with some basic connectivity between our CE and PE devices:

```
R5(config-router-af)#int lo0
R5(config-if)#no ip add
R5(config-if)#ipv6 add 2001:0:0:10::1/64
R5(config-if)#int gi 1/0
R5(config-if)#no ip add
R5(config-if)#ipv6 add 2001:1:1:1::1/64
R5(config-if)#no shut

R6(config-router-af)#int lo0
R6(config-if)#no ip add
R6(config-if)#ipv6 add 2001:0:0:20::1/64
R6(config)#int gi 1/0
R6(config-if)#no ip add
R6(config-if)#ipv6 add 2001:2:2:2::1/64
R6(config-if)#no shut
```

We have a couple of networks, which will be the loopback interfaces we have created. Interface Gi1/0 is the interface that will connect us to the MPLS network.

On the PE side, we need to assign an IPv6 address to our connecting interfaces (GI 4/0) and assign these (as we have done previously) to a VRF. We have seen that the default behavior in IOS is to remove all IPv4 addresses on an interface once that interface is assigned to a VRF. This is still the case wit IPv6, so it makes sense for us to create our IPv6 VRFs first.

Note that I have said IPv6 VRF. The commands for VRF creation in IPv6 are slightly different. We create a "vrf definition", which allows us to assign the route distinguisher and the route targets as we usually do, but the route targets are placed under an IPv6 address family:

```
PE1(config-router-af)#vrf definition BLUE2
PE1(config-vrf)#rd 100:6
PE1(config-vrf)#address-family ipv6
PE1(config-vrf-af)#route-target both 100:6

PE2(config-router-af)#vrf definition BLUE2
PE2(config-vrf)#rd 100:6
PE2(config-vrf)#address-family ipv6
PE2(config-vrf-af)#route-target both 100:6
```

We can actually always use the definition method. We can use it to create an IPv4 address family as well, instead of using the "ip vrf <vrf name>" command. Now, we can assign the interfaces to our IPv6 VRFs and add the IPv6 addresses:

```
PE1(config-vrf-af)#int gi 4/0
PE1(config-if)#vrf forwarding BLUE2
% Interface GigabitEthernet4/0 IPv6 disabled and address(es) removed
due to disabling VRF BLUE2
PE1(config-if)#
PE1(config-if)#ipv6 address 2001:1:1:1::2/64

PE2(config-vrf-af)#int gi 4/0
PE2(config-if)#vrf forwarding BLUE2
% Interface GigabitEthernet4/0 IPv6 disabled and address(es) removed
due to disabling VRF BLUE2
PE2(config-if)#
PE2(config-if)#ipv6 address 2001:2:2:2::2/64
```

We should now be able to ping from our CE devices to our PE devices:

```
R5(config-if)#do ping 2001:1:1:1::2
Type escape sequence to abort.
Sending 5, 100-byte ICMP Echos to 2001:1:1:1::2, timeout is 2
seconds:
!!!!!
Success rate is 100 percent (5/5)
R5(config-if)#exit

R6(config-if)#do ping 2001:2:2:2::2
Type escape sequence to abort.
Sending 5, 100-byte ICMP Echos to 2001:2:2:2::2, timeout is 2
seconds:
!!!!!
Success rate is 100 percent (5/5)
R6(config-if)#exit
```

For our customer connections, we don't actually have much in the way of options really. We are limited to a routing protocol that is VRF aware, which means either static routing, eBGP, or EIGRP, as these are all VRF aware.

So, let's push ahead and set up some eBGP peering between our CE and PE devices. To make life easier, we will use different AS numbers on R5 and on R6. This way we do not need to use "allow-as in" to overcome the issue with duplicate AS numbering:

```
PE1(config-if)#router bgp 100
PE1(config-router)#address-family ipv6 vrf BLUE2
PE1(config-router-af)#neigh 2001:1:1:1::1 remote-as 65530
PE1(config-router-af)#neigh 2001:1:1:1::1 activate

R5(config)#router bgp 65530
R5(config-router)#no bgp default ipv4-unicast
R5(config-router)#neigh 2001:1:1:1::2 remote-as 100
R5(config-router)#address-family ipv6
R5(config-router-af)#neigh 2001:1:1:1::2 activate
R5(config-router-af)#network 2001:0:0:10::/64
R5(config-router-af)#end
R5#
*Jul 26 10:35:00.939: %BGP-5-ADJCHANGE: neighbor 2001:1:1:1::2 Up

R6(config)#router bgp 65531
R6(config-router)#no bgp default ipv4-unicast
R6(config-router)#neigh 2001:2:2:2::2 remote-as 100
R6(config-router)#address-family ipv6
R6(config-router-af)#neigh 2001:2:2:2::2 activate
R6(config-router-af)#network 2001:0:0:20::/64
```

```
PE2(config-if)#router bgp 100
PE2(config-router)#address-family ipv6 vrf BLUE2
PE2(config-router-af)#neigh 2001:2:2:2::1 remote-as 65531
PE2(config-router-af)#neigh 2001:2:2:2::1 activate
*Jul 26 10:53:28.591: %BGP-5-ADJCHANGE: neighbor 2001:2:2:2::1 vpn
vrf BLUE2 Up
PE2(config-router-af)#
```

We can check that our PE to CE peerings are fully up using the command "sh ip bgp ipv6 unicast neighbors". From R5, we can see a peering to PE1, and from PE1, we can see a peering with PE2:

```
R5#sh ip bgp ipv6 unicast neighbors
BGP neighbor is 2001:1:1:1::2,  remote AS 100, external link
  BGP version 4, remote router ID 10.250.3.1
  BGP state = Established, up for 00:01:37

PE1#sh bgp vpnv6 unicast all neighbors
BGP neighbor is 10.250.4.1,  remote AS 100, internal link
  BGP version 4, remote router ID 10.250.4.1
  BGP state = Established, up for 01:00:38
```

If all is well and working as hoped, R5 and R6 should see the networks advertised by each other in their ipv6 routing table and have reachability from loopback to loopback:

```
R6#sh ipv6 route | sec e Codes
IPv6 Routing Table - default - 6 entries
B   2001:0:0:10::/64 [20/0]
     via FE80::C80C:4FF:FE1D:70, GigabitEthernet1/0
C   2001:0:0:20::/64 [0/0]
     via Loopback0, directly connected
L   2001:0:0:20::1/128 [0/0]
     via Loopback0, receive
C   2001:2:2:2::/64 [0/0]
     via GigabitEthernet1/0, directly connected
L   2001:2:2:2::1/128 [0/0]
     via GigabitEthernet1/0, receive
L   FF00::/8 [0/0]
     via Null0, receive
R6#ping ipv6 2001:0:0:10::1 so lo0
Type escape sequence to abort.
Sending 5, 100-byte ICMP Echos to 2001:0:0:10::1, timeout is 2
seconds:
Packet sent with a source address of 2001:0:0:20::1
!!!!!
```

```
Success rate is 100 percent (5/5)
R6#

R5#sh ipv6 route bgp | sec e Codes
IPv6 Routing Table - default - 6 entries
B   2001:0:0:20::/64 [20/0]
     via FE80::C80B:4FF:FE1D:70, GigabitEthernet1/0
R5#ping ipv6 2001:0:0:20::1 so lo0
Type escape sequence to abort.
Sending 5, 100-byte ICMP Echos to 2001:0:0:20::1, timeout is 2 seconds:
Packet sent with a source address of 2001:0:0:10::1
!!!!!
Success rate is 100 percent (5/5)
R5#
```

If we look at the VPNv6 routing table, we can see something interesting:

```
PE1#sh bgp vpnv6 unicast all | beg Network
   Network          Next Hop        Metric LocPrf Weight Path
Route Distinguisher: 100:6 (default for vrf BLUE2)
*> 2001:0:0:10::/64 2001:1:1:1::1        0             0 65530 i
*>i2001:0:0:20::/64 ::FFFF:10.250.4.1    0    100      0 65531 i
PE1#
```

The IPv6 VPN next hop has been "faked" by the PE1 router. There is no IPv6 running between PE1 and PE2, and the next hop for an IPv6 VPN address family must be an IPv6 address. Remember that this is a pure IPv4 MPLS core network; therefore, PE1 creates a fake address for PE2. It takes the remote router id and adds ::FFFF: to the beginning, so that the next hop becomes ::FFFF:10.250.4.1. Obviously, the next hop for R5 does not need to change anyway, and R5 does not need to change the next hop for PE1:

```
R5#sh bgp ipv6 unicast | beg Network
   Network          Next Hop        Metric LocPrf Weight Path
*> 2001:0:0:10::/64 ::                   0         32768 i
*> 2001:0:0:20::/64 2001:1:1:1::2                      0 100 65531 i
R5#
```

So, here we can see how an MPLS network overcomes the lack of IPv6 internal routing to transport IPv6 across a purely IPv4 core. As you can see, there is very little we need to do to transport IPv6 across our core network; MP-BGP looks after it. We just need to open it up to the IPv6 traffic, as well as ensuring basic connectivity and making sure we are using an appropriate (IPv6) VRF.

Essentially, there is little difference between an IPv4 VRF and an IPv6 VRF. Both do the same function, albeit with a slightly different syntax. We can use the same commands to look at our IPv4 VRFs as we do our IPv6 VRFs:

```
PE1#sh vrf
  Name                    Default RD           Protocols      Interfaces
  BLUE                    100:3                ipv4           Lo5
  BLUE2                   100:6                ipv6           Gi4/0
  INTERNET                100:200              ipv4           Gi6/0
  RED                     100:1                ipv4           Gi2/0
  WHITE                   100:2                ipv4           Gi3/0
PE1#
```

If we look at the detail for our BLUE2 VRF, we can see that the same command would work on an IPv4 VRF, as both address families are reported within the same output:

```
PE1#sh vrf detail BLUE2
VRF BLUE2 (VRF Id = 6); default RD 100:6; default VPNID <not set>
  Interfaces:
    Gi4/0
Address family ipv4 not active
Address family ipv6 (Table ID = 503316482 (0x1E000002)):
  Export VPN route-target communities
    RT:100:6
  Import VPN route-target communities
    RT:100:6
  No import route-map
  No export route-map
  VRF label distribution protocol: not configured
  VRF label allocation mode: per-prefix

PE1#
```

13.2 6PE

In a simplified environment, we can run 6PE. 6PE achieves the same goals, namely transporting IPv6 traffic across and IPv4 MPLS core; however, it is not necessarily concerned with customer routes. Therefore, there is no need for any logical separation of routes using VRFs.

Stepping away from our main topology for a moment, we have two sites (R1 and R2) connecting through pure IPv6:

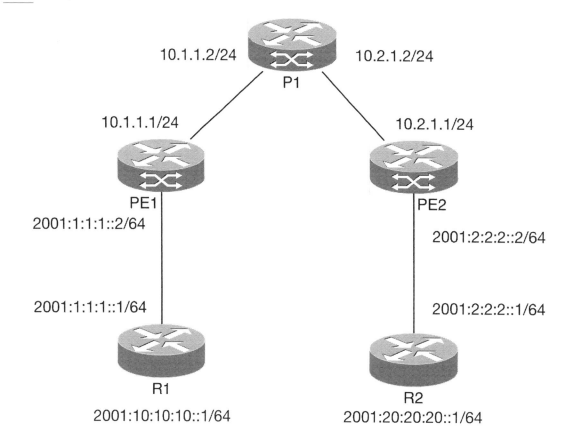

We start by creating the IPv4 MPLS core:

```
PE1(config)#int lo0
PE1(config-if)#ip add 1.1.1.1 255.255.255.255
PE1(config-if)#int gi 2/0
PE1(config-if)#ip add 10.1.1.1 255.255.255.0
PE1(config-if)#no shut
PE1(config-if)#mpls ip
PE1(config-if)#
PE1(config-if)#router ospf 1
PE1(config-router)#network 1.1.1.1 0.0.0.0 area 0
PE1(config-router)#network 10.1.1.0 0.0.0.255 area 0
PE1(config-router)#

P1(config)#int lo0
P1(config-if)#ip add 2.2.2.2 255.255.255.255
P1(config-if)#int gi 1/0
P1(config-if)#mpls ip
P1(config-if)#no shut
```

```
P1(config-if)#ip add 10.1.1.2 255.255.255.0
P1(config-if)#int gi 2/0
P1(config-if)#mpls ip
P1(config-if)#no shut
P1(config-if)#ip add 10.2.1.2 255.255.255.0
P1(config-if)#router ospf 1
P1(config-router)#network
P1(config-router)#network 2.2.2.2 0.0.0.0 area 0
P1(config-router)#network 10.1.1.0 0.0.0.255 area 0
P1(config-router)#network 10.2.1.0 0.0.0.255 area 0
P1(config-router)#

PE2(config)#int lo0
PE2(config-if)#ip add 3.3.3.3 255.255.255.255
PE2(config-if)#int gi 2/0
PE2(config-if)#no shut
PE2(config-if)#mpls ip
PE2(config-if)#ip add 10.2.1.1 255.255.255.0
PE2(config-if)#router ospf 1
PE2(config-router)#network 3.3.3.3 0.0.0.0 area 0
PE2(config-router)#network 10.2.1.0 0.0.0.255 area 0
PE2(config-router)#
```

Next in preparation for R1 and R2 to pass routes to each other, we will enable PE1 and PE2 for IPv6 and create the MP-BGP autonomous system:

```
PE1(config)#ipv6 unicast-routing
PE1(config)#router bgp 100
PE1(config-router)#no bgp default ipv4-unicast
PE1(config-router)#neigh 3.3.3.3 remote-as 100
PE1(config-router)#neigh 3.3.3.3 update-source lo0
PE1(config-router)#address-family ipv6
PE1(config-router-af)#neigh 3.3.3.3 activate
PE1(config-router-af)#neigh 3.3.3.3 send-label
PE1(config-router-af)#

PE2(config)#ipv6 unicast-routing
PE2(config)#router bgp 100
PE2(config-router)#no bgp default ipv4-unicast
PE2(config-router)#neigh 1.1.1.1 remote-as 100
PE2(config-router)#neigh 1.1.1.1 update-source lo0
PE2(config-router)#address-family ipv6
PE2(config-router-af)#neigh 1.1.1.1 activate
PE2(config-router-af)#neigh 1.1.1.1 send-label
PE2(config-router-af)#
```

Now, we move on to creating the connection between R1 and PE1:

```
R1(config)#ipv6 unicast-routing
R1(config)#int gi 1/0
R1(config-if)#ipv6 add 2001:1:1:1::1/64
R1(config-if)#no shut
R1(config-if)#

PE1(config)#int gi 1/0
PE1(config-if)#ipv6 add 2001:1:1:1::2/64
PE1(config-if)#no shut
PE1(config-if)#

R1#ping ipv6 2001:1:1:1::2
Type escape sequence to abort.
Sending 5, 100-byte ICMP Echos to 2001:1:1:1::2, timeout is 2
seconds:
!!!!!
Success rate is 100 percent (5/5)
R1#
```

Connectivity is good, so let's complete the other side of the network:

```
PE2(config)#int gi 1/0
PE2(config-if)#ipv6 add 2001:2:2:2::2/64
PE2(config-if)#no shut
PE2(config-if)#

R2(config)#ipv6 unicast-routing
R2(config)#int gi 1/0
R2(config-if)#ipv6 add 2001:2:2:2::1/64
R2(config-if)#no shut
R2(config-if)#end
R2#ping ipv6 2001:2:2:2::2
Type escape sequence to abort.
Sending 5, 100-byte ICMP Echos to 2001:2:2:2::2, timeout is 2
seconds:
!!!!!
Success rate is 100 percent (5/5)
R2#
```

The final step is to create our IGP processes for advertisement and redistribution. We will add a couple of loopback interfaces as well so that we have something to advertise:

```
R1(config)#ipv6 router ospf 1
R1(config-rtr)#router-id 10.10.10.10
R1(config-rtr)#int gi 1/0
R1(config-if)#ipv6 ospf 1 area 0
```

```
R1(config)#int lo0
R1(config-if)#ipv6 add 2001:10:10:10::1/64
R1(config-if)#ipv6 ospf 1 area 0
R1(config-if)#

R2(config)#ipv6 router ospf 1
R2(config-rtr)#router-id 20.20.20.20
R2(config-rtr)#int gi 1/0
R2(config-if)#ipv6 ospf 1 area 0
R2(config)#int lo0
R2(config-if)#ipv6 add 2001:20:20:20::1/64
R2(config-if)#ipv6 ospf 1 area 0
R2(config-if)#

PE1(config)#ipv6 router ospf 1
PE1(config-rtr)#int gi 1/0
PE1(config-if)#ipv6 ospf 1 area 0
PE1(config-if)#

PE2(config)#ipv6 router ospf 1
PE2(config-rtr)#int gi 1/0
PE2(config-if)#ipv6 ospf 1 area 0
PE2(config-if)#

PE1(config)#ipv6 router ospf 1
PE1(config-rtr)#redistribute bgp 100 metric 10 metric-type 1
PE1(config-rtr)#router bgp 100
PE1(config-router)#address-family ipv6
PE1(config-router-af)#redistribute ospf 1 metric 10
PE1(config-router-af)#

PE2(config)#ipv6 router ospf 1
PE2(config-rtr)#redistribute bgp 100 metric 10 metric-type 1
PE2(config-rtr)#router bgp 100
PE2(config-router)#address-family ipv6
PE2(config-router-af)#redistribute ospf 1 metric 10
PE2(config-router-af)#
```

With everything in place, we should have visibility and reachability between the loopback networks:

```
R1#sh ipv6 route ospf | beg 2001
OE1 2001:20:20:20::1/128 [110/11]
     via FE80::C803:30FF:FEB4:1C, GigabitEthernet1/0
R1#

R2#sh ipv6 route ospf | beg 2001
```

```
OE1 2001:10:10:10::1/128 [110/11]
     via FE80::C805:27FF:FEA0:1C, GigabitEthernet1/0
R2#

R2#ping ipv6 2001:10:10:10::1 so lo0
Type escape sequence to abort.
Sending 5, 100-byte ICMP Echos to 2001:10:10:10::1, timeout is 2
seconds:
Packet sent with a source address of 2001:20:20:20::1
!!!!!
Success rate is 100 percent (5/5)
R2#
```

As you can see, we have a fully working IPv6 network with an IPv4 only MPLS core! Let's go one step further and remove MPLS completely!

13.3 IPv6 and VRF-Lite

With EIGRPv6 and VRF-Lite, we can use the EIGRP named mode, which gives us the ability to create a named EIGRP process. Within that, we can create number processes for our VRFs.

Using the below topology, we will carry some routes from R1 to R2 within two VRFs; ALPHA and BETA:

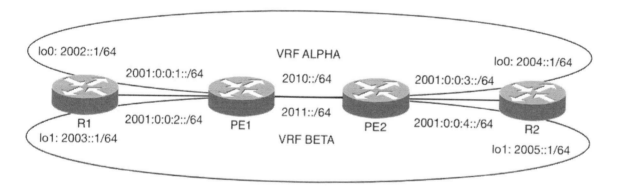

The initial configuration is below. We first enable IPv6 routing globally and then create our VRFs using the definition method (vrf definition <vrf name>). As usual, we are required to use a route-distinguisher, but as we will not be doing any form of redistribution we do not need to define any route targets for import or export. We will use sub interfaces for encapsulation and add a couple of loopback interfaces to test with:

```
R1(config)#ipv6 unicast-routing
```

```
R1(config)#vrf definition ALPHA
R1(config-vrf)#rd 100:100
R1(config-vrf)#address-family ipv6
R1(config-vrf-af)#exit
R1(config-vrf)#vrf def BETA
R1(config-vrf)#rd 200:200
R1(config-vrf)#address-family ipv6
R1(config-vrf)#int lo0
R1(config-if)#vrf for ALPHA
R1(config-if)#ipv6 add 2002::1/64
R1(config-if)#int lo1
R1(config-if)#vrf for BETA
R1(config-if)#ipv6 add 2003::1/64
R1(config-if)#int gi 1/0
R1(config-if)#no shut
R1(config-if)#int gi 1/0.1
R1(config-subif)#encap dot 100
R1(config-subif)#vrf for ALPHA
R1(config-subif)#ipv6 add 2001:0:0:1::1/64
R1(config-subif)#int gi 1/0.2
R1(config-subif)#encap dot 200
R1(config-subif)#vrf for BETA
R1(config-subif)#ipv6 add 2001:0:0:2::1/64
R1(config-subif)#
```

We can then move on to PE1 and check that we have basic connectivity:

```
PE1(config)#ipv6 unicast-routing
PE1(config)#vrf def ALPHA
PE1(config-vrf)#rd 100:100
PE1(config-vrf)#address-family ipv6
PE1(config-vrf-af)#vrf def BETA
PE1(config-vrf)#rd 200:200
PE1(config-vrf)#address-family ipv6
PE1(config-vrf-af)#exit
PE1(config-vrf)#int gi 1/0
PE1(config-if)#no shut
PE1(config-if)#int gi 1/0.1
PE1(config-subif)#encap dot 100
PE1(config-subif)#vrf for ALPHA
PE1(config-subif)#ipv6 add 2001:0:0:1::2/64
PE1(config-subif)#int gi 1/0.2
PE1(config-subif)#encap dot 200
PE1(config-subif)#vrf for BETA
PE1(config-subif)#ipv6 add 2001:0:0:2::2/64
PE1(config-subif)#do ping vrf ALPHA 2001:0:0:1::1
Type escape sequence to abort.
```

```
Sending 5, 100-byte ICMP Echos to 2001:0:0:1::1, timeout is 2
seconds:
!!!!!
Success rate is 100 percent (5/5)
PE1(config-subif)#
```

R1 has connectivity to PE1, so we can move on to R2 and PE2:

```
R2(config)#ipv6 unicast-routing
R2(config)#vrf def ALPHA
R2(config-vrf)#rd 100:100
R2(config-vrf)#address-family ipv6
R2(config-vrf-af)#vrf def BETA
R2(config-vrf)#rd 200:200
R2(config-vrf)#address-family ipv6
R2(config-vrf-af)#int lo0
R2(config-if)#vrf for ALPHA
R2(config-if)#ipv6 add 2004::1/64
R2(config-if)#int lo1
R2(config-if)#vrf for BETA
R2(config-if)#ipv6 address 2005::1/64
R2(config-if)#int gi 1/0
R2(config-if)#no shut
R2(config-if)#int gi 1/0.1
R2(config-subif)#encap dot 100
R2(config-subif)#vrf for ALPHA
R2(config-subif)#ipv6 add 2001:0:0:3::1/64
R2(config-subif)#int gi 1/0.2
R2(config-subif)#encap dot 200
R2(config-subif)#vrf for BETA
R2(config-subif)#ipv6 add 2001:0:0:4::1/64

PE2(config)#ipv6 unicast-routing
PE2(config)#vrf def ALPHA
PE2(config-vrf)#rd 100:100
PE2(config-vrf)#address-family ipv6
PE2(config-vrf-af)#vrf def BETA
PE2(config-vrf)#rd 200:200
PE2(config-vrf)#address-family ipv6
PE2(config-vrf-af)#int gi 1/0
PE2(config-if)#no shut
PE2(config-if)#int gi 1/0.1
PE2(config-subif)#encap dot 100
PE2(config-subif)#vrf for ALPHA
PE2(config-subif)#ipv6 add 2001:0:0:3::2/64
PE2(config-subif)#int gi 1/0.2
PE2(config-subif)#encap dot 200
```

```
PE2(config-subif)#vrf for BETA
PE2(config-subif)#ipv6 add 2001:0:0:4::2/64
PE2(config-subif)#do ping vrf ALPHA 2001:0:0:3::1
Type escape sequence to abort.
Sending 5, 100-byte ICMP Echos to 2001:0:0:3::1, timeout is 2
seconds:
!!!!!
Success rate is 100 percent (5/5)
PE2(config-subif)#
```

Now that we have basic connectivity, we can move on to creating the EIGRP IGP.

We first create a named EIGRP virtual instance called "MyVRF", and under this create an IPv6 address family for each of our VRFs. We can then associate interfaces with the EIGRP address family using the command "af-interface <interface name>":

R1's EIGRP config:

```
R1(config-subif)#router eigrp MyVRF
R1(config-router)#address-family ipv6 unicast vrf ALPHA autonomous-
system 100
R1(config-router-af)#af-interface lo0
R1(config-router-af-interface)#exit
R1(config-router-af)#af-interface Gi 1/0.1
R1(config-router-af-interface)#exit
R1(config-router-af)#eigrp router-id 1.1.1.1
R1(config-router-af)#exit
R1(config-router)#address-family ipv6 unicast vrf BETA autonomous-
system 200
R1(config-router-af)#af-interface lo1
R1(config-router-af-interface)#exit
R1(config-router-af)#af-interface Gi 1/0.2
R1(config-router-af-interface)#exit
R1(config-router-af)#eigrp router-id 1.1.1.1
R1(config-router-af)#end
```

We do not have to specify "unicast" in the address-family command, as that is the default. Nor do we need to specify interfaces using the af-interface command, so we can achieve the same results on R2 using less commands:

```
R2(config-subif)#router eigrp MyVRF
R2(config-router)#address-family ipv6 vrf ALPHA auto 100
R2(config-router-af)#eigrp router-id 4.4.4.4
R2(config-router-af)#exit
R2(config-router)#address-family ipv6 vrf BETA auto 200
R2(config-router-af)#eigrp router-id 4.4.4.4
```

```
R2(config-router-af)#exit
```

EIGRP named mode has three different configuration sub menus; the first of these being address-family configuration mode, where we can set our EIGRP router id (as shown above), set up our neighbors, specify networks to advertise, as well as other settings such as our metrics and timers. From here, we can drop down into the address-family interface configuration mode and the address-family topology configuration mode. In the interface command set we can set our adjacency forming parameters, such as our hello timers and hold timers, set an interface to be passive or maybe set a summary address. The topology command set is where we would enable redistribution. Say, for instance, we were using MPLS; here, we would redistribute between BGP and EIGRP. Under the topology command set, we can also set our variance commands, traffic sharing and our offset or redistribute lists.

PE1 and PE2 can also take the smaller command sequence:

```
PE1(config-subif)#router eigrp MyVRF
PE1(config-router)#address-family ipv6 vrf ALPHA auto 100
PE1(config-router-af)#eigrp router-id 2.2.2.2
PE1(config-router-af)#exit
PE1(config-router)#address-family ipv6 vrf BETA auto 200
PE1(config-router-af)#eigrp router-id 2.2.2.2
PE1(config-router-af)#

PE2(config-subif)#router eigrp MyVRF
PE2(config-router)#address-family ipv6 vrf ALPHA auto 100
PE2(config-router-af)#eigrp router-id 3.3.3.3
PE2(config-router-af)#exit
PE2(config-router)#address-family ipv6 vrf BETA auto 200
PE2(config-router-af)#eigrp router-id 3.3.3.3
PE2(config-router-af)#
```

The last step is to create the connections between PE1 and PE2:

```
PE1(config-router-af)#int gi 2/0
PE1(config-if)#no shut
PE1(config-if)#int gi 2/0.1
PE1(config-subif)#encap dot 100
PE1(config-subif)#vrf for ALPHA
PE1(config-subif)#ipv6 add 2010::2/64
PE1(config-subif)#int gi 2/0.2
PE1(config-subif)#encap dot 200
PE1(config-subif)#vrf for BETA
PE1(config-subif)#ipv6 add 2011::2/64
```

```
PE2(config-router-af)#int gi 2/0
PE2(config-if)#no shut
PE2(config-if)#int gi 2/0.1
PE2(config-subif)#encap dot 100
PE2(config-subif)#vrf for ALPHA
PE2(config-subif)#ipv6 add 2010::1/64
PE2(config-subif)#int gi 2/0.2
PE2(config-subif)#encap dot 200
PE2(config-subif)#vrf for BETA
PE2(config-subif)#ipv6 add 2011::1/64
```

Although I have not included the EIGRP adjacency console messages, we now have a fully connected network.

Here, we can see that R1 can reach R2's VRF ALPHA loopback interface (2004::1) from its Gi1/0.1 interface and also from its own loopback interface:

```
R1#sh ipv6 route vrf ALPHA eigrp | sec exc Codes:
IPv6 Routing Table - ALPHA - 8 entries
D   2001:0:0:3::/64 [90/20480]
     via FE80::C803:41FF:FE94:1C, GigabitEthernet1/0.1
D   2004::/64 [90/21120]
     via FE80::C803:41FF:FE94:1C, GigabitEthernet1/0.1
D   2010::/64 [90/15360]
     via FE80::C803:41FF:FE94:1C, GigabitEthernet1/0.1

R1#ping vrf ALPHA ipv6 2004::1
Type escape sequence to abort.
Sending 5, 100-byte ICMP Echos to 2004::1, timeout is 2 seconds:
!!!!!
Success rate is 100 percent (5/5)
R1#ping vrf ALPHA ipv6 2004::1 so lo0
Type escape sequence to abort.
Sending 5, 100-byte ICMP Echos to 2004::1, timeout is 2 seconds:
Packet sent with a source address of 2002::1%ALPHA
!!!!!
Success rate is 100 percent (5/5)
R1#
```

The same is true for VRF BETA. Lastly, we have a failed ping attempt from VRF BETA to VRF ALPHA, which is exactly how it should be, as the two should by design be kept completely separate:

```
R1#sh ipv6 route vrf BETA eigrp | sec exc Codes:
IPv6 Routing Table - BETA - 8 entries
D   2001:0:0:4::/64 [90/20480]
```

```
         via FE80::C803:41FF:FE94:1C, GigabitEthernet1/0.2
D    2005::/64 [90/21120]
         via FE80::C803:41FF:FE94:1C, GigabitEthernet1/0.2
D    2011::/64 [90/15360]
         via FE80::C803:41FF:FE94:1C, GigabitEthernet1/0.2

R1#ping vrf BETA ipv6 2005::1
Type escape sequence to abort.
Sending 5, 100-byte ICMP Echos to 2005::1, timeout is 2 seconds:
!!!!!
Success rate is 100 percent (5/5)
R1#ping vrf BETA ipv6 2005::1 so lo1
Type escape sequence to abort.
Sending 5, 100-byte ICMP Echos to 2005::1, timeout is 2 seconds:
Packet sent with a source address of 2003::1%BETA
!!!!!
Success rate is 100 percent (5/5)
R1#ping vrf BETA ipv6 2005::1 so lo0
% No valid source address for destination
R1#
```

Now, as we are getting close to the end, we'll have a look at a few tricks we need to know. Then, we will finish off with some troubleshooting.

14. Tweaking MPLS

This is one of those kind of chapters that is filled with those smaller aspects of MPLS that could have been inserted into previous chapters, but it seems better that they were kept separate. For ease of following along with this, we will use the main topology for practice, with just R1 and R2 and the MPLS core routers switched on.

This chapter is all about those little tweaks that we can do to MPLS, either because we are asked to in an exam or because it makes sense from an administrative or usability point of view. We will cover some things we can do with the labels that we assign, the timers that we use in our network, setting up security within MPLS, and tweaking the performance of our VPNs.

14.1 Tweaking MLPS labels

Recall from chapter 10.1 when we looked at loop prevention using the OSPF down bit. In that configuration, we used the commands "mpls label range" followed by a number range, such as a starting number of 100. Then, allowing the range to go up to and including 199, we issue the full command "mpls label range 100 199."

So, what is the purpose of fixing the label ranges, apart from because we are told to do so? Firstly, it makes label allocation easier to work out when looking at the forwarding table. Secondly, when two LSRs speak to each other, they swap label information; therefore, each router will already be using a very separate set of ranges.

We can do this on our routers. Firstly, let's have a look at the current forwarding tables of PE1 and PE2:

```
PE1#sh mpls forwarding-table
Local   Outgoing    Prefix            Bytes Label   Outgoing      Next Hop
Label   Label       or Tunnel Id      Switched      interface
16      Pop Label   10.10.4.0/24      0             Gi5/0         10.10.3.2
17      Pop Label   10.250.2.0/24     0             Gi5/0         10.10.3.2
18      Pop Label   10.10.2.0/24      0             Gi1/0         10.10.1.1
19      19          10.250.4.0/24     0             Gi1/0         10.10.1.1
        19          10.250.4.0/24     0             Gi5/0         10.10.3.2
20      Pop Label   10.250.1.0/24     0             Gi1/0         10.10.1.1
21      No Label    10.1.1.0/24[V]    0             aggregate/RED
22      No Label    192.168.1.0/24[V] \
                                      0             Gi2/0         10.1.1.2
23      No Label    192.168.20.0/24[V] \
```

```
 24    No Label    10.1.3.0/24[V]    0             Gi2/0       10.1.1.2
 25    Pop Label   2.2.2.5/32[V]     776           aggregate/WHITE
PE1#                                               aggregate/BLUE
```

```
PE2#sh mpls forwarding-table
Local   Outgoing   Prefix              Bytes Label   Outgoing    Next Hop
Label   Label      or Tunnel Id        Switched      interface
16      Pop Label  10.10.3.0/24        0             Gi5/0       10.10.4.2
17      Pop Label  10.250.2.0/24       0             Gi5/0       10.10.4.2
18      Pop Label  10.10.1.0/24        0             Gi1/0       10.10.2.1
19      17         10.250.3.0/24       0             Gi1/0       10.10.2.1
        17         10.250.3.0/24       0             Gi5/0       10.10.4.2
20      Pop Label  10.250.1.0/24       0             Gi1/0       10.10.2.1
21      No Label   10.2.2.0/24[V]      0             aggregate/RED
22      No Label   172.20.1.0/24[V]    0             Gi2/0       10.2.2.2
23      Pop Label  2.2.2.6/32[V]       840           aggregate/BLUE
PE2#
```

Both PE1 and PE2 have the same label numbers used, and these may or may not correspond to the same IPv4 prefix. We can set the label ranges using the following:

```
PE1(config)#mpls label range 100 199

P1(config)#mpls label range 200 299

P2(config)#mpls label range 300 399

PE2(config)#mpls label range 400 499
```

Now, when we look at the forwarding tables again, we can see that there can be no chance of any overlap. This did require a reboot of the routers in order to get the updated label numbers. New prefixes introduced into the forwarding table would be issued with a label from our configured range, but existing ones would not, hence the requirement for a reload of the router:

```
PE1#sh mpls forwarding-table
Local   Outgoing   Prefix              Bytes Label   Outgoing    Next Hop
Label   Label      or Tunnel Id        Switched      interface
100     Pop Label  10.10.2.0/24        0             Gi1/0       10.10.1.1
101     Pop Label  10.250.1.0/24       0             Gi1/0       10.10.1.1
102     Pop Label  10.10.4.0/24        0             Gi5/0       10.10.3.2
103     201        10.250.4.0/24       0             Gi1/0       10.10.1.1
        301        10.250.4.0/24       0             Gi5/0       10.10.3.2
104     Pop Label  10.250.2.0/24       0             Gi5/0       10.10.3.2
105     No Label   10.1.1.0/24[V]      0             aggregate/RED
```

```
106        No Label    192.168.1.0/24[V]   \
                                           0          Gi2/0        10.1.1.2
107        No Label    192.168.20.0/24[V]  \
                                           0          Gi2/0        10.1.1.2
108        No Label    10.1.3.0/24[V]      0          aggregate/WHITE
109        Pop Label   2.2.2.5/32[V]       776        aggregate/BLUE
PE1#

PE2#sh mpls forwarding-table
Local      Outgoing    Prefix              Bytes Label  Outgoing    Next Hop
Label      Label       or Tunnel Id        Switched     interface
400        Pop Label   10.10.3.0/24        0            Gi5/0       10.10.4.2
401        Pop Label   10.250.2.0/24       0            Gi5/0       10.10.4.2
402        Pop Label   10.10.1.0/24        0            Gi1/0       10.10.2.1
403        Pop Label   10.250.1.0/24       0            Gi1/0       10.10.2.1
404        203         10.250.3.0/24       0            Gi1/0       10.10.2.1
           303         10.250.3.0/24       0            Gi5/0       10.10.4.2
405        No Label    10.2.2.0/24[V]      0            aggregate/RED
406        No Label    172.20.1.0/24[V]    0            Gi2/0       10.2.2.2
407        Pop Label   2.2.2.6/32[V]       840          aggregate/BLUE
PE2#
```

We can also specify static labels for specific IPv4 addresses. If we wished to set the static label for the 192.168.1.0/24 prefix to 599 and tried to do this now we would get the following error message:

```
PE1(config)#mpls static binding ipv4 vrf RED 192.168.1.0
255.255.255.0 ?
  <>   <static label range not configured>
```

We actually need to make a slight change to our label range command, by specifying a second set of labels to use for our static ranges, this is done by appending the word static to the range command we used previously:

```
PE1(config)#mpls label range 100 199 static ?
  <16-99>         Lower minimum static label value
  <200-1048575>   Upper minimum static label value
```

We can see that the IOS is being clever and offering us two sets of ranges. There are those we are permitted to use before our configured range and those we are permitted to use afterwards. We will set it to use 500 - 599:

```
PE1(config)#mpls label range 100 199 static 500 599
```

Now, we can try the same command again and can see that we can select a number between 500 and 599:

```
PE1(config)#mpls static binding ipv4 vrf RED 192.168.1.0
255.255.255.0 ?
  <500-599>  Label Value <500 - 599>
  input      Incoming (local) label

PE1(config)#mpls static binding ipv4 vrf RED 192.168.1.0
255.255.255.0 599
PE1(config)#
```

The forwarding table on PE1 looks like this:

```
PE1#sh mpls forwarding-table
Local   Outgoing    Prefix              Bytes Label   Outgoing      Next Hop
Label   Label       or Tunnel Id        Switched      interface
100     Pop Label   10.10.2.0/24        0             Gi1/0         10.10.1.1
101     Pop Label   10.250.1.0/24       0             Gi1/0         10.10.1.1
102     Pop Label   10.10.4.0/24        0             Gi5/0         10.10.3.2
103     201         10.250.4.0/24       0             Gi1/0         10.10.1.1
        301         10.250.4.0/24       0             Gi5/0         10.10.3.2
104     Pop Label   10.250.2.0/24       0             Gi5/0         10.10.3.2
108     No Label    10.1.3.0/24[V]      0             aggregate/WHITE
109     Pop Label   2.2.2.5/32[V]       776           aggregate/BLUE
110     No Label    10.1.1.0/24[V]      0             aggregate/RED
111     No Label    192.168.20.0/24[V]  \
                                        0             Gi2/0         10.1.1.2
599     No Label    192.168.1.0/24[V]   \
                                        0             Gi2/0         10.1.1.2
PE1#
```

We can check what label ranges we are using through the command "sh mpls label range":

```
PE1#sh mpls label range
Downstream Generic label region: Min/Max label: 100/199
Range for static labels: Min/Max label: 500/599

PE1#
```

Likewise, we can see the information in BGP:

```
PE1#sh ip bgp vpnv4 vrf RED labels
   Network           Next Hop       In label/Out label
Route Distinguisher: 100:1 (RED)
```

```
10.1.1.0/24       10.1.1.2        110/nolabel
10.1.3.0/24       0.0.0.0         nolabel/nolabel(RED)
10.2.2.0/24       10.250.4.1      nolabel/408
172.20.1.0/24     10.250.4.1      nolabel/409
192.168.1.0       10.1.1.2        599/nolabel
192.168.20.0      10.1.1.2        111/nolabel
PE1#
```

We can completely change the way that the labels are allocated. Throughout the book, the default behavior has been to allocate a label per prefix. Well, we can actually allocate labels based on an entire VRF, either for one VRF or for all VRFs. Let's see how to do this for VRF RED on PE1:

```
PE1(config)#mpls label mode vrf RED protocol bgp-vpnv4 per-vrf
```

The result is that we now have a different entry in the forwarding table:

```
PE1#sh mpls forwarding-table
Local   Outgoing    Prefix              Bytes Label  Outgoing      Next Hop
Label   Label       or Tunnel Id        Switched     interface
100     Pop Label   10.10.2.0/24        0            Gi1/0         10.10.1.1
101     Pop Label   10.250.1.0/24       0            Gi1/0         10.10.1.1
102     Pop Label   10.10.4.0/24        0            Gi5/0         10.10.3.2
103     201         10.250.4.0/24       0            Gi1/0         10.10.1.1
        301         10.250.4.0/24       0            Gi5/0         10.10.3.2
104     Pop Label   10.250.2.0/24       0            Gi5/0         10.10.3.2
106     Pop Label   IPv4 VRF[V]         0            aggregate/RED
108     No Label    10.1.3.0/24[V]      0            aggregate/WHITE
109     Pop Label   2.2.2.5/32[V]       776          aggregate/BLUE
599     No Label    192.168.1.0/24[V]   \
                                        0            Gi2/0         10.1.1.2
PE1#
```

Our static entry for the 192.168.1.0/24 prefix has not been overridden. Instead of an entry for 10.1.1.0/24 (which had label 110 previously), we now have one entry (106) for "IPv4 VRF", which corresponds to VRF RED. If we look at PE2, we can see that the VRF label allocation mode is still per-prefix:

```
PE2#sh vrf detail RED
VRF RED (VRF Id = 5); default RD 100:1; default VPNID <not set>
  Interfaces:
    Gi2/0
Address family ipv4 (Table ID = 5 (0x5)):
  Export VPN route-target communities
```

```
        RT:100:1
    Import VPN route-target communities
      RT:100:1                     RT:100:2                          RT:100:20
      RT:100:200
    No import route-map
    Export route-map: VRF-RED-SUBNETS
    VRF label distribution protocol: not configured
    VRF label allocation mode: per-prefix
  Address family ipv6 not active

  PE2#
```

Yet, on PE1, we can see that it is now per-vrf, using label 106:

```
  PE1#sh vrf detail RED
  VRF RED (VRF Id = 5); default RD 100:1; default VPNID <not set>
    Interfaces:
      Gi2/0
  Address family ipv4 (Table ID = 5 (0x5)):
    Export VPN route-target communities
      RT:100:1
    Import VPN route-target communities
      RT:100:1                     RT:100:2                          RT:100:20
      RT:100:200
    No import route-map
    Export route-map: VRF-RED-INTERNET
    VRF label distribution protocol: not configured
    VRF label allocation mode: per-vrf (Label 106)
  Address family ipv6 not active

  PE1#
```

Naturally, this does not affect the customer in anyway, and they still have reachability:

```
  R1#ping 172.20.1.1
  Type escape sequence to abort.
  Sending 5, 100-byte ICMP Echos to 172.20.1.1, timeout is 2 seconds:
  !!!!!
  Success rate is 100 percent (5/5)
  R1#ping 172.20.1.1 so lo0
  Type escape sequence to abort.
  Sending 5, 100-byte ICMP Echos to 172.20.1.1, timeout is 2 seconds:
  Packet sent with a source address of 192.168.1.1
  !!!!!
  Success rate is 100 percent (5/5)
  R1#
```

14.2 Tweaking MPLS timers

In chapter 6, we looked at how the LSP, the Label Switched Path, is created. A number of timers are used in the set up of the LSP. These are the Hello interval (default is 5 seconds), Hello holdtime (15 seconds) and the LDP backoff (15 seconds initial, 120 seconds maximum backoff). We can check these using the command "sh mpls ldp parameters":

```
PE1#sh mpls ldp parameters
LDP Feature Set Manager: State Initialized
  LDP features:
    Basic
    IP-over-MPLS
    TDP
    IGP-Sync
    Auto-Configuration
    TCP-MD5-Rollover
Protocol version: 1
Session hold time: 180 sec; keep alive interval: 60 sec
Discovery hello: holdtime: 15 sec; interval: 5 sec
Discovery targeted hello: holdtime: 90 sec; interval: 10 sec
Downstream on Demand max hop count: 255
LDP for targeted sessions
LDP initial/maximum backoff: 15/120 sec
LDP loop detection: off
PE1#
```

We can set our interval to 20 seconds and our holdtime to 60 seconds using the following commands:

```
PE1(config)#mpls ldp discovery hello interval 20
PE1(config)#mpls ldp discovery hello holdtime 60
```

The LDP backoff can be set to an initial 10 seconds and a maximum of 25 seconds using the following:

```
PE1(config)#mpls ldp backoff ?
  <5-2147483>  Initial session backoff time (seconds)

PE1(config)#mpls ldp backoff 10 ?
  <5-2147483>  Maximum session backoff time (seconds)

PE1(config)#mpls ldp backoff 10 25
```

```
PE1(config)#
```

These changes are all immediate:

```
PE1#sh mpls ldp parameters
LDP Feature Set Manager: State Initialized
  LDP features:
    Basic
    IP-over-MPLS
    TDP
    IGP-Sync
    Auto-Configuration
    TCP-MD5-Rollover
Protocol version: 1
Session hold time: 180 sec; keep alive interval: 60 sec
Discovery hello: holdtime: 60 sec; interval: 20 sec
Discovery targeted hello: holdtime: 90 sec; interval: 10 sec
Downstream on Demand max hop count: 255
LDP for targeted sessions
LDP initial/maximum backoff: 10/25 sec
LDP loop detection: off
PE1#
```

14.3 Tweaking MPLS security

We can set MD5 password security between LDP neighbors using the command "mpls ldp neigh <neighbor ID> password <password>". Here, we will set PE1 to require a password of "802101.com" from P1 but for it to be optional from P2:

```
PE1(config)#mpls ldp neigh 10.250.1.1 password 802101.com
```

This alone does not mean that a password is required:

```
PE1(config)#do sh mpls ldp neigh password current
    Peer LDP Ident: 10.250.1.1:0; Local LDP Ident 10.250.3.1:0
        TCP connection: 10.250.1.1.646 - 10.250.3.1.19429
        Password: not required, none, in use
        State: Oper; Msgs sent/rcvd: 75/72
    Peer LDP Ident: 10.250.2.1:0; Local LDP Ident 10.250.3.1:0
        TCP connection: 10.250.2.1.646 - 10.250.3.1.29884
        Password: not required, none, in use
        State: Oper; Msgs sent/rcvd: 21/21
```

We can force the router to require a password using the command "mpls ldp password required". This, however, forces the setting on all neighbors, which tears down their connections:

```
PE1(config)#mpls ldp password required
*Aug 15 18:23:43.319: %LDP-5-NBRCHG: LDP Neighbor 10.250.1.1:0 (1) is
DOWN (Session's MD5 password changed)
*Aug 15 18:23:43.323: %LDP-5-NBRCHG: LDP Neighbor 10.250.2.1:0 (2) is
DOWN (Session's MD5 password changed)
PE1(config)#
*Aug 15 18:23:45.899: %LDP-4-PWD: MD5 protection is required for peer
10.250.1.1:0, no password configured
PE1(config)#
*Aug 15 18:24:16.759: %LDP-4-PWD: MD5 protection is required for peer
10.250.2.1:0, no password configured
PE1(config)#
```

We set the password on P1 in the same manner as before, and the LDP adjacency forms again:

```
P1(config)#mpls ldp neigh 10.250.3.1 password 802101.com

PE1(config)#
*Aug 15 18:31:37: %LDP-5-NBRCHG: LDP Neighbor 10.250.1.1:0 (1) is UP
PE1(config)#
```

The steps also need to be performed on P2 and on PE1 for the connection to P2:

```
P2(config)#mpls ldp neigh 10.250.3.1 password 802101.com

PE1(config)#mpls ldp neigh 10.250.2.1 password 802101.com
```

With this, the LDP connection to P2 comes back up again:

```
*Aug 15 18:32:51.427: %LDP-4-PWD: MD5 protection is required for peer
10.250.2.1:0, no password configured
PE1(config)#
*Aug 15 18:32:55.455: %LDP-5-NBRCHG: LDP Neighbor 10.250.2.1:0 (2) is
UP
PE1(config)#do sh mpls ldp neigh password current
    Peer LDP Ident: 10.250.1.1:0; Local LDP Ident 10.250.3.1:0
        TCP connection: 10.250.1.1.646 - 10.250.3.1.26591
        Password: required, neighbor, in use
        State: Oper; Msgs sent/rcvd: 14/16
    Peer LDP Ident: 10.250.2.1:0; Local LDP Ident 10.250.3.1:0
```

```
            TCP connection: 10.250.2.1.646 - 10.250.3.1.54700
            Password: required, neighbor, in use
            State: Oper; Msgs sent/rcvd: 12/12
    PE1(config)#
```

We can see that PE1 requires a password from both its neighbors, but P1 is a little more relaxed:

```
    P1#sh mpls ldp neigh pass curr
        Peer LDP Ident: 10.250.4.1:0; Local LDP Ident 10.250.1.1:0
            TCP connection: 10.250.4.1.16042 - 10.250.1.1.646
            Password: not required, none, in use
            State: Oper; Msgs sent/rcvd: 84/82
        Peer LDP Ident: 10.250.3.1:0; Local LDP Ident 10.250.1.1:0
            TCP connection: 10.250.3.1.26591 - 10.250.1.1.646
            Password: not required, neighbor, in use
            State: Oper; Msgs sent/rcvd: 17/15
    P1#
```

So here, we have not really fulfilled the requirements. Both P1 and P2 are required to authenticate with a password, whereas our goal was just for P1 to be required. Let's turn off the requirement for the moment:

```
    PE1(config)#no mpls ldp password required
    PE1(config)#do sh mpls ldp neigh pass curr
        Peer LDP Ident: 10.250.1.1:0; Local LDP Ident 10.250.3.1:0
            TCP connection: 10.250.1.1.646 - 10.250.3.1.52555
            Password: not required, neighbor, in use
            State: Oper; Msgs sent/rcvd: 13/15
        Peer LDP Ident: 10.250.2.1:0; Local LDP Ident 10.250.3.1:0
            TCP connection: 10.250.2.1.646 - 10.250.3.1.19932
            Password: not required, neighbor, in use
            State: Oper; Msgs sent/rcvd: 13/13
    PE1(config)#
```

What options do we have then? Well, clearly, neighbor commands are designed to be on a per neighbor basis, so let's step back a bit and look at the global commands for "mpls ldp password":

```
    PE1(config)#mpls ldp password ?
      fallback  Specifies a fallback password will follow
      option    LDP password options
      required  MD5 password is required for the peer
      rollover  LDP password rollover parameters

    PE1(config)#mpls ldp password
```

There is an option for "required", which if we look at we can see that we can specify an access-list of neighbors to who we want to force the password to be required:

```
PE1(config)#mpls ldp password required ?
  for  IP access-list specifying control on LDP peers
  <cr>

PE1(config)#mpls ldp password required
```

We can set this access list up very easily:

```
PE1(config)#ip access-list standard RequireP1
PE1(config-std-nacl)#permit 10.250.1.1
PE1(config-std-nacl)#exit
```

Lastly, we just need to apply it to the "required for" command:

```
PE1(config)#mpls ldp password required for RequireP1
```

The result of this is exactly as we would hope. The password is required for P1, but not for P2:

```
PE1(config)#do sh mpls ldp neigh pass curr
    Peer LDP Ident: 10.250.1.1:0; Local LDP Ident 10.250.3.1:0
        TCP connection: 10.250.1.1.646 - 10.250.3.1.52555
        Password: required, neighbor, in use
        State: Oper; Msgs sent/rcvd: 18/20
    Peer LDP Ident: 10.250.2.1:0; Local LDP Ident 10.250.3.1:0
        TCP connection: 10.250.2.1.646 - 10.250.3.1.19932
        Password: not required, neighbor, in use
        State: Oper; Msgs sent/rcvd: 18/18
PE1(config)#
```

14.4 Tweaking MPLS performance

MPLS performance tuning is a large subject, very much embedded in the world of MPLS Traffic Engineering (TE). We will discuss performance tuning here, but only briefly, as TE is tackled in greater depth in the Service Provider exam syllabus than the Routing and Switching exam. There are a couple of ways that we can implement performance enhancements, which we will look at as well as discussing what the future has in store.

We have already looked at MPLS Traffic Engineering in chapter 12.2 when we looked at tunnels in conjunction with AToM. We also saw that we could have multiple tunnels. A component of MPLS TE is Fast Reroute (FRR). There are a number of requirements for fast reroute. The main one being two working tunnels (i.e., both are up, one to act as a primary, the other to be the backup). Next is the the tunnel that needs to be rerouted is configured with the command "tunnel mpls traffic-eng fast-reroute". The backup tunnel is configured with the command "mpls traffic-eng backup-path".

FRR allows an LSP to be protected from failure by "repairing" that LSP at the point of failure, allowing data to flow interrupted whilst the routers establish new end-to-end LSPs.

In terms of redundancy, FRR works very well. However, the rerouted path can take a route that is less than optimal. The responsibility again falls on the network administrator to work out the best path and formulate the tunnel paths accordingly.

So, we have an automatic ability to recover from a failure and a manual process of path tuning, but what about an automatic process of path tuning? Well, this would be the future aspect of MPLS, and indeed the future of all networking, which is the concept of Software Defined Networking.

Software Defined Networking (SDN) separates the Control Plane (which looks after the configuration, management and exchange of routing information, building the RIB or LIB, and other aspects, such as the ARP table and stacking) from the Forwarding Plane (which decides what to do with packets based on the information in the routing table, as well as managing QoS, filtering and the encapsulation of packets).

An SDN controller (such as OpenDaylight or Cisco's OnePK) sits between an API (Application Programming Interface) and the devices, such as routers and switches. This allows for the for the API to make changes based on certain events through a protocol, such as OpenFlow, or Cisco's ONE. SDN is a burgeoning technology, yet companies such as Cisco, Arista, HP and Juniper, to name but a few, have been backing it for some time. At the time of writing, Cisco have just published details of a new exam track concentrating on network programmability.

In terms of MPLS and SDN, it means that in the future an MPLS core may become more responsive to sub-optimal conditions. In the event of a path becoming congested and a less congested backup path being available, the backup path could be used. The flow of packets could then switch back to the primary path once the congestion eases. All this would happen without intervention from network staff.

That pretty much wraps up the odds and ends chapter. Let's move on to the next chapter, in which we will look at a few troubleshooting scenarios.

15. Troubleshooting MPLS

A junior technician is looking to enhance his MPLS skills and has come to you for help. He has been doing a bit of networking and has set up a topology, but it has several issues, which he has asked you to help him fix.

During this chapter, we will break each troubleshooting step down into trouble tickets. You will be presented with some output showing a symptom of the issue. Then, we will look at ways of diagnosing the issue, finding the cause and implementing a fix.

If you are following along with GNS3, load up the Troubleshooting MPLS Lab files. The topology looks like this:

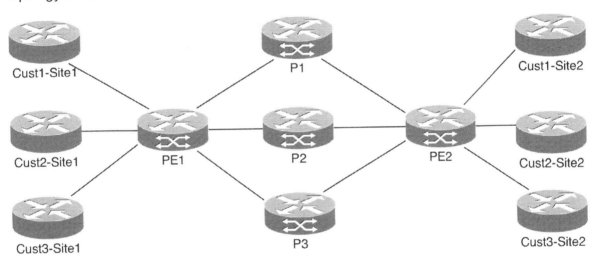

All interfaces will have the appropriate descriptions added to them to help identify connections between routers. Several faults have been injected into the topology, the number of faults is listed in the ticket information. To follow the core tickets, you will need to "turn off" two of the P routers, to simulate this just shutdown the Gi1/0 and Gi2/0 interfaces. At the beginning of each of the tickets (1 – 3), there is a table of which interfaces should be shut down and those that should be up. All P routers can be up for ticket 4.

Remember to "no shut" the interfaces when we need the relevant P router and to turn the unused one "off".

Using "sh run" should be a last resort!

Troubleshooting the Core

Ticket 1

Router	Int Gi 1/0	Int Gi 2/0
P1	Admin Down	Admin Down
P2	Admin Down	Admin Down
P3	Up	Up

It was found that with the P1 and P2 routers shut down there is no label exchange. There is 1 fault in this ticket. We will be using P3 only.

```
PE1#sh mpls forwarding-table
Local  Outgoing   Prefix            Bytes Label  Outgoing     Next Hop
Label  Label      or Tunnel Id      Switched     interface
16     No Label   192.168.1.1/32    0            Gi3/0        10.3.1.1
17     No Label   3.3.3.3/32        0            drop
18     No Label   30.2.3.0/24       0            drop
19     No Label   30.2.1.0/24       0            drop
22     No Label   30.30.30.0/24     0            drop
23     No Label   30.2.2.0/24       0            drop
PE1#

PE2#sh mpls forwarding-table
Local  Outgoing   Prefix            Bytes Label  Outgoing     Next Hop
Label  Label      or Tunnel Id      Switched     interface
17     No Label   1.1.1.1/32        0            drop
20     Pop Label  30.1.3.0/24       0            Gi6/0        30.2.3.2
21     No Label   30.1.2.0/24       0            drop
22     No Label   30.1.1.0/24       0            drop
23     Pop Label  30.30.30.0/24     0            Gi6/0        30.2.3.2
PE2#
```

We start with basic connectivity tests:

```
P3#sh ip int bri | i up
GigabitEthernet1/0       30.1.3.2       YES manual up                    up
GigabitEthernet2/0       30.2.3.2       YES manual up                    up
Loopback0                30.30.30.1     YES manual up                    up
P3#sh int desc | i up
Gi1/0                             up          up          link to PE1
Gi2/0                             up          up          link to PE2
```

```
Lo0                                  up                  up
P3#ping 30.1.3.2
Type escape sequence to abort.
Sending 5, 100-byte ICMP Echos to 30.1.3.2, timeout is 2 seconds:
!!!!!
Success rate is 100 percent (5/5)
P3#ping 30.2.3.2
Type escape sequence to abort.
Sending 5, 100-byte ICMP Echos to 30.2.3.2, timeout is 2 seconds:
!!!!!
Success rate is 100 percent (5/5)
P3#
```

We have connectivity between P3 and PE1 and PE2. So, we should start to look at the underlying requirements of MPLS, such as is CEF running?

```
P3#sh ip cef
Prefix                  Next Hop            Interface
0.0.0.0/0               no route
0.0.0.0/8               drop
0.0.0.0/32              receive
3.3.3.3/32              30.2.3.1            GigabitEthernet2/0
30.1.3.0/24             attached            GigabitEthernet1/0
30.1.3.0/32             receive             GigabitEthernet1/0
30.1.3.1/32             attached            GigabitEthernet1/0
30.1.3.2/32             receive             GigabitEthernet1/0
30.1.3.255/32           receive             GigabitEthernet1/0
30.2.1.0/24             30.2.3.1            GigabitEthernet2/0
30.2.2.0/24             30.2.3.1            GigabitEthernet2/0
30.2.3.0/24             attached            GigabitEthernet2/0
30.2.3.0/32             receive             GigabitEthernet2/0
30.2.3.1/32             attached            GigabitEthernet2/0
30.2.3.2/32             receive             GigabitEthernet2/0
30.2.3.255/32           receive             GigabitEthernet2/0
30.30.30.0/24           attached            Loopback0
30.30.30.0/32           receive             Loopback0
30.30.30.1/32           receive             Loopback0
30.30.30.255/32         receive             Loopback0
127.0.0.0/8             drop
224.0.0.0/4             drop
224.0.0.0/24            receive
240.0.0.0/4             drop
255.255.255.255/32      receive
P3#
```

CEF is running, so is MPLS enabled on the interfaces?

```
P3#sh mpls interfaces
Interface                IP          Tunnel    BGP Static Operational
GigabitEthernet1/0       Yes (ldp)   No        No  No     Yes
GigabitEthernet2/0       Yes (ldp)   No        No  No     Yes
P3#
```

We have CEF and the respective interfaces are enabled for MPLS, so do we have LDP connectivity?

```
P3#sh mpls ldp neigh
    Peer LDP Ident: 3.3.3.3:0; Local LDP Ident 30.30.30.1:0
    TCP connection: 3.3.3.3.646 - 30.30.30.1.53641
    State: Oper; Msgs sent/rcvd: 29/31; Downstream
    Up time: 00:08:58
    LDP discovery sources:
      GigabitEthernet2/0, Src IP addr: 30.2.3.1
        Addresses bound to peer LDP Ident:
          30.2.1.1         30.2.2.1         30.2.3.1        2.2.2.2
          3.3.3.3
P3#
```

It would appear that we only have an LDP adjacency between P3 and PE2; therefore, the issue is between P3 and PE1. We have checked basic connectivity between the two, which was fine, but we need to be able to reach the loopback interfaces that form the LDP router-id. Do we have a route to PE1's loopback interface?

```
P3#sh ip route ospf | beg Gate
Gateway of last resort is not set

      3.0.0.0/32 is subnetted, 1 subnets
O        3.3.3.3 [110/2] via 30.2.3.1, 00:13:08, GigabitEthernet2/0
      30.0.0.0/8 is variably subnetted, 8 subnets, 2 masks
O        30.2.1.0/24 [110/2] via 30.2.3.1, 00:13:08, Gi2/0
O        30.2.2.0/24 [110/2] via 30.2.3.1, 00:13:08, Gi2/0
P3#
```

No, we don't. What's more is that we have nothing coming from PE1. We can confirm this by looking at the OSPF neighbors:

```
P3#sh ip ospf neighbor

Neighbor ID     Pri   State       Dead Time   Address         Interface
3.3.3.3           1   FULL/DR     00:00:36    30.2.3.1        Gi2/0
P3#
```

We can look at the interface as it is seen by OSPF:

```
P3#sh ip ospf interface gi 1/0
GigabitEthernet1/0 is up, line protocol is up
  Internet Address 30.1.3.2/24, Area 0, Attached via Network Statement
  Process ID 1, Router ID 30.30.30.1, Network Type BROADCAST, Cost: 1
  Topology-MTID    Cost    Disabled    Shutdown    Topology Name
        0            1        no          no          Base
  Transmit Delay is 1 sec, State DR, Priority 1
  Designated Router (ID) 30.30.30.1, Interface address 30.1.3.2
  No backup designated router on this network
  Timer intervals configured, Hello 10, Dead 40, Wait 40, Retransmit 5
    oob-resync timeout 40
    No Hellos (Passive interface)
  Supports Link-local Signaling (LLS)
  Cisco NSF helper support enabled
  IETF  NSF helper support enabled
  Index 1/2, flood queue length 0
 Next 0x0(0)/0x0(0)
 Last flood scan length is 0, maximum is 0
 Last flood scan time is 0 msec, maximum is 0 msec
 Neighbor Count is 0, Adjacent neighbor count is 0
 Suppress hello for 0 neighbor(s)
P3#
```

Here, we can see that the interface is showing as a passive interface. If we look at the connecting interface from PE1, we can see that this is not set to passive:

```
PE1#sh ip ospf interface gi 6/0
GigabitEthernet6/0 is up, line protocol is up
  Internet Address 30.1.3.1/24, Area 0, Attached via Network Statement
  Process ID 1, Router ID 1.1.1.1, Network Type BROADCAST, Cost: 1
  Topology-MTID    Cost    Disabled    Shutdown    Topology Name
        0            1        no          no          Base
  Transmit Delay is 1 sec, State DR, Priority 1
  Designated Router (ID) 1.1.1.1, Interface address 30.1.3.1
  No backup designated router on this network
  Timer intervals configured, Hello 10, Dead 40, Wait 40, Retransmit 5
    oob-resync timeout 40
    Hello due in 00:00:07
  Supports Link-local Signaling (LLS)
```

```
      Cisco NSF helper support enabled
      IETF NSF helper support enabled
      Index 4/4, flood queue length 0
     Next 0x0(0)/0x0(0)
     Last flood scan length is 0, maximum is 1
     Last flood scan time is 0 msec, maximum is 4 msec
     Neighbor Count is 0, Adjacent neighbor count is 0
     Suppress hello for 0 neighbor(s)
   PE1#
```

Now, we know that the GigabitEthernet interface 1/0 on P3 must be set as a passive interface, which will prevent it taking part in the exchange of EIGRP messages. Let's remove this setting:

```
   P3(config)#int gi 1/0
   P3(config-if)#router ospf 1
   P3(config-router)#no passive-interface Gi1/0
```

Straight away, we can see our EIGRP adjacency form, as well as our LDP adjacency:

```
   P3(config-router)#
   *Aug 25 18:18:51.063: %OSPF-5-ADJCHG: Process 1, Nbr 1.1.1.1 on
   GigabitEthernet1/0 from LOADING to FULL, Loading Done
   P3(config-router)#
   P3(config-router)#
   *Aug 25 18:19:10.367: %LDP-5-NBRCHG: LDP Neighbor 1.1.1.1:0 (1) is UP
   P3(config-router)#
```

Lastly, we can check that the MPLS forwarding table is looking healthier:

```
   PE1#sh mpls forwarding-table
   Local  Outgoing    Prefix          Bytes Label  Outgoing    Next Hop
   Label  Label       or Tunnel Id    Switched     interface
   16     No Label    192.168.1.1/32  0            Gi3/0       10.3.1.1
   17     17          3.3.3.3/32      0            Gi6/0       30.1.3.2
   18     Pop Label   30.2.3.0/24     0            Gi6/0       30.1.3.2
   19     22          30.2.1.0/24     0            Gi6/0       30.1.3.2
   22     Pop Label   30.30.30.0/24   0            Gi6/0       30.1.3.2
   23     23          30.2.2.0/24     0            Gi6/0       30.1.3.2
   PE1#
```

Ticket 2

Router	Int Gi 1/0	Int Gi 2/0
P1	Admin Down	Admin Down
P2	Up	Up
P3	Admin Down	Admin Down

With P1 and P3 shut down, there is no label exchange (2 faults).

```
PE1#sh mpls forwarding-table
Local  Outgoing     Prefix            Bytes Label  Outgoing    Next Hop
Label  Label        or Tunnel Id      Switched     interface
16     No Label     192.168.1.1/32    0            Gi3/0       10.3.1.1
17     18           3.3.3.3/32        0            Gi5/0       30.1.2.2
18     22           30.2.3.0/24       0            Gi5/0       30.1.2.2
19     21           30.2.1.0/24       0            Gi5/0       30.1.2.2
21     Pop Label    20.20.20.1/32     0            Gi5/0       30.1.2.2
22     No Label     30.30.30.0/24     0            drop
23     20           30.2.2.0/24       0            Gi5/0       30.1.2.2
PE1#


PE2#sh mpls forwarding-table
Local  Outgoing     Prefix            Bytes Label  Outgoing    Next Hop
Label  Label        or Tunnel Id      Switched     interface
17     No Label     1.1.1.1/32        0            Gi5/0       30.2.2.2
19     No Label     20.20.20.1/32     0            Gi5/0       30.2.2.2
20     No Label     30.1.3.0/24       0            Gi5/0       30.2.2.2
21     No Label     30.1.2.0/24       0            Gi5/0       30.2.2.2
22     No Label     30.1.1.0/24       0            Gi5/0       30.2.2.2
23     No Label     30.30.30.0/24     0            drop
PE2#
```

It looks like we have more issues on the side connecting to PE2.

```
PE2#sh ip int bri | i up
GigabitEthernet1/0   20.1.1.2      YES manual up             up
GigabitEthernet2/0   20.2.1.2      YES manual up             up
GigabitEthernet3/0   20.3.1.2      YES manual up             up
GigabitEthernet4/0   30.2.1.1      YES manual up             up
GigabitEthernet5/0   30.2.2.1      YES manual up             up
GigabitEthernet6/0   30.2.3.1      YES manual up             up
Loopback0            2.2.2.2       YES manual up             up
Loopback1            3.3.3.3       YES manual up             up
PE2#sh int desc | i up
Interface            Status        Protocol Description
```

```
    Gi1/0           up          up          Connection to Cust1-Site2
    Gi2/0           up          up          Connection to Cust2-Site2
    Gi3/0           up          up          Connection to Cust3-Site2
    Gi4/0           up          up          link to P1
    Gi5/0           up          up          link to P2
    Gi6/0           up          up          link to P3
    Lo0             up          up
    Lo1             up          up
    PE2#ping 30.2.2.1
    Type escape sequence to abort.
    Sending 5, 100-byte ICMP Echos to 30.2.2.1, timeout is 2 seconds:
    !!!!!
    Success rate is 100 percent (5/5)
    PE2#
```

How much can we deduce from PE2 alone? Well, we can see that PE2 is transmitting LDP messages but nor receiving any:

```
    PE2#sh mpls ldp discovery
      Local LDP Identifier:
        3.3.3.3:0
        Discovery Sources:
        Interfaces:
        GigabitEthernet4/0 (ldp): xmit
        GigabitEthernet5/0 (ldp): xmit
        GigabitEthernet6/0 (ldp): xmit
    PE2#
```

Compare this to PE1:

```
    PE1#sh mpls ldp discovery
      Local LDP Identifier:
        1.1.1.1:0
        Discovery Sources:
        Interfaces:
        GigabitEthernet4/0 (ldp): xmit
        GigabitEthernet5/0 (ldp): xmit/recv
            LDP Id: 20.20.20.1:0
        GigabitEthernet6/0 (ldp): xmit
    PE1#
```

So, we know that we are not expecting to see any traffic on Gi 4/0 or 6/0, but we should see something on Gi 5/0 (like we do for PE1).

Now, we should move on to P2:

```
P2#sh mpls ldp discovery
 Local LDP Identifier:
    20.20.20.1:0
    Discovery Sources:
    Interfaces:
   GigabitEthernet1/0 (ldp): xmit/recv
       LDP Id: 1.1.1.1:0
P2#
```

OK, so from this, it looks like Gi2/0 is not taking part in LDP. We can confirm this as well:

```
P2#sh mpls interfaces
Interface              IP          Tunnel   BGP Static Operational
GigabitEthernet1/0     Yes (ldp)   No       No  No     Yes
P2#
```

This is an easy fix:

```
P2(config)#int gi 2/0
P2(config-if)#mpls ip
P2(config-if)#
*Aug 25 18:41:06.763: %LDP-5-NBRCHG: LDP Neighbor 3.3.3.3:0 (1) is UP
P2(config-if)#
```

We can see that the interface is taking part in MPLS and that PE2 is now receiving LDP messages on Gi 5/0:

```
P2#sh mpls interfaces
Interface              IP          Tunnel   BGP Static Operational
GigabitEthernet1/0     Yes (ldp)   No       No  No     Yes
GigabitEthernet2/0     Yes (ldp)   No       No  No     Yes
P2#

PE2#sh mpls ldp discovery
 Local LDP Identifier:
    3.3.3.3:0
    Discovery Sources:
    Interfaces:
   GigabitEthernet4/0 (ldp): xmit
   GigabitEthernet5/0 (ldp): xmit/recv
       LDP Id: 20.20.20.1:0
   GigabitEthernet6/0 (ldp): xmit
PE2#
```

The forwarding table on PE2 also looks better now.

```
PE2#sh mpls forwarding-table
Local   Outgoing   Prefix          Bytes Label   Outgoing    Next Hop
Label   Label      or Tunnel Id    Switched      interface
17      25         1.1.1.1/32      0             Gi5/0       30.2.2.2
19      Pop Label  20.20.20.1/32   0             Gi5/0       30.2.2.2
20      16         30.1.3.0/24     0             Gi5/0       30.2.2.2
21      19         30.1.2.0/24     0             Gi5/0       30.2.2.2
22      24         30.1.1.0/24     0             Gi5/0       30.2.2.2
PE2#
```

We have resolved the first problem. We still have another to fix. If we look at the forwarding table for P2 we can see a similar issue:

```
P2#sh mpls forwarding-table
Local   Outgoing   Prefix          Bytes Label   Outgoing    Next Hop
Label   Label      or Tunnel Id    Switched      interface
16      No Label   30.1.3.0/24     0             drop
18      No Label   3.3.3.3/32      0             drop
19      No Label   30.1.2.0/24     0             drop
20      No Label   30.2.2.0/24     0             drop
21      No Label   30.2.1.0/24     0             drop
22      No Label   30.2.3.0/24     0             drop
24      No Label   30.1.1.0/24     0             drop
25      No Label   1.1.1.1/32      0             drop
P2#
```

We do not have any Outgoing labels, and we have a "drop" action.

Let's do another comparison with PE2:

```
PE2#sh mpls forwarding-table detail
Local   Outgoing   Prefix          Bytes Label   Outgoing    Next Hop
Label   Label      or Tunnel Id    Switched      interface
17      25         1.1.1.1/32      0             Gi5/0       30.2.2.2
        MAC/Encaps=14/18, MRU=1500, Label Stack{25}
        CA1101FB0038CA0F01FB008C8847 00019000
        No output feature configured
19      Pop Label  20.20.20.1/32   0             Gi5/0       30.2.2.2
        MAC/Encaps=14/14, MRU=1504, Label Stack{}
        CA1101FB0038CA0F01FB008C8847
        No output feature configured
20      16         30.1.3.0/24     0             Gi5/0       30.2.2.2
        MAC/Encaps=14/18, MRU=1500, Label Stack{16}
        CA1101FB0038CA0F01FB008C8847 00010000
        No output feature configured
21      19         30.1.2.0/24     0             Gi5/0       30.2.2.2
```

```
     MAC/Encaps=14/18, MRU=1500, Label Stack{19}
     CA1101FB0038CA0F01FB008C8847 00013000
     No output feature configured
22      24           30.1.1.0/24      0              Gi5/0      30.2.2.2
     MAC/Encaps=14/18, MRU=1500, Label Stack{24}
     CA1101FB0038CA0F01FB008C8847 00018000
     No output feature configured
PE2#

P2#sh mpls forwarding-table detail
Local   Outgoing    Prefix           Bytes Label   Outgoing    Next Hop
Label   Label       or Tunnel Id     Switched      interface
16      No Label    30.1.3.0/24      0             drop
   MAC/Encaps=0/0, MRU=0, Label Stack{}
   No output feature configured
18      No Label    3.3.3.3/32       0             drop
   MAC/Encaps=0/0, MRU=0, Label Stack{}
   No output feature configured
19      No Label    30.1.2.0/24      0             drop
   MAC/Encaps=0/0, MRU=0, Label Stack{}
   No output feature configured
20      No Label    30.2.2.0/24      0             drop
   MAC/Encaps=0/0, MRU=0, Label Stack{}
   No output feature configured
21      No Label    30.2.1.0/24      0             drop
   MAC/Encaps=0/0, MRU=0, Label Stack{}
   No output feature configured
22      No Label    30.2.3.0/24      0             drop
   MAC/Encaps=0/0, MRU=0, Label Stack{}
   No output feature configured
24      No Label    30.1.1.0/24      0             drop
   MAC/Encaps=0/0, MRU=0, Label Stack{}
   No output feature configured
25      No Label    1.1.1.1/32       0             drop
   MAC/Encaps=0/0, MRU=0, Label Stack{}
   No output feature configured
P2#
```

P2 is missing the CA values that PE2 has. So, what are the CA values? Have a look at the output from "sh adjacency detail" from PE2:

```
PE2#sh adjacency detail
Protocol Interface                    Address
TAG      GigabitEthernet4/0           30.2.1.2(2)
                                      0 packets, 0 bytes
                                      epoch 0
                                      sourced in sev-epoch 0
```

```
                                      Encap length 14
                                      CA1001FB0038CA0F01FB00708847
                                      ARP
IP         GigabitEthernet5/0         30.2.2.2(12)
                                      7 packets, 630 bytes
                                      epoch 0
                                      sourced in sev-epoch 0
                                      Encap length 14
                                      CA1101FB0038CA0F01FB008C0800
                                      ARP
```

I have only included 2 entries from the output, but it's enough to get an idea for what the issue is. Notice one protocol says TAG and one says IP. In the output from "sh mpls forwarding-table detail" for PE2, we see that PE2 had a number of "CA" entries ending in 8847. These would be CEF entries. Remember that we require CEF for MPLS to work. Well, the lack of these in the forwarding table on P2 would denote an issue with CEF.

Recall from the first ticket that we checked our CEF table for P3. Well, this check was deliberately omitted. If we check it on P2, we can see:

```
P2# sh ip cef
%IPv4 CEF not running
P2#
```

So, let's enable it and see what happens:

```
P2#conf t
P2(config)#ip cef
P2(config)#
```

Straight away, our mpls forwarding table looks much healthier:

```
P2#sh mpls forwarding-table
Local   Outgoing    Prefix          Bytes Label   Outgoing    Next Hop
Label   Label       or Tunnel Id    Switched     interface
16      Pop Label   30.1.3.0/24     0             Gi1/0       30.1.2.1
18      Pop Label   3.3.3.3/32      216           Gi2/0       30.2.2.1
21      Pop Label   30.2.1.0/24     0             Gi2/0       30.2.2.1
22      Pop Label   30.2.3.0/24     0             Gi2/0       30.2.2.1
24      Pop Label   30.1.1.0/24     0             Gi1/0       30.1.2.1
25      Pop Label   1.1.1.1/32      232           Gi1/0       30.1.2.1
P2#
```

If we look at the detail for our forwarding table, we can see that we also have it populated with the CA values that we were previously missing:

```
P2#sh mpls forwarding-table detail
Local   Outgoing    Prefix           Bytes Label    Outgoing    Next Hop
Label   Label       or Tunnel Id     Switched       interface
16      Pop Label   30.1.3.0/24      0              Gi1/0       30.1.2.1
   MAC/Encaps=14/14, MRU=1504, Label Stack{}
   CA0E01FB008CCA1101FB001C8847
   No output feature configured
18      Pop Label   3.3.3.3/32       486            Gi2/0       30.2.2.1
   MAC/Encaps=14/14, MRU=1504, Label Stack{}
   CA0F01FB008CCA1101FB00388847
   No output feature configured
21      Pop Label   30.2.1.0/24      0              Gi2/0       30.2.2.1
   MAC/Encaps=14/14, MRU=1504, Label Stack{}
   CA0F01FB008CCA1101FB00388847
   No output feature configured
22      Pop Label   30.2.3.0/24      0              Gi2/0       30.2.2.1
   MAC/Encaps=14/14, MRU=1504, Label Stack{}
   CA0F01FB008CCA1101FB00388847
   No output feature configured
24      Pop Label   30.1.1.0/24      0              Gi1/0       30.1.2.1
   MAC/Encaps=14/14, MRU=1504, Label Stack{}
   CA0E01FB008CCA1101FB001C8847
   No output feature configured
25      Pop Label   1.1.1.1/32       522            Gi1/0       30.1.2.1
   MAC/Encaps=14/14, MRU=1504, Label Stack{}
   CA0E01FB008CCA1101FB001C8847
   No output feature configured
P2#
```

Ticket 3

Router	Int Gi 1/0	Int Gi 2/0
P1	Up	Up
P2	Admin Down	Admin Down
P3	Admin Down	Admin Down

With P2 and P3 shut down, there is no label exchange (1 fault).

```
PE1#sh mpls forwarding-table
Local   Outgoing    Prefix           Bytes Label    Outgoing    Next Hop
Label   Label       or Tunnel Id     Switched       interface
16      No Label    192.168.1.1/32   0              Gi3/0       10.3.1.1
17      No Label    10.10.10.1/32    0              Gi4/0       30.1.1.2
```

```
18      No Label    30.2.1.0/24         0           Gi4/0       30.1.1.2
19      No Label    3.3.3.3/32          0           Gi4/0       30.1.1.2
20      No Label    30.2.3.0/24         0           Gi4/0       30.1.1.2
21      No Label    30.2.2.0/24         0           Gi4/0       30.1.1.2
PE1#

PE2#sh mpls forwarding-table
Local   Outgoing    Prefix              Bytes Label Outgoing    Next Hop
Label   Label       or Tunnel Id        Switched    interface
16      No Label    10.10.10.1/32       0           Gi4/0       30.2.1.2
17      No Label    1.1.1.1/32          0           Gi4/0       30.2.1.2
18      No Label    30.1.3.0/24         0           Gi4/0       30.2.1.2
19      No Label    30.1.2.0/24         0           Gi4/0       30.2.1.2
20      No Label    30.1.1.0/24         0           Gi4/0       30.2.1.2
PE2#
```

As always, we start by checking basic connectivity:

```
PE1#sh int desc
Interface           Status          Protocol  Description
Fa0/0               admin down      down
Gi1/0               up              up        Connection to Cust1-Site1
Gi2/0               up              up        Connection to Cust2-Site1
Gi3/0               up              up        Connection to Cust3-Site1
Gi4/0               up              up        link to P1
Gi5/0               up              up        link to P2
Gi6/0               up              up        link to P3
Lo0                 up              up
PE1#sh ip int bri | i up
GigabitEthernet1/0          10.1.1.2        YES NVRAM   up          up
GigabitEthernet2/0          10.2.1.2        YES NVRAM   up          up
GigabitEthernet3/0          10.3.1.2        YES NVRAM   up          up
GigabitEthernet4/0          30.1.1.1        YES NVRAM   up          up
GigabitEthernet5/0          30.1.2.1        YES NVRAM   up          up
GigabitEthernet6/0          30.1.3.1        YES NVRAM   up          up
Loopback0                   1.1.1.1         YES NVRAM   up          up
PE1#ping 30.1.1.2
Type escape sequence to abort.
Sending 5, 100-byte ICMP Echos to 30.1.1.2, timeout is 2 seconds:
!!!!!
Success rate is 100 percent (5/5)
PE1#

PE2#ping 30.2.1.1
Type escape sequence to abort.
Sending 5, 100-byte ICMP Echos to 30.2.1.1, timeout is 2 seconds:
!!!!!
```

```
Success rate is 100 percent (5/5)
PE2#
```

Do we have IGP based connectivity?

```
PE1#sh ip route ospf | beg Gate
Gateway of last resort is not set

      3.0.0.0/32 is subnetted, 1 subnets
O        3.3.3.3 [110/3] via 30.1.1.2, 00:07:14, GigabitEthernet4/0
      10.0.0.0/8 is variably subnetted, 3 subnets, 2 masks
O        10.10.10.1/32 [110/2] via 30.1.1.2, 00:07:24, Gi4/0
      30.0.0.0/8 is variably subnetted, 9 subnets, 2 masks
O        30.2.1.0/24 [110/2] via 30.1.1.2, 00:07:14, Gi4/0
O        30.2.2.0/24 [110/3] via 30.1.1.2, 00:07:14, Gi4/0
O        30.2.3.0/24 [110/3] via 30.1.1.2, 00:07:14, Gi4/0
PE1#

PE2#sh ip route ospf | beg Gate
Gateway of last resort is not set

      1.0.0.0/32 is subnetted, 1 subnets
O        1.1.1.1 [110/3] via 30.2.1.2, 00:08:10, GigabitEthernet4/0
      10.0.0.0/32 is subnetted, 1 subnets
O        10.10.10.1 [110/2] via 30.2.1.2, 00:08:10, Gi4/0
      30.0.0.0/8 is variably subnetted, 9 subnets, 2 masks
O        30.1.1.0/24 [110/2] via 30.2.1.2, 00:08:10, Gi4/0
O        30.1.2.0/24 [110/3] via 30.2.1.2, 00:08:10, Gi4/0
O        30.1.3.0/24 [110/3] via 30.2.1.2, 00:08:10, Gi4/0
PE2#
```

We are receiving OSPF routes, so that's our IGP ruled out from the problem. Let's check CEF, as that has been an issue in the past:

```
P1#sh ip cef summary
IPv4 CEF is enabled and running
VRF Default
 25 prefixes (25/0 fwd/non-fwd)
 Table id 0x0
 Database epoch:        0 (25 entries at this epoch)

P1#
```

CEF is OK, so let's check MPLS:

```
PE1#sh mpls ldp discovery
```

```
   Local LDP Identifier:
     1.1.1.1:0
     Discovery Sources:
     Interfaces:
       GigabitEthernet4/0 (ldp): xmit
       GigabitEthernet5/0 (ldp): xmit
       GigabitEthernet6/0 (ldp): xmit
PE1#

PE2#sh mpls ldp discovery
   Local LDP Identifier:
     3.3.3.3:0
     Discovery Sources:
     Interfaces:
       GigabitEthernet4/0 (ldp): xmit
       GigabitEthernet5/0 (ldp): xmit
       GigabitEthernet6/0 (ldp): xmit
PE2#
```

So, neither are receiving LDP packets from P1. Is P1 enabled for MPLS?

```
P1#sh mpls interfaces
Interface              IP          Tunnel   BGP  Static Operational
GigabitEthernet1/0     Yes (tdp)   No       No   No     Yes
GigabitEthernet2/0     Yes (tdp)   No       No   No     Yes
P1#
```

Yes, it is. What about comparing PE1 and PE2?

```
PE1#sh mpls interfaces
Interface              IP          Tunnel   BGP  Static Operational
GigabitEthernet4/0     Yes (ldp)   No       No   No     Yes
GigabitEthernet5/0     Yes (ldp)   No       No   No     Yes
GigabitEthernet6/0     Yes (ldp)   No       No   No     Yes
PE1#

PE2#sh mpls interfaces
Interface              IP          Tunnel   BGP  Static Operational
GigabitEthernet4/0     Yes (ldp)   No       No   No     Yes
GigabitEthernet5/0     Yes (ldp)   No       No   No     Yes
GigabitEthernet6/0     Yes (ldp)   No       No   No     Yes
PE2#
```

P1 is running TDP instead of LDP. Let's fix this and see what happens:

```
P1(config)#mpls label protocol ldp
```

```
P1(config)#
*Aug 26 07:23:09.971: %LDP-5-NBRCHG: LDP Neighbor 1.1.1.1:0 (1) is UP
*Aug 26 07:23:09.975: %LDP-5-NBRCHG: LDP Neighbor 3.3.3.3:0 (2) is UP
P1(config)#
```

Our LDP neighbors appear, and our forwarding tables look good:

```
PE1#sh mpls forwarding-table
Local  Outgoing    Prefix            Bytes Label   Outgoing    Next Hop
Label  Label       or Tunnel Id      Switched      interface
16     No Label    192.168.1.1/32    0             Gi3/0       10.3.1.1
17     Pop Label   10.10.10.1/32     0             Gi4/0       30.1.1.2
18     Pop Label   30.2.1.0/24       0             Gi4/0       30.1.1.2
19     17          3.3.3.3/32        0             Gi4/0       30.1.1.2
20     21          30.2.3.0/24       0             Gi4/0       30.1.1.2
21     20          30.2.2.0/24       0             Gi4/0       30.1.1.2
PE1#

PE2#sh mpls forwarding-table
Local  Outgoing    Prefix            Bytes Label   Outgoing    Next Hop
Label  Label       or Tunnel Id      Switched      interface
16     Pop Label   10.10.10.1/32     0             Gi4/0       30.2.1.2
17     16          1.1.1.1/32        0             Gi4/0       30.2.1.2
18     19          30.1.3.0/24       0             Gi4/0       30.2.1.2
19     18          30.1.2.0/24       0             Gi4/0       30.2.1.2
20     Pop Label   30.1.1.0/24       0             Gi4/0       30.2.1.2
PE2#
```

Ticket 4

There is no BGP neighborship between PE1 and PE2 (2 faults).

We start by confirming the issue:

```
PE1#sh ip bgp neigh | i (remote|state)
BGP neighbor is 2.2.2.2,  remote AS 100, internal link
  BGP version 4, remote router ID 0.0.0.0
  BGP state = Idle
PE1#

PE2#sh ip bgp neigh | i (remote|state)
BGP neighbor is 1.1.1.1,  remote AS 100, internal link
  BGP version 4, remote router ID 0.0.0.0
```

```
     BGP state = Idle
PE2#
```

The above check also rules out a number of possible faults. Firstly, we can see that both are in agreement about the other sides AS number (AS 100), secondly we know we are using the same BGP version, and thirdly, we can see what our neighbor is.

Starting with the basic checks, can we reach the peering IP addresses? Firstly, what are the peering IP addresses?

```
PE1#sh ip bgp summary
BGP router identifier 1.1.1.1, local AS number 100
BGP table version is 1, main routing table version 1

Neighbor   V   AS MsgRcvd MsgSent TblVer  InQ OutQ Up/Down  State/PfxRcd
2.2.2.2    4  100       0       0       1    0    0 never    Idle
PE1#
```

Well, it is probably the loopback interface, but you can never 100% guarantee. We are justified in using "sh run | i neighbor 2.2.2.2" here on PE1:

```
PE1#sh run | i neighbor 2.2.2.2
 neighbor 2.2.2.2 remote-as 100
 neighbor 2.2.2.2 update-source Loopback0
 neighbor 2.2.2.2 activate
 neighbor 2.2.2.2 send-community extended
PE1#
```

Similarly, we can run this on PE2:

```
PE2#sh run | i neighbor 1.1.1.1
 neighbor 1.1.1.1 remote-as 100
 neighbor 1.1.1.1 update-source Loopback1
PE2#
```

The first thing that stands out is that we have more entries on PE1 than we do on PE2. From this limited output, it would appear that we are missing an address family on PE2.

Before we come to that though, we should confirm that we have reachability to the loopback interfaces of the other router from our own loopback interfaces.

Lets get the ip addresses:

```
PE1#sh ip int bri | i Loopback0
```

```
    Loopback0              1.1.1.1         YES NVRAM  up         up
PE1#

PE2#sh ip int bri | i Loopback1
    Loopback1              3.3.3.3         YES NVRAM  up         up
PE2#
```

Well, loopback 1 on PE1 has a different IP address to the one set on PE1's BGP configuration. So, which is correct? Well, if PE2 has a loopback with IP address 2.2.2.2, we should use that instead.

```
PE2#sh ip int bri | i Loopback0
    Loopback0              2.2.2.2         YES NVRAM  up         up
PE2#
```

Does PE1 have reachability to this IP address?

```
PE1#ping 2.2.2.2 so lo0
Type escape sequence to abort.
Sending 5, 100-byte ICMP Echos to 2.2.2.2, timeout is 2 seconds:
Packet sent with a source address of 1.1.1.1
.....
Success rate is 0 percent (0/5)
PE1#sh ip route 2.2.2.2
% Network not in table
PE1#
```

No, it does not. PE2, however, can see PE1's loopback interface:

```
PE2#sh ip route 1.1.1.1
Routing entry for 1.1.1.1/32
  Known via "ospf 1", distance 110, metric 3, type intra area
  Last update from 30.2.1.2 on GigabitEthernet4/0, 00:41:49 ago
  Routing Descriptor Blocks:
  * 30.2.1.2, from 1.1.1.1, 00:41:49 ago, via GigabitEthernet4/0
      Route metric is 3, traffic share count is 1
PE2#
```

At this stage, we should check our IGP configuration. Are we advertising lo0 from PE2?

```
PE2#sh ip ospf interface lo0
%OSPF: OSPF not enabled on Loopback0
PE2#
```

If we compare this to PE1, we can see that it is working in OSPF:

```
PE1#sh ip ospf interface lo0
Loopback0 is up, line protocol is up
  Internet Address 1.1.1.1/32, Area 0, Attached via Interface Enable
  Process ID 1, Router ID 1.1.1.1, Network Type LOOPBACK, Cost: 1
  Topology-MTID    Cost    Disabled    Shutdown    Topology Name
        0           1         no          no           Base
  Enabled by interface config, including secondary ip addresses
  Loopback interface is treated as a stub Host
PE1#
```

In order to add the interface into OSPF, we need to first make sure adding it to the correct process and area. We know that PE1 can reach the networks advertised in OSPF from PE2 through its physical interface. We can test this by pinging PE2's Gi 4/0 interface:

```
PE1#sh ip route ospf | beg Gate
Gateway of last resort is not set

      3.0.0.0/32 is subnetted, 1 subnets
O        3.3.3.3 [110/3] via 30.1.1.2, 00:51:49, Gi4/0
      10.0.0.0/8 is variably subnetted, 3 subnets, 2 masks
O        10.10.10.1/32 [110/2] via 30.1.1.2, 00:51:59, Gi4/0
      30.0.0.0/8 is variably subnetted, 9 subnets, 2 masks
O        30.2.1.0/24 [110/2] via 30.1.1.2, 00:51:49, Gi4/0
O        30.2.2.0/24 [110/3] via 30.1.1.2, 00:51:49, Gi4/0
O        30.2.3.0/24 [110/3] via 30.1.1.2, 00:51:49, Gi4/0
PE1#

PE2#sh ip int bri | i up
Interface              IP-Address      OK? Method Status    Protocol
GigabitEthernet1/0     20.1.1.2        YES NVRAM  up        up
GigabitEthernet2/0     20.2.1.2        YES NVRAM  up        up
GigabitEthernet3/0     20.3.1.2        YES NVRAM  up        up
GigabitEthernet4/0     30.2.1.1        YES NVRAM  up        up
GigabitEthernet5/0     30.2.2.1        YES NVRAM  up        up
GigabitEthernet6/0     30.2.3.1        YES NVRAM  up        up
Loopback0              2.2.2.2         YES NVRAM  up        up
Loopback1              3.3.3.3         YES NVRAM  up        up
PE2#

PE1#ping 30.2.1.1
Type escape sequence to abort.
Sending 5, 100-byte ICMP Echos to 30.2.1.1, timeout is 2 seconds:
!!!!!
Success rate is 100 percent (5/5)
PE1#
```

Now that we know that this works, we can look at Gi4/0 and put Lo0 in the same process and area:

```
PE2#sh ip ospf interface Gi 4/0 | i (Area|Process)
  Internet Address 30.2.1.1/24, Area 0, Attached via Network
Statement
  Process ID 1, Router ID 3.3.3.3, Network Type BROADCAST, Cost: 1
PE2#
```

Here, we can see that the interface should be in process 1 and area 0:

```
PE2(config)#int lo0
PE2(config-if)#ip ospf 1 area 0
PE2(config-if)#
```

Now, PE1 has an route to 2.2.2.2:

```
PE1#sh ip route 2.2.2.2
Routing entry for 2.2.2.2/32
  Known via "ospf 1", distance 110, metric 3, type intra area
  Last update from 30.1.1.2 on GigabitEthernet4/0, 00:00:28 ago
  Routing Descriptor Blocks:
  * 30.1.1.2, from 3.3.3.3, 00:00:28 ago, via GigabitEthernet4/0
      Route metric is 3, traffic share count is 1
PE1#ping 2.2.2.2 so lo0
Type escape sequence to abort.
Sending 5, 100-byte ICMP Echos to 2.2.2.2, timeout is 2 seconds:
Packet sent with a source address of 1.1.1.1
!!!!!
Success rate is 100 percent (5/5)
PE1#
```

We have connectivity, so we can now fix our BGP configuration:

```
PE2(config)#router bgp 100
PE2(config-router)#neigh 1.1.1.1 update-source lo0
PE2(config-router)#
*Aug 26 19:22:11.563: %BGP-5-ADJCHANGE: neighbor 1.1.1.1 Up
PE2(config-router)#
```

Lastly, we need to add the vpnv4 address family to BGP and assign our neighbor to it:

```
PE2(config)#router bgp 100
PE2(config-router)#address-family vpnv4
```

```
PE2(config-router-af)#neigh 1.1.1.1 activate
PE2(config-router-af)#neigh 1.1.1.1 send-community bo
```

Our BGP adjacencies should look healthy now:

```
PE1#sh ip bgp summary
BGP router identifier 1.1.1.1, local AS number 100
BGP table version is 1, main routing table version 1

Neighbor   V   AS MsgRcvd MsgSent TblVer  InQ OutQ Up/Down   Sta/PfxRcd
2.2.2.2    4 100       5       5      1    0    0 00:00:34            0
PE1#

PE2#sh ip bgp summ
BGP router identifier 3.3.3.3, local AS number 100
BGP table version is 1, main routing table version 1

Neighbor   V   AS MsgRcvd MsgSent TblVer  InQ OutQ Up/Down   Sta/PfxRcd
1.1.1.1    4 100       5       6      1    0    0 00:00:51            0
PE2#
```

Troubleshooting the Customer environment

Ticket 1

Customer 1 is not receiving any routes. (2 faults).

```
Cust1-Site1#sh ip route | beg Gate
Gateway of last resort is not set

      10.0.0.0/8 is variably subnetted, 2 subnets, 2 masks
C        10.1.1.0/24 is directly connected, GigabitEthernet1/0
L        10.1.1.1/32 is directly connected, GigabitEthernet1/0
      192.168.1.0/32 is subnetted, 1 subnets
C        192.168.1.1 is directly connected, Loopback0
Cust1-Site1#

Cust1-Site2#sh ip route | beg Gate
Gateway of last resort is not set

      20.0.0.0/8 is variably subnetted, 2 subnets, 2 masks
C        20.1.1.0/24 is directly connected, GigabitEthernet1/0
```

```
L         20.1.1.1/32 is directly connected, GigabitEthernet1/0
      172.16.0.0/32 is subnetted, 1 subnets
C         172.16.1.1 is directly connected, Loopback0
Cust1-Site2#
```

We start by checking reachability:

```
Cust1-Site1#ping 10.1.1.2
Type escape sequence to abort.
Sending 5, 100-byte ICMP Echos to 10.1.1.2, timeout is 2 seconds:
.!!!!
Success rate is 80 percent (4/5)
Cust1-Site1#
```

Next, we check to see if the connecting interface is enabled for EIGRP:

```
Cust1-Site1#sh ip eigrp interfaces
EIGRP-IPv4 Interfaces for AS(100)
                Xmit Queue   Mean Pacing Time   Multicast   Pending
Interface Peers Un/Reliable  SRTT Un/Reliable   Flow Timer  Routes
Gi1/0      0    0/0          0    0/1           0           0
Lo0        0    0/0          0    0/1           0           0
Cust1-Site1#
```

We can see that the customer router is enabled for EIGRP in AS 100. What AS are we set up for?

```
PE1#sh run vrf Cust1
Building configuration...

Current configuration : 336 bytes
ip vrf Cust1
 rd 100:100
 route-target export 100:100
 route-target import 100:100
!
!
interface GigabitEthernet1/0
 description Connection to Cust1-Site1
 ip vrf forwarding Cust1
 ip address 10.1.1.2 255.255.255.0
 negotiation auto
!
router bgp 100
 !
 address-family ipv4 vrf Cust1
```

```
    redistribute eigrp 10
  exit-address-family
 !
end

PE1#
```

We are forwarding on the correct interface. We are importing and exporting routes, and we have the BGP address family defined. We can see a difference though, and this is that we are redistributing EIGRP AS 10. The Customer router is using AS 100.

We can change their EIGRP AS number:

```
Cust1-Site1(config)#no router eigrp 100
Cust1-Site1(config)#router eigrp 10
Cust1-Site1(config-router)#network 10.1.1.0 0.0.0.255
Cust1-Site1(config-router)#network 192.168.1.0
Cust1-Site1(config-router)#end
Cust1-Site1#
```

We still have no adjacency. When we did "sh run vrf Cust1", we did not see any EIGRP configuration for vrf Cust1. We are still missing the address family within EIGRP:

```
PE1(config)#router eigrp 10
PE1(config-router)#address-family ipv4 vrf Cust1
PE1(config-router-af)#network 10.1.1.0 0.0.0.255
PE1(config-router-af)#end
%Warning: EIGRP Autonomous-System number must be provided
PE1#
```

Another little gotcha here; recall that autonomous-system needs to be set:

```
PE1(config)#router eigrp 10
PE1(config-router)#address-family ipv4 vrf Cust1
PE1(config-router-af)#autonomous-system 10
PE1(config-router-af)#
*Aug 26 20:08:00.131: %DUAL-5-NBRCHANGE: EIGRP-IPv4 10: Neighbor
10.1.1.1 (GigabitEthernet1/0) is up: new adjacency
PE1(config-router-af)#
```

Let's run through the same corrections on PE2:

```
PE2(config)#router eigrp 10
PE2(config-router)#address-family ipv4 vrf Cust1
PE2(config-router-af)#autonomous-system 10
```

```
PE2(config-router-af)#network 20.1.1.0 0.0.0.255
PE2(config-router-af)#
*Aug 26 20:11:16.831: %DUAL-5-NBRCHANGE: EIGRP-IPv4 10: Neighbor
20.1.1.1 (GigabitEthernet1/0) is up: new adjacency
PE2(config-router-af)#
```

We still do not have any new routes:

```
Cust1-Site1#sh ip route | beg Gate
Gateway of last resort is not set

      10.0.0.0/8 is variably subnetted, 2 subnets, 2 masks
C        10.1.1.0/24 is directly connected, GigabitEthernet1/0
L        10.1.1.1/32 is directly connected, GigabitEthernet1/0
      192.168.1.0/32 is subnetted, 1 subnets
C        192.168.1.1 is directly connected, Loopback0
Cust1-Site1#
```

This is because we have not added any redistribution to our EIGRP address family for vrf Cust1:

```
PE1(config-router-af)#redistribute bgp 100 metric 1000 10 100 1 1500

PE2(config-router-af)#redistribute bgp 100 metric 1000 10 100 1 1500
```

Now, we have a full routing table:

```
Cust1-Site1#sh ip route | beg Gate
Gateway of last resort is not set

      10.0.0.0/8 is variably subnetted, 2 subnets, 2 masks
C        10.1.1.0/24 is directly connected, GigabitEthernet1/0
L        10.1.1.1/32 is directly connected, GigabitEthernet1/0
      20.0.0.0/24 is subnetted, 1 subnets
D EX     20.1.1.0 [170/2562816] via 10.1.1.2, 00:01:20, Gi1/0
      172.16.0.0/32 is subnetted, 1 subnets
D        172.16.1.1 [90/131072] via 10.1.1.2, 00:01:20, Gi1/0
      192.168.1.0/32 is subnetted, 1 subnets
C        192.168.1.1 is directly connected, Loopback0
Cust1-Site1#

Cust1-Site2#sh ip route | beg Gate
Gateway of last resort is not set

      10.0.0.0/24 is subnetted, 1 subnets
D        10.1.1.0 [90/3072] via 20.1.1.2, 00:01:25, Gi1/0
```

```
                 20.0.0.0/8 is variably subnetted, 2 subnets, 2 masks
C                20.1.1.0/24 is directly connected, GigabitEthernet1/0
L                20.1.1.1/32 is directly connected, GigabitEthernet1/0
              172.16.0.0/32 is subnetted, 1 subnets
C                172.16.1.1 is directly connected, Loopback0
              192.168.1.0/32 is subnetted, 1 subnets
D                192.168.1.1 [90/131072] via 20.1.1.2, 00:01:25, Gi1/0
Cust1-Site2#
```

The final step is to check reachability:

```
Cust1-Site2#ping 192.168.1.1 so lo0
Type escape sequence to abort.
Sending 5, 100-byte ICMP Echos to 192.168.1.1, timeout is 2 seconds:
Packet sent with a source address of 172.16.1.1
!!!!!
Success rate is 100 percent (5/5)
Cust1-Site2#
```

Ticket 2

Customer 2 are not receiving their routes either (2 faults).

This time, you ask the junior tech if he created the address family for the eigrp process. He says no, so you start to create them:

```
PE1(config)#router eigrp 20
PE1(config-router)#address-family ipv4 vrf Cust2
PE1(config-router-af)#network 10.2.1.0 0.0.0.255
PE1(config-router-af)#autonomous-system 20
PE1(config-router-af)#
*Aug 30 11:25:24.943: %DUAL-5-NBRCHANGE: EIGRP-IPv4 20: Neighbor
10.2.1.1 (GigabitEthernet2/0) is up: new adjacency
PE1(config-router-af)#
PE1(config-router-af)#redistribute bgp 100 metric 1000 10 100 1 1500

PE2(config)#router eigrp 20
PE2(config-router)#address-family ipv4 vrf Cust2
PE2(config-router-af)#autonomous-system 20
PE2(config-router-af)#network 20.2.1.0 0.0.0.255
PE2(config-router-af)#
*Aug 30 11:29:06.215: %DUAL-5-NBRCHANGE: EIGRP-IPv4 20: Neighbor
20.2.1.1 (GigabitEthernet2/0) is up: new adjacency
```

```
PE2(config-router-af)#
PE2(config-router-af)#redistribute bgp 100 metric 1000 10 100 1 1500
```

We should make sure that we are redistributing properly in BGP as well. We can do this from the vrf or from BGP:

```
PE1#sh run vrf Cust2
Building configuration...

Current configuration : 509 bytes
ip vrf Cust2
 rd 200:200
 route-target export 200:200
 route-target import 200:200
!
!
interface GigabitEthernet2/0
 description Connection to Cust2-Site1
 ip vrf forwarding Cust2
 ip address 10.2.1.2 255.255.255.0
 negotiation auto
!
router bgp 100
 !
 address-family ipv4 vrf Cust2
  redistribute eigrp 20
 exit-address-family
!
router eigrp 20
!
address-family ipv4 vrf Cust2
  redistribute bgp 100 metric 1000 10 100 1 1500
  network 10.2.1.0 0.0.0.255
  autonomous-system 20
 exit-address-family
!
end

PE1#


PE2#sh run | sec bgp
   redistribute bgp 100 metric 1000 10 100 1 1500
  redistribute bgp 100
   redistribute bgp 100 metric 1000 10 100 1 1500
  redistribute bgp 100
  redistribute bgp 100
```

```
router bgp 100
 bgp log-neighbor-changes
 neighbor 1.1.1.1 remote-as 100
 neighbor 1.1.1.1 update-source Loopback0
 !
 address-family vpnv4
  neighbor 1.1.1.1 activate
  neighbor 1.1.1.1 send-community both
 exit-address-family
 !
 address-family ipv4 vrf Cust1
  redistribute eigrp 10
 exit-address-family
 !
 address-family ipv4 vrf Cust2
  redistribute eigrp 200
 exit-address-family
 !
 address-family ipv4 vrf Cust3
  redistribute eigrp 30
 exit-address-family
PE2#
```

We can see that PE2 is trying to redistribute the incorrect EIGRP AS, so let's fix that:

```
PE2(config)#router bgp 100
PE2(config-router)#address
PE2(config-router)#address-family ipv4 vrf Cust2
PE2(config-router-af)#no redistribute eigrp 200
PE2(config-router-af)#redistribute eigrp 20
PE2(config-router-af)#
```

At this stage, all our address families and redistribution commands are correct, but neither of the customer routers are getting any routes:

```
Cust2-Site1#sh ip route | beg Gate
Gateway of last resort is not set

      10.0.0.0/8 is variably subnetted, 2 subnets, 2 masks
C        10.2.1.0/24 is directly connected, GigabitEthernet1/0
L        10.2.1.1/32 is directly connected, GigabitEthernet1/0
      192.168.1.0/32 is subnetted, 1 subnets
C        192.168.1.1 is directly connected, Loopback0
Cust2-Site1#

Cust2-Site2#sh ip route | beg Gate
Gateway of last resort is not set
```

```
        20.0.0.0/8 is variably subnetted, 2 subnets, 2 masks
C          20.2.1.0/24 is directly connected, GigabitEthernet1/0
L          20.2.1.1/32 is directly connected, GigabitEthernet1/0
        172.16.0.0/32 is subnetted, 1 subnets
C          172.16.1.1 is directly connected, Loopback0
Cust2-Site2#
```

This looks like an issue with our MPLS core (mainly because everything else is working).

We know we are forwarding and that we are forwarding on the correct interfaces:

```
PE1#sh ip vrf Cust2
  Name                         Default RD              Interfaces
  Cust2                        200:200                 Gi2/0
PE1#

PE2#sh ip vrf Cust2
  Name                         Default RD              Interfaces
  Cust2                        200:200                 Gi2/0
PE2#
```

Let's see what BGP is telling us:

```
PE1#sh ip bgp vpnv4 vrf Cust2 192.168.1.1
BGP routing table entry for 200:200:192.168.1.1/32, version 15
Paths: (1 available, best #1, table Cust2)
  Advertised to update-groups:
     2
  Local
    10.2.1.1 from 0.0.0.0 (1.1.1.1)
      Origin incomplete, metric 130816, localpref 100, weight 32768,
 valid, sourced, best
      Extended Community: RT:200:200 Cost:pre-bestpath:128:130816
        0x8800:32768:0 0x8801:20:128256 0x8802:65281:2560
0x8803:65281:1500
        0x8806:0:3232235777
      mpls labels in/out 26/nolabel
PE1#
```

Looks fine there.

```
PE2#sh ip bgp vpnv4 vrf Cust2 172.16.1.1
BGP routing table entry for 200:200:172.16.1.1/32, version 15
Paths: (1 available, best #1, table Cust2)
  Advertised to update-groups:
```

```
                3
         Local
            20.2.1.1 from 0.0.0.0 (3.3.3.3)
              Origin incomplete, metric 130816, localpref 100, weight 32768,
      valid, sourced, best
              Extended Community: RT:20:20 Cost:pre-bestpath:128:130816
                0x8800:32768:0 0x8801:20:128256 0x8802:65281:2560
      0x8803:65281:1500
                0x8806:0:2886729985
              mpls labels in/out 24/nolabel
      PE2#
```

So, both are on the same table version and are being advertised out. Both are considered best and valid. On PE2, we can see an issue though; we are using different RT values to PE1

```
      PE1#sh ip bgp vpnv4 vrf Cust2 192.168.1.1 | i RT
            Extended Community: RT:200:200 Cost:pre-bestpath:128:130816
      PE1#

      PE2#sh ip bgp vpnv4 vrf Cust2 172.16.1.1 | i RT
            Extended Community: RT:20:20 Cost:pre-bestpath:128:130816
      PE2#
```

Let's change PE2.

```
      PE2(config)#ip vrf Cust2
      PE2(config-vrf)#no route-target import 20:20
      PE2(config-vrf)#no route-target export 20:20
      PE2(config-vrf)#route-target bo 200:200
      PE2(config-vrf)#
```

Now how do things look?

```
      Cust2-Site1#sh ip route | beg Gate
      Gateway of last resort is not set

            10.0.0.0/8 is variably subnetted, 2 subnets, 2 masks
      C        10.2.1.0/24 is directly connected, GigabitEthernet1/0
      L        10.2.1.1/32 is directly connected, GigabitEthernet1/0
            20.0.0.0/24 is subnetted, 1 subnets
      D        20.2.1.0 [90/3072] via 10.2.1.2, 00:00:01, Gi1/0
            172.16.0.0/32 is subnetted, 1 subnets
      D        172.16.1.1 [90/131072] via 10.2.1.2, 00:00:01, Gi1/0
            192.168.1.0/32 is subnetted, 1 subnets
      C        192.168.1.1 is directly connected, Loopback0
```

```
Cust2-Site1#

Cust2-Site2#sh ip route | beg Gate
Gateway of last resort is not set

         10.0.0.0/24 is subnetted, 1 subnets
D           10.2.1.0 [90/3072] via 20.2.1.2, 00:00:23, Gi1/0
         20.0.0.0/8 is variably subnetted, 2 subnets, 2 masks
C           20.2.1.0/24 is directly connected, GigabitEthernet1/0
L           20.2.1.1/32 is directly connected, GigabitEthernet1/0
         172.16.0.0/32 is subnetted, 1 subnets
C           172.16.1.1 is directly connected, Loopback0
         192.168.1.0/32 is subnetted, 1 subnets
D           192.168.1.1 [90/131072] via 20.2.1.2, 00:00:23, Gi1/0
Cust2-Site2#

Cust2-Site1#ping 172.16.1.1 so lo0
Type escape sequence to abort.
Sending 5, 100-byte ICMP Echos to 172.16.1.1, timeout is 2 seconds:
Packet sent with a source address of 192.168.1.1
!!!!!
Success rate is 100 percent (5/5)
Cust2-Site1#
```

Looking good! Let's move on.

Ticket 3

Customer 3 is also not receiving any routes (2 faults).

Starting with the PE routers, let's see what kind of connectivity we have:

```
PE1#sh ip route vrf Cust3 | beg Gate
Gateway of last resort is not set

PE1#

PE2#sh ip route vrf Cust3 | beg Gate
Gateway of last resort is not set

         20.0.0.0/8 is variably subnetted, 2 subnets, 2 masks
C           20.3.1.0/24 is directly connected, GigabitEthernet3/0
L           20.3.1.2/32 is directly connected, GigabitEthernet3/0
```

PE2#

PE2 has the better output, so let's start with that. Base on the assumption that the junior technician didn't add in the eigrp address families, this is where you start:

```
PE2(config)#router eigrp 30
PE2(config-router)#address-family ipv4 vrf Cust3
PE2(config-router-af)#network 20.3.1.0 0.0.0.255
PE2(config-router-af)#autonomous-system 30
PE2(config-router-af)#redistribute bgp 100 metric 1000 10 100 1 1500
PE2(config-router-af)#end
PE2#
*Aug 30 11:52:50.483: %DUAL-5-NBRCHANGE: EIGRP-IPv4 30: Neighbor
20.3.1.1 (GigabitEthernet3/0) is up: new adjacency
PE2#

PE2#sh ip route vrf Cust3 | beg Gate
Gateway of last resort is not set

      20.0.0.0/8 is variably subnetted, 2 subnets, 2 masks
C        20.3.1.0/24 is directly connected, GigabitEthernet3/0
L        20.3.1.2/32 is directly connected, GigabitEthernet3/0
      172.16.0.0/32 is subnetted, 1 subnets
D        172.16.1.1 [90/130816] via 20.3.1.1, 00:00:25, Gi3/0
PE2#
```

PE2 is looking better already. Let's try the same for PE1:

```
PE1(config)#router eigrp 30
PE1(config-router)#address-family ipv4 vrf Cust3
PE1(config-router-af)#network 10.3.1.0 0.0.0.255
PE1(config-router-af)#autonomous-system 30
PE1(config-router-af)#redistribute bgp 100 metric 1000 10 100 1 1500
PE1(config-router-af)#end
```

We still do not see an EIGRP adjacency yet, and the routing table for the VRF is still empty:

```
PE1#sh ip route vrf Cust3 | beg Gate
Gateway of last resort is not set

PE1#
```

Now, usually there would be at least something listed, so let's make sure that we have physical connectivity:

```
Cust3-Site1#ping 10.3.1.2
Type escape sequence to abort.
Sending 5, 100-byte ICMP Echos to 10.3.1.2, timeout is 2 seconds:
!!!!!
Success rate is 100 percent (5/5)
Cust3-Site1#
```

Looks ok, but remember we are dealing with two separate routing tables on the PE routers. If we ping the customer router in site 2 from PE2, we need to specify the vrf:

```
PE2#ping vrf Cust3 20.3.1.1
Type escape sequence to abort.
Sending 5, 100-byte ICMP Echos to 20.3.1.1, timeout is 2 seconds:
!!!!!
Success rate is 100 percent (5/5)
PE2#
```

If we try the same for site 1, we get this error:

```
PE1#ping vrf Cust3 10.3.1.1
% VRF Cust3 does not have a usable source address
PE1#
```

We can see from the list of VRFs that we do not have an interface assigned to vrf Cust3:

```
PE1#sh ip vrf
  Name                          Default RD           Interfaces
  Cust1                         100:100              Gi1/0
  Cust2                         200:200              Gi2/0
  Cust3                         300:300
PE1#
```

Let's fix that

```
PE1(config)#int gi 3/0
PE1(config-if)#ip vrf for Cust3
% Interface GigabitEthernet3/0 IPv4 disabled and address(es) removed
due to enabling VRF Cust3
PE1(config-if)#
*Aug 30 12:00:08.527: %DUAL-5-NBRCHANGE: EIGRP-IPv4 30: Neighbor
10.3.1.1 (GigabitEthernet3/0) is down: interface down
PE1(config-if)#ip add 10.3.1.2 255.255.255.0
PE1(config-if)#
*Aug 30 12:00:23.331: %DUAL-5-NBRCHANGE: EIGRP-IPv4 30: Neighbor
10.3.1.1 (GigabitEthernet3/0) is up: new adjacency
```

```
PE1(config-if)#
```

Now, PE1 is receiving routes from Customer3:

```
PE1#sh ip route vrf Cust3 | beg Gate
Gateway of last resort is not set

     10.0.0.0/8 is variably subnetted, 2 subnets, 2 masks
C       10.3.1.0/24 is directly connected, GigabitEthernet3/0
L       10.3.1.2/32 is directly connected, GigabitEthernet3/0
     192.168.1.0/32 is subnetted, 1 subnets
D       192.168.1.1 [90/130816] via 10.3.1.1, 00:00:24, Gi3/0
PE1#
```

How do things look from the customer router perspective?

```
Cust3-Site1#sh ip route | beg Gate
Gateway of last resort is not set

     10.0.0.0/8 is variably subnetted, 2 subnets, 2 masks
C       10.3.1.0/24 is directly connected, GigabitEthernet1/0
L       10.3.1.1/32 is directly connected, GigabitEthernet1/0
     192.168.1.0/32 is subnetted, 1 subnets
C       192.168.1.1 is directly connected, Loopback0
Cust3-Site1#

Cust3-Site2#sh ip route | beg Gate
Gateway of last resort is not set

     10.0.0.0/24 is subnetted, 1 subnets
D EX    10.3.1.0 [170/2562816] via 20.3.1.2, 00:00:08, Gi1/0
     20.0.0.0/8 is variably subnetted, 2 subnets, 2 masks
C       20.3.1.0/24 is directly connected, GigabitEthernet1/0
L       20.3.1.1/32 is directly connected, GigabitEthernet1/0
     172.16.0.0/32 is subnetted, 1 subnets
C       172.16.1.1 is directly connected, Loopback0
     192.168.1.0/32 is subnetted, 1 subnets
D       192.168.1.1 [90/131072] via 20.3.1.2, 00:00:08, Gi1/0
Cust3-Site2#
```

Site 2 looks ok, but site1 looks pretty sparse. So, let us use BGP to tell us what is going on inside the core:

```
PE1#sh ip bgp vpnv4 vrf Cust3 | beg Network
   Network          Next Hop            Metric LocPrf Weight Path
Route Distinguisher: 300:300 (default for vrf Cust3)
```

```
*> 10.3.1.0/24       0.0.0.0                    0          32768 ?
*> 192.168.1.1/32    10.3.1.1              130816          32768 ?
PE1#


PE2#sh ip bgp vpnv4 vrf Cust3 | beg Network
   Network          Next Hop          Metric LocPrf Weight Path
Route Distinguisher: 300:300 (default for vrf Cust3)
*>i10.3.1.0/24      1.1.1.1                    0    100      0 ?
*> 20.3.1.0/24      0.0.0.0                    0          32768 ?
*> 172.16.1.1/32    20.3.1.1              130816          32768 ?
*>i192.168.1.1/32   1.1.1.1               130816    100      0 ?
PE2#
```

It looks like we are exporting fine from PE1 and importing into PE2, as these are being seen from PE2. Yet, the routes that are on PE2 are not being seen in the BGP table on PE1.

Assuming that we should be importing and exporting from both PE1 and PE2 with the same set of RT values, then we know we are exporting correctly from PE1 and importing correctly on PE2. Therefore, the issue is either with importing on PE1 or exporting on PE2.

So, let's dig in a bit using the detail option for "sh ip vrf":

```
PE2#sh ip vrf detail Cust3
VRF Cust3 (VRF Id = 3); default RD 300:300; default VPNID <not set>
  Interfaces:
    Gi3/0
VRF Table ID = 3
  No Export VPN route-target communities
  Import VPN route-target communities
    RT:300:300
  No import route-map
  No export route-map
  VRF label distribution protocol: not configured
  VRF label allocation mode: per-prefix

PE2#

PE1#sh ip vrf detail Cust3
VRF Cust3 (VRF Id = 3); default RD 300:300; default VPNID <not set>
  Interfaces:
    Gi3/0
VRF Table ID = 3
  Export VPN route-target communities
    RT:300:300
  Import VPN route-target communities
```

```
        RT:300:300
  No import route-map
  No export route-map
  VRF label distribution protocol: not configured
  VRF label allocation mode: per-prefix

PE1#
```

On PE2, we can see that we are not exporting any RT communities:

```
PE2#sh ip vrf detail Cust3 | i Export
  No Export VPN route-target communities
PE2#
```

To get the pertinent information, we could also use:

```
PE1#sh ip vrf detail Cust3 | i (Export|Import|RT)
  Export VPN route-target communities
    RT:300:300
  Import VPN route-target communities
    RT:300:300
PE1#

PE2#sh ip vrf detail Cust3 | i (Export|Import|RT)
  No Export VPN route-target communities
  Import VPN route-target communities
    RT:300:300
PE2#
```

To fix, we just need to make sure we export the same RT values as PE1 is trying to import:

```
PE2(config)#ip vrf Cust3
PE2(config-vrf)#route-target export 300:300
PE2(config-vrf)#
```

Finally, we have visibility and end-to-end reachability:

```
Cust3-Site1#sh ip route | beg Gate
Gateway of last resort is not set

      10.0.0.0/8 is variably subnetted, 2 subnets, 2 masks
C        10.3.1.0/24 is directly connected, GigabitEthernet1/0
L        10.3.1.1/32 is directly connected, GigabitEthernet1/0
      20.0.0.0/24 is subnetted, 1 subnets
D        20.3.1.0 [90/3072] via 10.3.1.2, 00:00:04, Gi1/0
```

```
         172.16.0.0/32 is subnetted, 1 subnets
D           172.16.1.1 [90/131072] via 10.3.1.2, 00:00:04, Gi1/0
         192.168.1.0/32 is subnetted, 1 subnets
C           192.168.1.1 is directly connected, Loopback0
Cust3-Site1#

Cust3-Site1#ping 172.16.1.1 so lo0
Type escape sequence to abort.
Sending 5, 100-byte ICMP Echos to 172.16.1.1, timeout is 2 seconds:
Packet sent with a source address of 192.168.1.1
!!!!!
Success rate is 100 percent (5/5)
Cust3-Site1#
```

Now, the junior technician has learnt a lot about MPLS and is very thankful to you for your help. Naturally, you suggest he do a little more reading and maybe not test his skills out on production equipment just yet.

16. This book and the CCIE v5.0

Unlike the CCNP exams, which require a valid CCNA certification, there are no requirements for taking the CCIE exams. The exams come in two parts; the 2-hour written exam and the 8-hour lab exam.

The v5.0 blueprint lists the following topics that are required for MPLS. Along side it is the section or chapter that you will find this covered in.

Written	Lab	Title	In this book
1.1b		Identify Cisco Express Forwarding concepts	Chapter 4.
1.1b (i)		RIB, FIB, LFIB, Adjacency table	Chapter 4.
3.3	2.3	Fundamental routing concepts	
3.3.f	2.3.f	Implement and troubleshoot VRF-lite	Chapter 11.
4.0	3.0	VPN Technologies	
4.1	3.1	Tunneling	Chapter 15.
4.1.a	3.1.a	Implement and troubleshoot MPLS operations	
4.1.a (i)	3.1.a (i)	Label stack, LSR, LSP	Chapter 4.
4.1a (ii)	3.1.a (ii)	LDP	Chapter 4.
4.1.a (iii)	3.1.a (iii)	MPLS ping, MPLS traceroute	Chapter 15.
4.1.b	3.1.b	Implement and troubleshoot basic MPLS L3VPN	Chapter 5.
4.1.b (i)	3.1.b (i)	L3VPN, CE, PE, P	Chapter 5.
4.1.b (ii)	3.1.b (ii)	Extranet (route leaking)	Chapter 9.
4.1.g		Describe basic layer 2 VPN — wireline	
4.1.g (i)		L2TPv3 general principals	Chapter 12.
4.1.g (ii)		ATOM general principals	Chapter 12.
4.1.h		Describe basic L2VPN — LAN services	

Written	Lab	Title	In this book
4.1.h (i)		MPLS-VPLS general principals	Chapter 12.
4.1.h (ii)		OTV general principals	Chapter 12.

Alternative syllabi

The official CCIE syllabus for MPLS is pretty vague. The INE expanded blueprint gives a very good idea about the topics to study. Topics marked with a * are for written exams only (no different to the official syllabus on this topics). Neither syllabus specifically mentions IPv6 in the contact of MPLS. This is not to say that it is not included, hence the inclusion of it in this book.

Section	Title	In this book
4.1	MPLS	
4.1.1	VRF Lite	Chapter 11.
4.1.2	MPLS LDP	Chapter 4.
4.1.3	MPLS Ping - troubleshooting	Chapter 15.
4.1.4	MPLS Traceroute - troubleshooting	Chapter 15.
4.1.5	MPLS Label Filtering	Chapter 10.
4.1.6	MP-BGP VPNv4	Chapter 5.
4.1.7	MP-BGP Prefix Filtering	Chapter 10.
4.1.8	PE-CE Routing with RIP	Chapter 8.
4.1.9	PE-CE Routing with OSPF	Chapter 8.
4.1.10	OSPF Sham-Link	Chapter 8.
4.1.11	PE-CE Routing with EIGRP	Chapter 8.
4.1.12	EIGRP Site-of-Origin	Chapter 10.
4.1.13	PE-CE Routing with BGP	Chapter 8.

Section	Title	In this book
4.1.14	BGP SoO Attribute	Chapter 10.
4.1.15	Internet Access	Chapter 9.
4.1.16	Route Leaking	Chapter 9.
4.1.17	MPLS VPN Performance Tuning	Chapter 14.
4.1.18	AToM*	Chapter 12.
4.1.19	L2TPV3*	Chapter 12.
4.1.20	VPLS*	Chapter 12.

17. Further reading

BGP

Aside from MPLS specific links, the only extra protocols really needed to know for MPLS is BGP. The previous volume in this series covered BGP, so is well worth a read:

BGP for Cisco Networks, by Stuart Fordham (available via Amazon)

The original RFC for MP-BGP is covered here: http://tools.ietf.org/html/rfc4760

MPLS

MPLS Fundamentals, by Luc De Ghein
MPS Configuration on Cisco IOS Software, by Lancy Lobo & Umesh Lakshman
MPLS and VPN Architectures, by Ivan Pepelnjak & Jim Guichard
MPLS and VPN Architectures Volume 2, by Ivan Pepelnjak, Jim Guichard & Jeff Apcar

VPLS

Layer 2 VPN Architectures, by Wei Luo, Carlos Pignataro, Dmitry Bokotey, & Anthony Chan

http://www.cisco.com/c/en/us/td/docs/switches/lan/catalyst6500/ios/15-0SY/configuration/guide/15_0_sy_swcg/vpls.pdf

OTV

http://www.cisco.com/c/en/us/td/docs/solutions/Enterprise/Data_Center/DCI/whitepaper/DCI3_OTV_Intro.pdf

http://tools.ietf.org/html/draft-hasmit-otv-03

http://tools.ietf.org/html/rfc4364

MPLS & IPv6

http://www.cisco.com/c/en/us/td/docs/ios-xml/ios/mp_l3_vpns/configuration/15-mt/mp-l3-vpns-15-mt-book/ip6-mpls-6vpn.html

Made in the USA
San Bernardino, CA
19 April 2018